Queer Sites

Queer Sites is a history of gay space in seven of the world's major cities from the early modern period to the present. The book focuses on the changing nature of queer experience in London, Amsterdam, Rio de Janeiro, San Francisco, Paris, Lisbon and Moscow, and examines the transition from the sexual furtiveness of centuries when male homosexual behaviour was criminal, to the open affirmation of gay identities in the 1990s.

The book provides an interdisciplinary analysis of extensive source material, including diaries, poems, legal accounts and journalistic material. Original in its comparative approach to gay urban history, the work reveals the differences between the American model of gay male life and that of cities in other societies, and the impact of changing regimes. By concentrating on the importance of the city and varied meeting places such as parks, river walks, bathing places, the street, bars and even churches, the essays explore the extent to which gay space existed and the degree of social collectiveness felt by those who used this space. *Queer Sites* offers compelling individual histories and discusses the gay past beyond living witnesses.

David Higgs is Professor of History at the University of Toronto.

Queer Sites

Gay urban histories since 1600

Edited by David Higgs

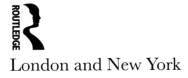

London and New York

First published 1999
by Routledge
11 New Fetter Lane, London EC4P 4EE

Simultaneously published in the USA and Canada
by Routledge
29 West 35th Street, New York, NY 10001

Typeset in Baskerville by Routledge
Printed and bound in Great Britain by Biddles Ltd,
Guildford and King's Lynn

British Library Cataloguing in Publication Data
A catalogue record for this book is available from the British Library

Library of Congress Cataloging in Publication Data
Queer Sites: gay urban histories since 1600/ [edited by] David Higgs.
p. cm.
Includes bibliographical references and index.
1. Gay men   history. 2. Gay men   Social life and customs.
5. Urban parks   History. I. Higgs, David, 1939   .
HQ76.Q43 1999
305.38'96642 dc21   98 35022
CIP

ISBN   0–415–15897–4 (hbk)
ISBN   0–415–15898–2 (pbk)

Contents

Illustrations

Contributors

Dan Healey is Research Fellow at the Wellcome Unit for the History of Medicine at the University of Glasgow, UK. He has published scholarly articles on Russian history, and a broad range of gay journalism. Email>DDHEALEY@modernhistory.dundee.ac.uk

Gert Hekma is a lecturer in Gay and Lesbian Studies at the University of Amsterdam in the Netherlands. He has published widely on the history of sexuality. Email>hekma@pscw.uva.nl

David Higgs, a Professor of History at University College of the University of Toronto, Canada, has published on aspects of French, Portuguese and Brazilian social history. Email>dhiggs@chass.utoronto.ca

Michael D. Sibalis is an Associate Professor of History at Wilfrid Laurier University, Canada. He has published a variety of articles and book chapters on French social history. Email>msibalis@mach1.wlu.ca

Randolph Trumbach, Professor of History at Baruch College, City University of New York, USA, has published a variety of books and studies on sexuality.

Les Wright, Associate Professor of Humanities and English at Mount Ida College, Massachussetts, USA, has published on the history of sexuality, is a past co-chair of the Gay and Lesbian Historical Society of Northern California and the Committee on Lesbian and Gay History, and presently serves as book review editor for the CLGH. Email>codybear@bear history.com

Acknowledgements

The authors thank the many friends and colleagues who provided them with information and suggestions and who remain innocent of any mistakes which may have reached the printed page.

Introduction

David Higgs

The writing of histories of cities is an old idea, particularly dating from the age of dynastic seats. Dynasties have been as decisive in shaping capital cities as nationality, climate or geography. European capitals like Vienna and Berlin eclipsed centers like Lyons, Frankfurt and Nuremberg that lacked a resident ruling family (Mansel 1995: xi). The seven cities considered in this book were not all of the same antiquity and did not always house ruling dynasties: Lisbon was the oldest, founded in approximately 1200 BC, London and Paris had settlements by 200 BC, and the walls of the latter were in place 400 years later around the year 250AD. Amsterdam was founded in 1225, and Moscow was a settlement before 1300. Rio de Janeiro was founded in 1565, but a royal household was only resident from 1808 to 1889. Rio is three centuries older than San Francisco which dated from 1839 and was never home to a ruling monarch. Thus the seven cities include three with settlement for more than 2,000 years, two with almost a millennium, and the two American cities which are each less than 500 years of age.

If the palaces of ruling dynasties often figured prominently in historical accounts of cities scant attention was paid in those chronicles to the urban population of homosexuals. Royal households were often said to be hothouses of homosexual behaviors. Dynasties rise and fall but homosexual activities are a more permanent feature of city life. This book examines seven cities in order to trace the development of dissident sexualities in them over the last four centuries. The title of this book was inspired by an international conference held at the University of Toronto in May 1993 in which several of the authors took part and which explored 'Queer Sites: Bodies at Work, Bodies at Play.'

Michael Sibalis opens this collection with Paris, for long the heart of the most populous monarchy of western Europe. Moscow (by Dan Healey) was an Orthodox metropolis dwelling within very different cultural traditions from those of Catholic Europe. Amsterdam (by Gert Hekma) like London (Randolph Trumbach) were major port cities with extensive maritime imperial connections for centuries. Lisbon (by David Higgs) was the leading city in the Portuguese-speaking world for many years and exported its cultural and social forms to the outpost of empire in Rio de Janeiro (by David Higgs). Rio was also a non-European city with its own distinctive forms of social development that owed much to Africa.

The book closes with an essay on the gay past of another city of the Americas, San Francisco (by Les Wright). Comparing the past of the seven cities may tell us more about differences in sexual cultures than to point to vague similarities in experience.

Queer city histories attract a readership because gay men are intensely urban. Few live by choice in the country on a permanent basis since they usually feel that cities offer a much greater variety of ways in which to enjoy one's life. Bonding with a city may also be bonding with a foreign place which was the site of special memories. More than one gay tourist undertook a nostalgic walking tour in a foreign city in daylight to photograph parks, railway stations, bars, cafés and apartments to make a visual record to remind himself of earlier experiences in those places. Like the Parisian mentioned by Sibalis, an American in another city in the 1960s laid a wreath on the snow which covered a demolished park 'tearoom' (Humphreys 1975: 14).

Time-frame

Homosexuality flourished most particularly in cities from antiquity to the present; more evidence on aspects of urban homosexual behavior has survived the centuries following 1600 than those before. The editor proposed that date as a convenient starting point. Historians of the seventeenth century have convincingly shown that it was an era of crisis and historical change in society not just in Europe but in other parts of the world (Aston 1965; Parker and Smith 1997).

Why male-centered?

The collection deals primarily with male experience. All seven cities had and have lesbian residents but the documentary evidence surviving from the past and the interpretation of it pose special questions best dealt with by separate studies. In early modern Europe, particularly at night, girls and women were subject to an informal curfew in the name of propriety. Even if a respectable girl or woman went out it was under the supervision of a chaperone or male protector. Indeed, in many societies only sex workers and abject women were encountered in the streets and outdoors after dark. The menfolk who controlled females watched over their vulnerability (Hufton 1995). This was evident in Europe and the Americas.

In some situations, particularly during the Belle Époque, cross-dressing lesbians and gay men associated in tourist amusements in Paris and elsewhere. In brothels for heterosexual men some of the prostitutes were lesbian in their personal affections, and in the same establishments men or boys sometimes dressed as women to provide sexual services for clients in search of novelty. Despite overlapping arenas of sexuality, and sometimes of sociability, between lesbians and gay men in some times and places the authors in the present collection kept their focus primarily on males because they have more evidence about the latter.

Figure 1 *Apollo and Cyperus* by Claude-Marie Dubufe (1790–1864), exhibited in the 1822
  Paris Salon. It shows Apollo's pity for a suicidal youth who had accidentally
  killed a cherished stag, but can simultaneously be viewed as a representation
  of homoeroticism.
Source: Avignon, Museum Calvet.

Elizabeth Kennedy and Madeline Davis made acknowledgements to personal informants over four and a half pages in their history of Lesbian Buffalo (Kennedy and Davis 1993). In the preface they wrote:

> We are forced to start in the 1930s because that is as far back as our narrator's memories reach.

It is difficult to test the existence in the past among males of what Kennedy and Davis affirm: 'community is key to the development of twentieth-century lesbian identity and consciousness.' Kennedy and Davis sought this from the group of people 'who regularly frequented lesbian bars and open or semi-open house parties during the 1940s and 1950s.'

Twentieth-century lesbians in the cities discussed here generally do not use parks and the outdoors like the gay men who enjoy outdoor cruising, and certainly did not do so in the past. So there is not the same sexualized use of outdoors. Even indoors there was less tendency for women to own their own housing and to live adjacent to other lesbians than is the case for gays in the emergent gay ghettos of the bigger US cities from the 1970s on. The socializing of lesbians and gays in a united community is, roughly speaking, a modern phenomenon, dating from the mid-century. It suggests non-genital activities and political solidarities which were unthinkable before 1900.

Methodological issues

No attempt is made by any of the authors to provide a sustained methodological discussion of past urban gay geographies because of the highly disparate historical sources available for that enterprise. Much more theorizing on geography and architecture that reflect same-sex desire is available for the contemporary period than that prior to 1900 (Bell and Valentine 1995; Betsky 1997).

Terminology

The language(s) of sexual labeling evolved in tandem with changes in city forms and continues to do so. Attitudes towards expressions of masculinity and femininity have also changed. Since any speaker or writer is in a dynamic relationship with her or his self-image and that of others the way in which terminology is used in text or inflected in speech is extremely complex, for sexuality as much as for race. An obvious example in North American English is the disappearance of the word 'negro' from African – American civil discourse, even though such heroes of the Civil Rights movement of the past as Booker T. Washington used it without embarrassment (Brotz 1992).

In a similar way in English and the other languages spoken in the seven cities of this book the words used by and about same-sex activities underwent frequent changes over centuries. Thus in English Canada in 1998 the word 'faggot' said with a smile can be a term of complicity among gays while pronounced with venom it is an abusive term. The head of psychiatry in a hospital would not usually talk about faggots among her patients but a new Judge of the Supreme Court (Binnie) spoke to law students of a 'faggoty dress-up party.' Although the North American use of 'faggot' to speak of homosexuals in a derogatory way began in the USA around 1914 the word meant a shrewish woman before that, and was recorded in dialect English from 1591 (*Shorter Oxford*). This was presumably transferred to an 'effeminate' man who wanted sex with other men.

The authors deliberately avoided encumbering their discussions with extensive digressions on shifting current and past vocabulary and linguistic usages, speech situations and changing definitions, but are entirely aware that terms used for same-sex practices have different values in different mouths at different times.

Documentation and evidence

Historians who work on gay urban history during the centuries out of reach of living witness – now essentially all time before 1900 – must turn to inanimate 'documents.' Records of urban male homosexual behaviors include derisive commentaries, like the pamphlet about the *bougres* (buggers) among the deputies of the National Assembly sitting in Paris in the 1790s. A 1906 book on libertinism in Rio de Janeiro used the neologism of 'Homosexualism' in the subtitle and took a medical stance. A gossipy Russian text described homosexuals in Saint Petersburg of 1908. Tabloids often commented on homosexual activities which were not mentioned in more serious newspapers.

An account of homosexuality in a city established through contemporary oral history gained from willing and loquacious informants is not available to the historian of earlier times. A narrative has frequently to be constructed out of mere scraps of information. Criminal records and scandal sheets have to be re-read with the imagined viewpoint of the prisoner or the denounced individual (Norton 1997). What Lévi-Strauss called the *bricolage* approach to information about behavior is necessary for the composition of gay urban histories. Bartlett (1988: 227) hailed two early writers on male homosexuality for their 'inspired queenly assemblage of fragments.' Attention to detail that perhaps others might not interpret in the same light was of the essence of same-sex practices.

Sites

The same-sex network of sexual encounters emerged as a subculture in urban settings with cruising sites such as the ruins of the Coliseum in Rome or places for sociability such as taverns and public baths. Furtive urban subcultures existed for centuries despite reprobation from the majority. As the subcultures extended in the growing urban context there was a commercial side of expenditures for drink, food, prostitution and entertainment.

Age groups and homosexuality

In the twentieth century the question of the exploitation of under-age partners in sexual activity became an issue for gay men. Many heterosexuals accused adult homosexuals of preying on the young and innocent and of perverting them. In 1922 a Portuguese doctor who advanced a typology of homosexual tastes thought that 5 per cent of male homosexuals were pedophiles and another 5 per cent were gerontophiles, while half of the remainder were ephebophiles (seeking partners aged 16–25) and the other half liked mature men, and were androphiles (Monteiro 1922: 251). From childhood to old age the individual with homosexual inclinations passed through changing targets of desire and perhaps himself revised the directions of his own lusts. In his travels in gay America during the 1970s one writer evoked cities where the *beau idéal* was no longer the 'beautiful boy' of 18 but the 'hot man' of 35 and he added that two of those hot men had become free to find each other attractive. He drew a contrast with an older paradigm frequently found in these pages that he associated with Kansas City:

The compliant, slightly nelly boy and the dominant, quietly masculine man form the usual couple. The age difference between them and their different degrees of assertiveness approximate the dimorphism of the heterosexual husband and wife, a model that the gays also emulate through a lot of role-playing.

(White 1986: 137)

In Europe and the Americas more choice of partners from across the spectrum of different age groups was usually found in cities.

Identity

In the 1960s the movement for homosexual rights between legal adults became highly vocal in a variety of capitalist countries in the West. This call for rights went beyond demanding the freedom for adult members of the subcultures to do in private what they pleased. An identity was asserted, founded on a sense of being a self-perceived group of people who hold in common a same-sex sexual orientation not shared by the majority with whom they are in contact. Stephen O. Murray wrote of a quasi-ethnic community (Murray 1979). As a result of shared responses to the 'heterosexual dictatorship,' as Christopher Isherwood put it, the identity was forged.

The gay identity of the 1960s on was accompanied in the Atlantic world by a fast build-up of businesses and institutions serving self-identifying gays. Intellectuals and historians who commented on this trajectory over time from sexual networks of partners often anonymous and silent, to subculture evolving into a public identity took a variety of postures. They ranged from theoretical commentaries on epistemology and discourses to simple efforts to amass information on how gay men lived over past centuries to the present.

Mass media in the 1960s began to carry non-judgmental reports on the urban sites and activities where lesbians and gays congregated. An annual festival parade started in 1970 as the commemoration of a riot in New York when lesbians and gays fought back against police raiding a bar. In 1978 a rainbow flag was devised and became an international symbol. The American usage of an adjective for happiness into a sexual label, 'gay,' supplanted local names for homosexual males in a variety of languages.

The general and the particular

The problem in making sweeping statements about the emergence of attitudes and sexual subcultures over time is not merely the parochial one of asking whether the relatively open political society of eighteenth-century England had the same sexual traditions as those of the Holy Roman Empire, or colonial Brazil or tsarist Russia. Why were there cyclical surges of calls for the repression of male homosexual activity? Various hypotheses can be advanced about 'moral panics' or fears driven by economic change (Bech 1997: 181–91).

In the 1990s people in the developed world in jurisdictions where same-sex activities between consenting adults are legal have totally polarized views about what should be permitted under the law, or what constitutes morally acceptable conduct. A 1995 survey of Canadian attitudes found that half of the population believed the practice of homosexuality to be wrong, but the number viewing homosexual relations as 'not wrong at all' or 'sometimes wrong' had risen to 48 per cent from 28 per cent in 1975.[1] A 1996 French survey found 67 per cent of the respondents thought homosexuality was a way to express one's sexuality like any other, 16 per cent thought it a sickness for which a cure should be found, while 15 per cent described homosexuality as a sexual perversion to be fought against.[2] Possibly such figures might be reversed subsequently according to respondents with different characteristics of age, ethnicity or residence.

As the essays in this book show, there were sharp cultural differences in how same-sex practices were manifested in the seven cities. San Francisco has in the 1990s a more vocal gay presence and a higher percentage of its population as self-identifying gay men than any of the other six cities. Self-identifying San Francisco gay men demanded safe streets and rights for co-resident couples with the same insistence as bourgeois heterosexuals. At the same time a swelling chorus of dissent arose among homosexuals against a glorification of the 'Adam and Steve' model projected by the US media. 'Adam and Steve' was inappropriate to various categories under the umbrella of the gay identity. The sadists and masochists, people of color, those who did not dwell in dyads and other clusters of diverse sexual agendas did not all recognize themselves in the media formulation of the gay life. The tacit imposition of a white, consumerist, US male couple as the appropriate paradigm for gay lives in urban Europe and elsewhere may not long continue into the third millennium.

At the end of the twentieth century about one-third of adult North American exclusively homosexual men are in some kind of sexual relationship and of that third a substantial number are co-residents. For the majority of homosexuals who for whatever reason are not in an ongoing relationship with another male the domestication of gay sex is now the theoretical ideal. That ideal contrasts with other realities, like that of the low-income solitary without children or a support group. Declining fertility, longer lives and heterosexual family breakdown rates mean that in future many men and women of all sexual persuasions will not be living in a couple for extended periods of their lives. Whether these generalizations hold equally true for all of the big cities of South America, Western and Eastern Europe is not easily answerable at this point of time. Latin-American familialism may inhibit same-sex cohabiting as much as housing shortages in Eastern Europe. However it appears undeniable that in those cities at the end of the second millennium the spaces for domestic and public gay male urban experiences have developed to an extent never previously known in history. Jane Jacobs told a lesbian and gay newspaper in Toronto that in any city she had ever been in she enjoyed 'what people call gay ghettos' and added: 'They really show evidence of people caring for the area and the community and each other.'[3]

The postmodern city with its predominance of tertiary economic activities counts considerable numbers of gay couples miming the co-resident nuclear family, affirming a same-sex version of romantic love, and displaying ongoing mutual support. Such couples may have only limited contacts with consanguine relatives and find their incomes from activities which are not directly dependent on their birth families. They often live in cities which are far from their birth-places and they have replaced the socialization network of their childhoods and early adolescence with new networks of friends and colleagues. Such men are frequently DINKS ('dual incomes and no kids') with higher household incomes than the median of heterosexual nuclear families. Just as in the case of hetero-sexuals their gay partnerships can be marked by physical violence, disputes over assets, withdrawal or expulsion of one or the other because of new sexual inter-ests. Nevertheless in all the cities considered in this book there are examples of co-resident male couples who live together in house or apartment over decades and until death. Such couples are increasingly impatient with the demeaning and dismissive attitudes towards them found not only among heterosexual bigots but some homosexuals married to wives.

In the second half of the twentieth century, particularly from the 1970s on, there was a quantum leap to the gay communities/villages in larger cities. There was also self- identification. This emergence of gay districts could even be recog-nized officially by urban authorities as in the case of Chicago in 1997.

The identification of a district as a focus of gay life permitted the prolifera-tion of sexual fantasies, tastes and pleasures: clones, S&M, transvestites, girth-and-mirth, ephebes, bears, leathermen and so forth. The diversity and differentiation in

Figure 2 A Gay Pride float entitled 'Latin Flavor' in a downtown parade on the main street of Toronto, June 1996.

the modern city is a function of the increase in scale and the absolute size of the membership of the urban gay community. The differentiation is reflected in the diversity of queer sites in large cities. Such variety was not, and is not, possible in small towns where the number of gay folk is small. Even in the capital cities of the past public authorities terrorized queer minorities and prevented the elaboration of sites of diversity. Sometimes, however, the police might extend limited forbearance with a view to milking blackmail victims.

At the end of the twentieth century lesbians and gays and other adult formulations of sexual desires enjoy more liberty than in the past in all of the cities considered in this book. In the 1980s a modish complaint of some older gays, at least among the white, gentrified professional bourgeoisie in the USA, was that gay liberation had taken the 'edge' out of gay life (White 1986: 156). One English entertainer in 1996 was wistful for a time before the clear identities of either straight or gay and said that half a century earlier he would have been married with three children and having affairs with men on the side. He thought he would probably be happier in the past than the present (David 1997: 269). Whether his putative wife, children and affairs would also share his felicity was unclear.

Growing acceptance of law-abiding homosexual behavior by adults robbed such conduct of the dangers and interdependencies which were, in some eyes, its charm in former days. The constant manipulation of deceptive protective stances made many a hapless individual homosexual in the past feel like a reproved outcast. In a society where adult sexuality *per se* is no reason for claiming distinction gay men must strive for status on other grounds. In knowing more about the furtive as well as the overt sexual histories of the seven cities in this book the reader will better understand how homosexual men sought to cope with the prohibitions of their days and to satisfy their needs and aspirations.

Notes

1 *Globe and Mail* (Toronto), 7 November 1995, A7.
2 *Le Monde*, 22 June 1996, 11.
3 *XTRA!* (Toronto), 9 October 1997, No. 338, 13.

1   Paris

Michael D. Sibalis

'Refugees from Sodom. – We know that the biblical fire did not destroy all the inhabitants of this corrupt city. Scattered over all the earth, they proliferated in Paris....'

(*La Petite Revue*, 15 October 1864)

Space, visibility and the gay identity

In 1895, André Raffalovich drew public attention to the clandestine homosexual subculture of Paris and other European urban centers with the warning that '[e]verywhere…Sodom exists, venal and menacing, the invisible city' (Raffalovich 1895: 447). One hundred years later, on Saturday afternoon, 24 June 1995, 80,000 Parisians celebrated *la Lesbian and Gay Pride* – the international commemoration of the Stonewall riots of June 1969 in New York City – with a parade along the boulevards of the Left Bank. Banners and placards raised high, balloons and flags afloat overhead and music blasting from a hundred loudspeakers, the jubilant crowd of men and women made its way along the 4-kilometer route from the Montparnasse Railway Station to the Place de la Bastille.

Parisians have observed Gay Pride in this way every June since 1982, but until recently the number of participants rarely exceeded 5,000–10,000. The unprecedented turnout in 1995 therefore marked a turning-point for France's gay community. 'Visible we chose to be…' exulted one gay journalist at the time. 'And numerous we were…' (Muhleisen 1995). Subsequent demonstrations have been even bigger. In 1996, 120,000 people showed up, and twice that number marched during the Europride celebrations of 1997, when (in the words of a leading newspaper) Paris became, for a few days at least, 'the European capital of homosexual visibility.' [1] Clearly, the denizens of Raffalovich's 'invisible city' have taken 'visibility' as their watchword.

Visibility is a very recent objective for French homosexuals. For many centuries, homosexually inclined men and women usually preferred to conceal their unconventional desires from a hostile society. Today's gay visibility is the culmination of a long process by which homosexuals not only created and expanded private gay space, but also struggled to secure a share of public space.

This effort to appropriate urban space for sexual activity has been the work of gay men in particular, whereas lesbians have tended to be more discreet and more private in the conduct of their sexual lives.

A sociological study of contemporary French male homosexuals published in 1984 has pointed out the paradoxes inherent in gay men's strategic use of urban space: 'Space is a very complicated thing. ...Because space is defined by an inside and outside, it excludes and includes, encloses and liberates.' Closed and private space – like clandestine or semi-clandestine commercial venues, but also personal networks of friends and acquaintances – protects, but at the cost of isolating men from the outside world. And yet closed space also creates new possibilities by bringing men together, ending their individual sense of isolation 'and confer[ring] a collective strength that allows people to be themselves in public.' Inversely, however, gay liberation (as 'being oneself in public' has come to be called) leads to a proliferation of exclusively gay spaces (like bars, clubs and cruising areas), which eventually creates gay-dominated enclaves (so-called 'gay ghettos') that can sometimes cut homosexuals off from the broader society in which they live. Ghettos set gay men apart from fellow citizens so that they run the risk of making their status as a scorned minority a permanent one (Cavailhes *et al.* 1984: 43–4).

Historically, Parisian gay spaces have been situated both literally and figuratively on the margins of city life. Thirty years ago, a rather unusual guidebook classed Paris's gay spaces among the city's many 'bad places' (*mauvais lieux*), which it defined as '[s]treet, business, quarter, residence, even public place, square, train station, riverbank that human evil and the force of circumstances have transformed into a chosen domain of sin and vice'(Bastiani 1968: 7). This equation of homosexuality with moral turpitude is typical of how most French people have traditionally regarded sexual relations between men or between women.

Terminology provides striking evidence of these negative public attitudes. Frenchmen who have sex with other men have been designated by many words over the years: 'sodomites,' 'buggers,' 'vile creatures' (*infâmes*) and 'anti-physicals' in the seventeenth and eighteenth centuries; 'pederasts' (still the most common term) from about 1740; 'uranians,' 'inverts' and especially 'homosexuals' since the late nineteenth century; and 'gays' (a term imported from the United States) beginning in the 1970s. As these words indicate, society at large has usually considered these men to be sinful, depraved, degenerate, sick or insane. Even today, although two-thirds of the French tell pollsters that homosexuality is 'just another way to live one's sexuality,'[2] the words *pédé* (slang for 'pederast' and equivalent to the American 'fag' or the British 'poofter') and *enculé* (literally, a man who is sodomized) are common taunts with an especially harsh sting.

'Gay Paree'

Urbanization is a precondition to emergence of a significant gay subculture. Paris is France's historic capital and has always been by far its largest city. It had perhaps 300,000 inhabitants in 1600, slightly less than half a million under

Louis XIV in the 1680s, and close to 600,000 on the eve of the French Revolution in 1789. The population reached 1 million by 1850 and 2 million by 1876. It peaked at 2.9 million in 1921. Only 2.2 million people live within city limits today, but the greater Paris region counts 11 million inhabitants, or about 20 per cent of the national population (Fierro 1996: 278–9). And yet a 1993 study of French sexual behaviour indicated that the region was home to 46 per cent of the country's homosexual men. The sample was small: 2,359 heterosexuals, 53 bisexuals, 52 homosexuals (Messian and Mouret-Fourme 1993). Gay men have apparently migrated to Paris from every part of the country.

Countless heterosexuals have also moved to Paris in search of work, professional advancement or a new life, but the city has almost certainly drawn a disproportionately high number of homosexuals. Until quite recently, even the largest of other French towns offered these men very little in the way of a gay subculture. Gay venues were (and in most cases still are) rare in provincial France, and strong social and familial constraints make it very difficult to live one's homosexuality openly there. As a result, as an American journalist explained in 1976:

> Gay Paris is the center of all homosexual life in France. A French homosexual will almost inevitably turn to the anonymity of the French capital to escape his fate in any one of thousands of provincial outposts. This makes Paris a privileged place no other city in the country can match.[3]

One gay journalist, now in his forties, recently recalled his move to the capital some twenty years ago: 'Paris to me meant freedom....Things became much easier for me. I knew...that I would end up living the life that I wanted.' And a much younger biologist, still in his twenties, remarked that 'in the provinces, there are very few places to meet someone....It's different in Paris. There are a lot more possibilities'(Minella and Angelotti 1996: 61–2).

Foreign homosexuals, too, have often seen Paris as a promised land of freedom. In the words of Dennis Altman:

> Paris occupies a special place in the homosexual imagination. It offers neither the tolerance of Amsterdam or San Francisco, nor the inexhaustible sensuality of New York. But we are reminded by such names as [Marcel] Proust, [André] Gide, [Jean] Cocteau, Colette, and [Jean] Genet that Paris has certainly been a major center for homosexual culture and a refuge from more repressive cultures for homosexuals such as Oscar Wilde, Radclyffe Hall, Gertrude Stein, and James Baldwin (who set *Giovanni's Room* there).[4]

The city's appeal to homosexuals undoubtedly extends well into its past. Of forty-six sodomites incarcerated in Bicêtre prison between 1701 and 1715, only twenty-one (45.7 per cent) were native-born Parisians. One hundred and fifty years later, the director of the city's vice squad reported that only 32.3 per cent of the pederasts arrested between 1860 and 1870 were born in Paris, whereas

58.5 per cent originated in the provinces and 9.2 per cent were foreigners (Carlier 1887: 444–5).[5]

The recorded history of Parisian homosexuality begins in the Middle Ages. An anonymous twelfth-century poet observed that 'Up to now Chartres and Paris have revelled / In the vice of Sodom,' while a clergyman lamented in the early thirteenth century that 'this shameful and abominable vice' was rampant in the city (Boswell 1980: 262; Lever 1985: 43). Allusions such as these to same-sex activity became more frequent as the centuries advanced. By the 1500s and 1600s, accusations of sodomy were standard weapons in the rhetorical arsenal of polemicists, who often alleged that foreigners (especially Italian courtiers) had first brought this strange taste for one's own sex into France and that it infected principally artists, clergymen and libertine noblemen, as well as the domestic servants whom they purportedly corrupted. Although men of every social class almost certainly did participate in same-sex activity, the surviving evidence from before the eighteenth century displays a marked bias toward the privileged elites. Consequently, to the extent that this can be determined, if seventeenth-century Paris had 'gay space' (a term that is surely anachronistic for the period), it was in the all-male schools run by the clergy, in aristocratic mansions and at the royal court, where in the 1680s many of the highest nobles in the land allegedly belonged to a secret 'Italian brotherhood' of sodomites (Lever 1985; Estrée 1902).

By the eighteenth century, however, there is substantial evidence of a more widespread and more socially diverse 'sodomitical subculture' in Paris among men whose sexual desires defined a collective identity and, some historians would claim, even a distinct 'lifestyle.' Maurice Lever, for instance, has argued that:

> [d]espite disparities of social class, the homosexual world [of eighteenth-century Paris] formed a community apart, with its own language, rules, codes, rivalries and clans. A closed society, secret by necessity, perhaps also by taste, situated on the margins of traditional society....For everybody, young or old, priests or laymen, great lords, financiers, workers, vagabonds, a single activity, devouring and obsessive: cruising for sex [*la drague*].
>
> (Lever 1985: 299)

If this subculture existed earlier, it has unfortunately left almost no trace in the archives. Police reports, the main source for the history of homosexual activity in the eighteenth and nineteenth centuries, do not exist for the period before 1700. It was only in 1667 that Paris got an effective police force to administer the growing city, control criminal activity, maintain good order and enforce public morals. In the early 1700s, special police agents began to patrol those parts of the city known to be frequented by sodomites, and harassed, entrapped and arrested the men they found there. Sodomy was a serious crime at the time and formal legal penalties harsh: death by fire until 1791. In practice, however, enforcement was almost always lenient. Only seven Parisian sodomites were burned at the stake in the entire eighteenth century, and five of them had other serious crimes, like rape and murder, on their conscience. The exceptions were a couple of hapless wretches executed by way of example in 1750, after the night watch caught them having sex in a darkened street. The police more usually released arrested sodomites with a warning or locked them up for a few weeks to teach them a lesson (Rey 1979–80).

In 1791, the French Revolution enacted a new penal code that decriminalized sodomy between consenting partners in private. A homosexual act was now criminal only when it occurred in public space, in which case it constituted an offense against public decency. The police consequently paid little heed to private and discreet homosexual conduct, but in 1817 a reconstituted vice squad resumed its rounds in the streets and parks (Sibalis 1996). These patrols continued into the early 1980s. The reports generated by policing constitute one very valuable source for the history of homosexual men and their use of Parisian space. Other kinds of sources also appeared in a gradually widening stream in the course of the nineteenth and twentieth centuries. Policemen, magistrates, clergymen and medical doctors – the pillars of the established order – expounded their expert (and generally hostile) opinions of homosexual behavior. Newspapers reported trials for public indecency and the occasional sensational scandal. Law courts kept records of such cases, which eventually found their way into the archives. And books, written for an insatiably curious reading public and sporting lurid titles like *Paris's Garbage* (1874), *Corruption in Paris* (1890), *Satan Leads the Ball* (1925), *Among the Bad Boys* (1937) and *The Underside of Paris* (1955), purported to expose the seamy side of Parisian life (including crime, prostitution and homosexuality), while clearly reveling in the accounts of the moral evils that they stigmatized (Urville 1874; Coffignon 1890; Georges-Anquetil 1925; Coglay 1937; Delpêche 1955).

Fiction, too, can be a useful historical source. The first French literary master-piece to deal extensively with homosexuality was Marcel Proust's seven-volume *A la recherche du temps perdu* (1913–27), translated into English as *Remembrance of Things Past*, which shocked many people with its panoramic view of Parisian homosexuality at the turn of the century. But even before Proust set pen to paper, minor novelists had already treated the subject and dozens more of varying talent would follow suit over the years. Some of their novels offer precious insights into past attitudes and sexual activities through their strong characterization of homosexual men and their vivid evocations of urban gay spaces.

For instance, 'Dr Luiz' (pseudonym of Paul Devaux), author of *Les Fellators* (1888), claimed that his mildly pornographic book was 'more a social study [of sexual perversion] than a novel.' Its main character, a beautiful Spaniard named Arthur, was one of 'those young men, models of elegance and good taste, who live in luxury and idleness,' spending their time in the fictional Café de la Guerre (standing in for the real Café de la Paix). Luiz told readers that he wanted to 'to aid you by dissipating your last doubts concerning those overly well-dressed ephebes.' Francis Carco's *Jésus-la-Caille* (1910) examined a very different but no less shocking milieu. In recounting the story of a teenage male hustler, Carco portrayed the world of crime, prostitution and homosexuality that flourished in the Montmartre district of early twentieth-century Paris. Montmartre was also the setting for *Adonis-Bar*, by Maurice Duplay (1928). The plot of this novel centered on a gay bar in the 1920s and sketched a realistic picture of the decadent lives of Horace, the middle-aged owner, and Fred, his much younger lover. The eponymous hero of Marcel Guersant's *Jean-Paul* (1953) dies at 23 after winning the struggle against his homosexual inclinations thanks to his recovered Catholic faith. Despite its moralizing tone, the book included realistic descriptions of homosexual cruising in Parisian streets in the mid-1930s. (For other French literary representations of homosexualities see Robinson, 1995; Summers 1995: 290–302).

As these few examples suggest, most novelists have demonstrated a marked antipathy toward their homosexual characters, often killing them off at the end of the story as if they had to die to atone for their deviance. This changed significantly only after the World War II and especially from the 1960s, when openly gay novelists began to produce a literature that celebrated their own experiences. The voice of homosexuals could be heard elsewhere as well, once they began speaking up, speaking out and speaking for themselves. *Arcadie*, a politically moderate 'homophile' review that appeared between 1954 and 1982, was the first long-lived gay publication, and dozens of more militant newspapers and magazines started up in later years.

Thus, police reports, newspapers, non-fictional books, novels and gay publications of all sorts offer the historian a wide range of valuable source material. If most Parisian homosexuals have managed to keep their personal life behind closed doors, where historians cannot easily go, surviving documents do make it possible to see how these same homosexuals have used both open public space and closed commercial space in the course of the last 300 years.

Public space

A 1969 'guide to Parisian pleasures' observed that for homosexuals '[i]n the streets, of course, there is every hazard but also every possibility.' Every possibility meant chance sexual encounters with 'young male models from the Faubourg Saint-Honoré, workmen in the Métro...students near the Sorbonne, sailors around the Gare Montparnasse...North Africans in the Barbès-Rochechouart district, Negroes almost everywhere, and everybody at Saint-Germain-des-Prés.' Police surveillance was the hazard (Rudorff 1969: 298).

For hundreds of years, homosexual men have sought sexual adventure in the streets, squares and parks of Paris, and they have often risked arrest to find it. This, for example, is the advice proffered by a guidebook for the gay visitor to Paris in 1995: 'swimming pools, public parks, the quays along the Seine, train stations and major tourist attractions all have potentials never imagined by their builders. Keep your eyes open' (Vichit-Vadakan 1995: 111). But homosexual 'cruising' is nothing new, as the following comments from 1826 demonstrate:

You can see these disgusting men move about Paris, at the Palais-Royal, in certain cafés, where an exquisite elegance almost always sets them apart.... In the evening, at the setting of the sun, you will notice a good number on the Quai Saint-Nicolas, the Quai du Louvre and the Quai de l'Archevêché; in the Place du Marché-Neuf and the Place de la Sorbonne and along the Champs-Élysées; and everywhere you will see with what assurance and with what shamelessness they dare to make you the most filthy propositions.

(Guyon 1826: 218)

One of the best-known places for cruising today is the Tuileries Garden. According to one recent guidebook, '[a]ll gay life is here, whispering on the benches, leaning against the balustrades, reading under trees, or sauntering around outside the former Orangerie museum – but all following a routine as mannered as anything out of Jane Austen's Bath society' (Phillips 1990: 155).

Parisian gays firmly believe that men have been coming here for centuries to meet other men and sometimes to have sex with them at night in the bushes or under the trees. In the words of one habitual visitor in 1987, 'The Tuileries, it's not even because of the tradition, it's naturally a place for cruising...you can't keep a guy from smelling it. There are always boys....'[6] As long ago as 1830, a writer observed that one specific corner of the garden near the antique statue of a wild boar (Figure 1.1) was 'the rallying point of our modern Antinouses' (Lamothe-Langon 1830: 20). (Antinous was the famed lover of the Roman emperor Hadrian.) The statue turns up again in a newspaper article of July 1845:

The section of the trees in the Tuileries Garden...at the center of which a marble statue of a wild boar stands on a pedestal, has for many years been known as one of the meeting places of those immoral creatures whose vice seems to be spreading at a frightful rate in Paris. It is above all on days of public festivities, when the garden stays open rather late at night, that these wretches gather at this spot, where the thick foliage keeps out the light.[7]

And yet the Tuileries Garden's reputedly timeless tradition is almost certainly not an unbroken one. Although the marble boar stood crumbling in place until finally restored and moved to shelter in the Louvre Museum in 1992, it had apparently lost all significance as a landmark by the 1850s. The Tuileries Garden itself almost entirely disappeared from descriptions of homosexual activity until the 1960s, when a Parisian tabloid newspaper called on the police to put an end to 'the scandal of the Tuileries,' which it presented as a recent development:

What goes on there every day, in the heart of Paris, in a place where children come to play, is revolting. The Tuileries Garden has become the number one meeting place for homosexuals in the capital....They come and go with their effeminate walk. One hears...their indecent giggling. There are dozens of them. They seek each other out. They wink, accost each other, arrange rendez-vous....It's appalling.[8]

Figure 1.1 Statue of a Wild Boar in the Tuileries Garden as it appeared in 1910
Source: Cabinet des Estampes, Bib. Nat.

Between 1850 and 1960, the principal cruising site in Paris was not the Tuileries Garden, but rather the Champs-Élysées. This does not refer to the famous avenue of that name, which was called the Avenue de Neuilly in the eighteenth and nineteenth centuries, but rather the 'Elysian Fields' themselves, meaning the wooded parkland along both sides of the avenue between the Place de la Concorde and the Rond-Point. The Champs-Élysées had been known for both heterosexual prostitution and homosexual cruising since the early eighteenth century. In 1845 a Parisian complained to the police about the 'hideous leprosy' that infected the Champs-Élysées every evening between nine and eleven o'clock: '[H]ere it's women, shameless in every way, who take you by the arm and try to drag you under the trees, further along it's some of those miserable creatures that one still calls men.' An agent with the vice squad explained in 1868 that 'no spot in Paris favors debauchery more than [the Champs-Élysées].'

This was because of 'the twisting paths in the shadows of the tall trees which a feeble ray of light barely penetrates' and 'the cafés installed amidst the clumps of trees along both sides of the avenue and which remain open until at least half past midnight.'[9]

One particular tree in the park achieved special renown by the 1880s:

> The headquarters of these pederasts in this corner of Paris…is called *the tree of love*…and it is located near the Café des Ambassadeurs [on the Avenue Gabriel]. Every evening around this tree, one can see vile rascals wandering about, easily recognizable by their clean-shaven face, their lifeless gaze and especially the peculiar way they sway their hips as they glide rather than walk over the ground.
>
> (Delcourt 1888: 285)

The public urinals installed amidst the trees and hedges made the park even more enticing to homosexuals. They prowled there nightly until they were scared off in the late 1950s, when, because of the Algerian War, the police tightened security around the Élysée Palace, the President's official residence, which backed onto the site.[10]

As well-known and well-frequented as they may have been since the early eighteenth century, the Tuileries Garden and the Champs-Élysées were just two cruising sites among countless others. The Grands Boulevards – the wide promenade laid out in the 1680s across northern Paris in a vast semi-circle along the line of the city's demolished fortifications and stretching between the Place de la Concorde and the Bastille – attracted pleasure seekers of every kind from their very inception. Pederasts and prostitutes walked these boulevards throughout the eighteenth, nineteenth and twentieth centuries. In 1850, for instance, an angry citizen wrote to the prefect of police that in the course of his evening stroll along the boulevards, he regularly witnessed 'scenes of a most shameful immorality…. I am speaking principally of those offered by those nameless creatures, those hideous hermaphrodites!…In short,…the boulevards are now a genuine den of thieves implanted in the heart of Sodom and Gomorrah.'[11]

Then there were the banks of the Seine. In the eighteenth century, pederasts often went down to the river to ogle (and sometimes pick up) the men who commonly bathed there naked. One official complained in 1724, 'It's a horrible scandal that a large number of libertine men swim in the nude in Paris in sight of so many people, principally of the opposite sex.…They also commit abominations with those of their own sex.' Men also went to the river bank at night, sometimes to urinate and defecate (public latrines being rare in those days) and sometimes to look for sex. Nude bathing within city limits ended in the early nineteenth century and the river's graveled shores became paved embankments, but the quays still drew men every evening, as the police noted in 1865: 'The river banks, the arches of the bridges and certain spots relatively rarely frequented will attract, on the pretext of satisfying their natural needs [to urinate or defecate], pederasts who will have an excuse for finding themselves there.'[12]

Changes to the urban landscape in the course of the nineteenth century created new cruising sites without eliminating the older ones. Among these new sites were the commercial arcades: enclosed galleries roofed over with glass, lit by gas and lined with shops, cafés and restaurants for well-to-do consumers. The first dates from 1791 and the last from 1860, but most were constructed between 1823 and 1846. The arcades provided sheltered public space for window shopping, dawdling and philandering, which brought throngs of idle strollers, including female prostitutes, the so-called *suiveurs* ('followers'), who accosted passing women, and, almost inevitably, pederasts who came looking for other men. Pederasts frequented three arcades in particular: the Galerie d'Orléans (Figure 1.2), built in 1828–30 at the south end of the Palais-Royal Garden, already a notorious site for debauchery and for male and female prostitution since the 1780s; the Passage des Panoramas (1799), which opened onto the south side of the Boulevard Montmartre; and the Passage Jouffroy (1847), which faced it from the opposite side of the boulevard. Shopkeepers complained that the presence of these men drove away customers, and in the mid-1840s the police began raiding the arcades to arrest 'these suspicious and vile prowlers with which the busiest galleries and passages swarm.'[13]

The public urinals installed in the Paris streets from about 1830 provided hundreds of additional spots for cruising. These *vespasiennes* (named for the emperor Vespasian who built public urinals in first-century Rome) were free-standing structures of sheet-metal that usually had room for three to six men (Figure 1.3). Paris had 500 of them by the early 1840s, and within a few decades

Figure 1.2 The Galerie d'Orléans in 1845
Source: Hoffbauer (1875–82).

they were ubiquitous along the streets and in the parks and squares (Guerrand 1985; Maillard 1967). The police regularly staked out those urinals most used by pederasts. An agent testifying at one scandalous trial in 1876, after he and his colleagues caught municipal councilor Charles de Germiny engaged in mutual masturbation in a public urinal with an unemployed 18-year-old worker, described the scene they had witnessed:

> The sixth of December [1876], at 10:40 p.m., I noticed Monsieur de Germiny exposing himself. He went into the same facilities six times. Suspect Chouart entered the same one as Monsieur de Germiny…. Glances were exchanged…. Both of them then went to sit on a [nearby] bench; I didn't see them speaking, but they undoubtedly understood each other and went back in together. Seeing then the unequivocal turn that events were taking, we put our hands on the shoulders of the two individuals [and arrested them].[14]

The police made 200–300 similar arrests almost every single year. It is no wonder that in 1910 an outraged newspaper columnist blasted the city's *vespasiennes* as 'a school of apprenticeship in the supreme vice' and railed against the graffiti scrawled inside them: 'With what disgraceful things they are covered inside…! Inverts are not satisfied with making them one of their meeting places, they write in them, using advertising to make converts by contagion.'[15]

An old ledger kept in the Paris police archives adds detail to an otherwise impressionistic picture of late nineteenth-century cruising. It records the names

Figure 1.3 Six-place urinal, Place de la Bourse, Paris, *c.* 1875–8
Source: Bib. Hist. de la ville de Paris.

of more than 900 men arrested between March 1873 and March 1879 for offenses against public decency with other males or for solicitation for the purposes of prostitution; it also gives the precise locations where the police arrested them.[16] The ledger probably does not indicate every single place in the city that pederasts went looking for sex, but only those spots that the police chose (for whatever reason) to keep under surveillance. Even so, the data are suggestive. First of all, they confirm the importance of the Champs-Élysées to the homosexual subculture. The police made 26.7 per cent of all their arrests there, and one-third of these occurred in and around one specific urinal located near the Café des Ambassadeurs on the Avenue Gabriel, making it the busiest cruising site in the entire city. The Grands Boulevards accounted for 9.8 per cent of arrests. The three arcades already watched by the police in the 1840s also remained busy: the Passage Jouffroy (8.4 per cent of arrests), the Passage des Panoramas (1.8 per cent) and the Galerie d'Orléans (2 per cent). Many of those arrested on the boulevards and in the arcades were young men whom the police subsequently charged with soliciting. They were presumably prostitutes, like the numerous women who plied their trade along the very same boulevards. That is what a journalist meant when he wrote in 1891 that 'from 11 p.m., sometimes even earlier, the boulevard, along a long stretch from the Rue du Faubourg-Montmartre to the Opera House, belongs to the "girls" and, alas!, even to the "boys".'[17] The police made another 11.6 per cent of their arrests along the quays of the Seine, either in the latrines installed there for the men who worked on the ports or under the sheltering arches of the many bridges that spanned the river.

All of these sites had been cruising places for decades, but newer ones also appear in the ledger. For example, the public urinals in the Place de la Bourse, site of the Stock Exchange, now accounted for 13.4 per cent of arrests, probably because the business quarter was conveniently deserted at night and also strategically situated halfway between the Galerie d'Orléans and the Grands Boulevards. As for railway stations, twenty arrests (2 per cent of the total) occurred in the public toilets at the Bastille terminus of the Vincennes Railroad Line, which took commuters between Paris and suburban Vincennes, and another six (0.6 per cent) at the Saint-Lazare Station, the busiest in Paris because of its heavy suburban traffic. On the other hand, the public parks seem to have been significantly less frequented in the 1870s than before 1850. Apart from the notorious Champs-Élysées, only Monceau Park, built in the 1860s, accounted for a significant number of arrests (twenty, or 2 per cent of the total). There were a mere three arrests in the Tuileries Garden, two in the Luxembourg Garden and six outside the city in Vincennes Woods.

The patterns established by the 1870s changed little until the 1950s or 1960s, except that cruising declined in the arcades, while it increased in other places of passage: railway, bus and subway stations, where men could offer police a believable excuse if stopped for loitering. To take a single example: from the 1940s into the 1970s, the Invalides Station, city terminus for the buses to and from Orly Airport, saw intensive homosexual activity. When a friend once spotted

Jean Genet there, the homosexual novelist, referring to the international travelers who passed through the terminus and whom he was trying to pick up, remarked, 'I'm doing a tour of the world'(White 1993: 350).

The most obvious change of all resulted from the gradual suppression of the city's *vespasiennes*. Municipal officials frankly admitted that they got rid of the urinals not only because they were unsightly and malodorous, but also 'for reasons of public order, when the improper use that is made of them [by homosexuals] becomes a real nuisance to the neighbors.' Paris, which still had more than 1,000 public urinals in the 1930s, had about 350 in 1961, 100 in 1980 and only 2 by the 1990s.[18] Many gay men lamented this loss. 'In the Place d'Iéna,' according to a 1969 guidebook, 'we have even seen a wreath laid on the pavement in honour of happy memories on the site of a former *vespasienne*' (Rudorf 1969: 298).

Gay guidebooks indicate with precision where men have been cruising since the 1960s. There is still always the possibility of an encounter on any street or boulevard, but without urinals to provide focal points, gay men increasingly turned back to the city's many public parks and gardens. The Tuileries Garden was only the busiest among many, and almost any dimly lit park would attract homosexuals looking for a pick-up or for quick on-the-spot sexual gratification. The late Pascal de Duve, a young novelist with a personal experience of Parisian parks in the 1990s, has described what went on there in striking albeit overblown prose:

> Parks are Dr. Jekylls and Mr. Hydes in ecological form. There, in the daytime, you see children, the elderly and young mothers with infants. At night, they are haunted by shadowy silhouettes drawing together and moving apart like moths engaged in a strange ballet. Sometimes the silhouettes merge in ephemeral couplings screened by a bush, from which a soft moan rises into the coolness of the night.
>
> (Duve 1994: 47)

The banks of the Seine remain as popular now as in the eighteenth century. Paris has 'a raunchy [nighttime] waterfront scene, like New York,' near the Austerlitz Railway Station on the Quai de la Gare, 'a large, dim boulevard peopled by spectres, hard, dangerous and anonymous,' where men can copulate amidst the concrete pillars that support the shipping sheds overhead.[19] And Parisian gays have dubbed the Quai des Tuileries, the embankment that runs along the edge of the Tuileries Garden, 'Tata Beach' (*tata* being slang for 'auntie'), because skimpily clad gay men regularly sunbathe there on sunny summer days. They also congregate there year round after dark.[20]

Despite all this activity, evidence suggests that outdoor cruising may have somewhat declined after the mid-1970s. 'Before,' one man explained in 1987, 'there were guys hanging around every Parisian bush. Now, it's over. AIDS scares us much more than the police do....The Tuileries aren't what they used to be.' But disease was hardly the only factor, any more than the marked increase in assaults by 'fag-bashers.' City Hall began fencing off the parks, installed bright lights in some spots to dispel the shadows and even instituted a special brigade to patrol the gardens in 1980.[21] Of at least equal importance has been the growth of alternative ways for gay men to meet each other. The gay press, especially after the magazine *Gai Pied* was launched in 1979, has featured personal advertisements by men seeking sexual partners for a night or a lifetime. The 1980s also saw the introduction of the minitel, a simple home-computer wired into the national telephone system and offered at minimal cost to every customer. The most successful commercial servers have been 'erotic' ones, which enable subscribers to post messages, communicate and eventually arrange intimate encounters (Duyves 1993: 193–203). Finally and most significantly, the development of an extensive network of bars, nightclubs and bath-houses has not only given men comfortable places to socialize, but also encouraged the formation of gay enclaves within the city and provided the infrastructure for a new gay community.

From gay commercial space to gay ghetto

Commercial establishments that cater to a predominantly homosexual clientele are nothing new. As long ago as the eighteenth century, Parisian homosexuals met together in specific taverns and cafés, where obliging publicans might even rent out private rooms for sexual encounters. Sources from the 1700s name many known hangouts for the city's sodomites. (Police reports mention eight different taverns in 1748 alone.) For example, at the Café Alexandre on the Boulevard du Temple, according to a pamphleteer in 1781, 'one finds only street-walkers, buggers and *bardaches* [passive sodomites]. In this café there occur vile acts and horrors that it is pointless to name…. The wisest and safest course would be to shut down this receptacle of lesbians and sodomites' (Rey 1979–1980: 65; see also Rey 1994: xii–xiv; Lever, 1985: 304; Mayeur Saint-Paul 1781: 38–9).

Nineteenth-century documents likewise indicate some of the various hotels, restaurants, lodging houses and taverns regularly patronized at one time or another by the city's pederasts. In 1822, for instance, the prefect of police noted that a man named Dupetit, who owned a café at the entrance to the Champs-Élysées since about 1805:

> has been reported to me for receiving, in small individual rooms of his café, depraved men, who come to indulge safely in the most shameful sort of debauchery. For some time Sieur Dupetit has encouraged these disgusting rendez-vous in his establishment.[22]

Fifty years later, the vice squad recorded that a certain Rousselot 'makes of his lodging-house [at 50 Rue Greneta] a den of pederasts' and that the Bamboulème restaurant at 1(bis) Rue de Bièvre was 'a [known] meeting place for pederasts'(Peniston 1996: 135–6).[23]

An exposé of Parisian 'corruption' published in 1890 explained that many pederasts:

meet together in special establishments, in wine shops, in dairy-shops, indeed in beer-halls....The owner is almost always a former pederast; when they have a foothold in an establishment of this kind, it is not easy to dislodge them except by using violence, which students have done on several occasions.

The book told the story of a small shop that sold fried potatoes on the Rue Monge in the Latin Quarter. The shopkeeper brought in a piano and:

began radically to transform not only the building, but the quarter, by letting his clients dance until two in the morning. And what clients! Men, nothing but men. Impossible, moreover, to know what went on inside. Every evening the shutters were closed, the transom-windows plugged up, the doorway curtained.

The distraught landlord, with no legal grounds for breaking the lease, was unwilling to hire thugs to throw out this undesirable tenant and in the end he had to pay the man to move away (Coffignon 1890: 347–8).

It would be difficult (even impossible) to map the precise location of these many venues, some of which remained open for no more than a few months. In a recent study of queer space, Aaron Betsky has concluded that most nineteenth-century gay bars throughout the world 'depended heavily on… darkness and a position on the edge of town. For middle-class men, the latter position meant a location at the point where their order broke down: in the slums (Betsky 1997: 157). This was certainly true of Paris. Most homosexual venues there seem to have been located on side streets in the poorer and seamier quarters of the city center, like those along the waterfront or close to Les Halles (the wholesale food market). Others were on the city's periphery, especially in the closest suburbs (absorbed into Paris in 1860), traditional places of cheap pleasure where Parisians had been going to drink, dine and dance since the seventeenth century. Still others were convenient to busy cruising areas like the Champs-Élysées.

A police raid in 1908 provides a rare glimpse into one homosexual venue of the period. Late on Sunday evening, 26 February 1908, the police descended on 'a small café of very respectable appearance' on the Quai de l'Hôtel de Ville, which allegedly served 'for overly amorous rendez-vous by sexual maniacs…from diverse social classes.' This was the Café des Ardennes, 'a small provincial café, with a discreet facade, whose windows are decorated with white cotton curtains brightened with simple lace....Along the length of the narrow room, whose walls are covered with a wallpaper with large red and green flowers, runs an unpolished bench, and a dozen tables with white marble tops press together as if to facilitate the clients' effusive and tender whispers…. Despite an unprepossessing appearance, the establishment did a very good business, but only in the evening. A neighbor told journalists that:

[a]ll day…the door of the bar stayed tightly shut; if the rare client entered by chance,…he had trouble getting served. But…the cabaret filled up from 9 p.m.…. You can imagine how surprised we were to see 'very chic' men get out of automobiles and consort in the bar with several workers and soldiers…

Couples formed in the café could adjourn to a hotel just around the corner on the Rue de l'Hôtel-de-Ville 'for more intimate tête-à-têtes.'[24] Parisian homosexuals were also frequenting bath-houses by the late nineteenth century. The tradition of public baths as 'the favored zone of debauchery, homosexuality, prostitution, [and] public indecencies' dates back to the Middle Ages, (Csergo 1988: 201), but the first recorded police raid on a Parisian bath-house took place only in 1876. Young men, most likely prostitutes, had been soliciting in the Galerie d'Orléans and then taking men back to the Bains de Gymnase, a bath-house located more than a mile away on the Rue du Faubourg-Poissonnière. The courts condemned the manager and two of his employees for 'facilitating pederasty in his establishment' and six working-class men, aged 14 to 22, for an offense against public decency.[25] In 1891 Parisian newspapers gave more extensive coverage to another raid on the Bains de Penthièvre, a bath-house on the Rue de Penthièvre, and to the subsequent trial of sixteen found-ins (twelve middle-class men, three domestic servants and the son of a British baronet). The newspapers tititlated readers with pointed allusions to the goings-on in the steam room, where naked clients committed unspecified acts 'that would make a monkey blush.'[26] An American expatriate and connoisseur of European homosexual life noted that by 1900 '[i]n Paris, [there] are at least a dozen baths that are homosexual rendezvous. Five or six are of wide popularity' (Mayne ?1908/1975: 440). This popularity has not faltered since. The Bains de Penthièvre itself remained in business until the late 1960s – an amazing and probably unmatched life span for a gay commercial establishment in Paris – and the latest gay guidebooks list a dozen exclusively gay bath-houses and saunas in the city today.

A small but significant gay commercial world comprising bath-houses, bars and restaurants had thus emerged in Paris by the early 1900s. A satirical magazine declared in 1909, with an allusion to a famous dancing boy:

How the times have changed! In our Third Republic, Bathyllus reigns in Paris as he once reigned in [ancient] Rome. Under the tolerant eye of our police, select bars, dedicated to the new cult, receive, every evening, a public of sick people, perverts, snobs, provincials and foreigners….[27]

An accompanying illustration (Figure 1.4) depicted a rather posh bar and its youthful, stylish and patently effeminate clients.

Three short articles published in *The Archives of Criminal Anthropology* at about the same time compared the homosexual underground of Paris and Berlin. The articles mentioned the Parisian bath-houses and several sordid restaurants, frequented by the lowest class of homosexuals, on the Rue des Vertus, not far

Figure 1.4 A Parisian gay bar in 1908–9
Source: *Fantasio* vol. 3.

from Les Halles, but reported that otherwise Paris's homosexuals, unlike Berlin's, tended to go to the same establishments as other citizens: 'In the Grand Café on the Boulevard de la Madeleine numerous homosexuals meet, or at least used to meet a few years ago, but absolutely mixed in with other persons. It's the same for certain other known cafés or restaurants….'[28] Other sources, however, suggest that spatial segregation might sometimes occur within ostensibly mixed venues, like the fashionable Café de la Paix on the Boulevard des Capucines. This café had two outdoor terraces, and in the 1920s and 1930s the one facing the Opera House became known as the 'ladies' side' (*côté des dames*), because well-to-do 'inverts' congregated there every evening (Raynaud 1934: 148).

Sometimes, too, pederasts used heterosexual venues for their own purposes. The standing galleries (*promenoirs*) in Parisian theaters and early movie houses provided cheap entry to anybody who wanted inexpensive entertainment. Pederasts, however, looked on the standing galleries primarily as crowded places where they could take liberties in the dark. A complaint to the prefect of police in 1840 indicated that among the many theater-goers who bought the standing-room tickets 'are some who, addicted to the vice of pederasty, come there on purpose to satisfy their unnatural desires on the men next to them.' The advent of moving pictures changed nothing. The narrator in one autobiographical novel recounted how in 1913 a friend 'took me to the promenade of a very big cinema, the fashionable meeting place of our secret brotherhood. We spent feverish evenings there, amidst a jostling crowd, the heat and stimulus of which impelled me to commit a thousand follies under cover of darkness' (Portal n.d.: 129).[29]

As specifically homosexual venues multiplied, they began to cluster in certain neighborhoods. Between 1880 and 1910, the district of Montmartre in northern Paris emerged as the center of anarchism, bohemianism and illicit sexuality, including prostitution, lesbianism and male homosexuality (Varias 1996: 29–40; Wilson 1991: 195–222).

A newspaper, reporting in June 1909 on two police raids on Mauri's Bar on the Rue Duperré and Le Bar Palmyre on the Place Blanche, commented that '[s]everal establishments in Montmartre have for some time been the theater of scandalous scenes. An entirely homosexual clientele frequented them and didn't hesitate to engage publicly in their favorite practices.' By the eve of the First World War, Montmartre had acquired a reputation as 'the land of cocaine, bars for pederasts and all-night restaurants' (Willette 1919: 105).[30]

After the war, Parisian homosexuality stepped even more boldly into the open. Sisley Huddleston, an Englishman then resident in the city, described the 'tendency to make the abnormal the normal' as 'a most important phenomenon in post-war France.' Citing authors like Marcel Proust and André Gide, Huddleston condemned '[a] whole literature…which is tainted with homosexuality.' 'That there should be tolerated special cafés in Paris, is an affair of the police,' he pontificated. 'What is serious…is that writers and artists should publicly proclaim with complacence and sympathy the prevalence of (to use the current expression) the love that dare not speak its name' (Huddleston 1928: 270–2).

The emblematic event of homosexual life in Paris in the inter-war years was a series of masked balls held annually during Carnival on *Mardi Gras* (Shrove Tuesday) and *Mi-Carême* (Thursday of Mid-Lent) at Magic-City Dancing, an immense dance-hall on the Rue de l'Université, near the Eiffel Tower. Carnival merrymaking traditionally encouraged people to give free rein to all their fantasies. Carnival had consequently always been 'the holiday of sexual marginals, [and] most particularly pederasts,' many of whom used the occasion to wear women's clothes in public, transvestism having been outlawed by police ordinance during the rest of the year (Faure 1978: 77). Private 'fags' balls' (*bals de tapettes* or *bals de tantes*) were held during Carnival throughout the nineteenth century. Between 1922 and 1939, thousands of men, most costumed and many in extravagant female drag, attended the balls at Magic-City every year. 'On this night,' wrote a journalist in 1931, 'all of Sodom's grandsons scattered throughout the world…seem to have rebuilt their accursed city for an evening. The presence of so many of their kind makes them forget their abnormality.' [31] Gyula Brassaï, whose photographs have immortalized these fabulous balls, described the 'immense, warm, impulsive fraternity' at Magic-City:

> The cream of Parisian inverts was to meet there, without distinction as to class, race or age. And every type came, faggots, cruisers, chickens, old queens, famous antique dealers and young butcher boys, hairdressers and elevator boys, well-known dress designers and drag queens…
>
> (Brassaï 1976)

On the other hand, one homosexual novelist described himself as 'humiliated' by the effeminacy of this 'equivocal masquerade.' 'Why did those young men ape a sex of which they ought to have been the enemies? Why did the most adorable youths…simper in that manner?…When a man gives himself to another man, he ought not to forget that he is a man' (Portal n.d.: 142).

The Magic-City balls were only the most conspicuous manifestation of Paris's thriving homosexual subculture in the 1920s and 1930s. And yet the city probably could not compare in this respect to Berlin before the rise of Hitler in 1933, a fact bemoaned by one Parisian bar-owner in the mid-1920s: 'Isn't it shameful for Paris to be so far behind: in Berlin they have 150 establishments like this one, and here there are barely ten!' (Georges-Anquetil 1925: 237). Nevertheless, there were in fact many specialized bars and nightclubs for gay men, lesbians and their friends on the Left Bank at Montparnasse, on the Champs-Élysées and still (and most especially) in Montmartre. Some venues were very elegant, like Le Boeuf sur le Toit, which opened in January 1922 on the Rue Boissy-d'Anglas, just off the Champs-Élysées. Contrary to rumor, the writer Jean Cocteau did not own this bar, although he and his circle patronized it regularly. Cocteau himself said that the place was 'not a bar at all, but a kind of club…– everybody met everybody at the Boeuf (Steegmuller 1970: 282–3). One of his biographers has described Le Boeuf as:

> an 'in spot' where the smart set met for drinks after dinner and stayed until the early morning' and where "high tone' consisted of sexual ambiguity, campy spoofing, brashness and quid pro quos.…Homosexuality had become 'chic,' and Le Boeuf its stronghold.
>
> (Brown 1968: 212–14)

Homosexuality in Montmartre, however, was far from chic. In 1932 one magazine took readers on a journalistic tour of 'the dives of the new Sodom' on the Rue Germain-Pilon, the Passage de l'Élysée-des-Beaux-Arts and the Boulevard de Clichy, which were much frequented by male prostitutes, their pimps and their customers.[32] One of the most famous venues in the district was La Chaumière on the Rue Gabrielle, where night-owls mingled with drag-queens: 'On the hill, at the foot of the funicular, dropped there like a turd, the little thatched cottage sits majestically…– vice is master here – the men are mistresses. There are wooden tables…a moth-eaten carpet, the hint of a table-cloth and a lot of dust' (Georges-Anquetil, 1925: 226). Another was Graff's, a busy tavern and restaurant on the Place Blanche, a few steps along the sidewalk from the world-famous Moulin Rouge. Graff's turned into a homosexual venue late every night. 'At 9 p.m. Graff's was still only bourgeois,' wrote one novelist who frequented the place. 'Later, when the theaters and the movie houses let out, a tumultuous throng of boys invaded it, shrieking like old ladies…' (Du Dognon 1948: 56). Montmartre of the 1930s was a murky world of thieves and whores portrayed so graphically by the novelist Jean Genet (Divine, the prostitute in *Our Lady of the Flowers*, took tea at 2 a.m. in Graff's – 'overcrowded and foundering in smoke' – and hustled on the Boulevard de Clichy and in the Place Blanche), although a recent biographer has suggested that Genet 'may have been depicting, as so many outsiders do, more a realm of the imagination than an actual district…' (Genet 1963: 81ff; White 1993: 209).

The boundaries of gay Paris in the inter-war years stretched well beyond Montmartre. So many homosexuals went to the working-class dance-halls (*bals musette*) on the dark and squalid Rue de Lappe near the Place de la Bastille that one wit joked in 1927 that the city planned to rename it the Rue de Loppe (Fag Street) (Willy 1927: 162; Dubois 1997: 218–24). A Dutch visitor to Paris in 1932 wrote: 'One of the dance-halls in the Rue de Lappe has a special character and also caters to a special kind of clientele; here the prohibition against men dancing together is not enforced. It is a terrible evil, which is getting worse and worse in these working-class neighborhoods…' (Faust and Schiphorst n.d.: 119). Fifty years later, a regular customer fondly recalled these dance-halls as 'tiny nightclubs where there were accordionists and a small band on a balcony.' 'These were sexual clubs and not homosexual clubs,' he explained, 'but there was a great deal of permissiveness in them.…Homosexuality and heterosexuality rubbed elbows on the Rue de Lappe without any problems' (Guérin in Barbedette and Carassou 1981: 48–9). Another popular dance-hall, located across the river in the Latin Quarter, was the Bal de la Montagne-Sainte-Geneviève, where 'Sodom and Gomorrah – or Lesbos, rather – got along beautifully together…' Men and women flocked to it from across the city, but also:

> Once in a while one would see [there] butchers from the neighborhood – rather common in appearance, but with hearts full of feminine longings – forming surprising couples. They would hold hands – thick, calloused hands – like timid children, and would waltz solemnly together, their eyes down-cast, blushing wildly.
>
> ('The Bal de la Montagne-Sainte-Geneviève,' in Brassaï, 1976 unpaginated)

After World War II, French intellectual life, dominated by existentialism, set up headquarters in the cafés of Saint-Germain-des-Prés on the Left Bank. The district's bars and clubs were soon the focus of the city's vibrant nightlife. They drew so many gay men and lesbians that guidebooks labeled Saint-Germain-des-Prés 'a world center for all such [homosexual] activities' and 'the kingdom of "queens"' (Rudorff 1969: 300; Bastiani 1968: 115). The most famous gay venue there was Le Fiacre on the Rue du Cherche-Midi, which advertised with the slogan: 'The place is not very big, but the entire world meets there and treasures it'.[33] Le Fiacre did indeed enjoy an international reputation. Its upstairs restaurant served a cosmopolitan elite that included international stars of stage and screen, while its ground-floor gay bar welcomed more plebeian customers (Martel 1996: 83–4). The English novelist Christopher Isherwood went there in 1955 and found himself 'jammed into a crowd so dense you could only sway with it like seaweed in water.' His visit occurred on New Year's Eve, but the bar was always full of people and in summer the overflow spilled out into the street (Isherwood 1997: 563).

Le Fiacre was only one of many gay bars, nightclubs and restaurants that prospered in Saint-Germain-des-Prés in the 1950s and 1960s. A tabloid newspaper warned readers in 1961 that 'Saint-Germain-des-Prés has become a degenerate district....Let's have to courage the say it: Saint-Germain-des-Prés has been invaded by the Third Sex.' It quoted hostile comments by Paul Boubal, owner of the Café de Flore, celebrated as the place where the philosophers Jean-Paul Sartre and Simone de Beauvoir once held court:

> It's a veritable scourge. Of course, there were already some [homosexuals] a few years ago. But they were few, courteous, polite, discreet....But today, it's become a real nightmare....On my terrace, there is nothing else. Do you know what people call my upstairs room? '*La salle des mignons* ['the pretty boys' room'].

The tabloid urged the police to clean up the quarter, because 'Paris must not become Berlin of 1925.'[34]

In the 1970s, gay night life migrated across the Seine to the district between the Palais Royal and the Opera House, and most notably to one street in particular: the Rue Sainte-Anne. In both Montmartre and Saint-Germain-des-Prés, the homosexual subculture had been part of a more general ambiance of unconventionality and bohemianism. The Rue Saint-Anne, in contrast, was in an ordinarily tranquil residential and business district in central Paris. It was almost deserted after the workday's end, which may well have been what first attracted gay venues at a time when many customers put a priority on secrecy. A gay restaurant and a gay nightclub had already opened in the quarter in the mid-1950s, while Le Royal Opéra, a large café on the Avenue de l'Opéra, stayed open all night and attracted nighthawks ranging from taxi drivers to men who cruised the nearby Tuileries Garden. Then, in 1964, a former barman named Fabrice Emaer (1935–83) opened Le Pimm's Bar at 3 Rue Sainte-Anne. In late 1968, he inaugurated Le Club Sept, a ground-floor restaurant and basement discotheque at number seven of the same street. Le Sept was an immediate hit, described by one guidebook as 'one of the home ports of fashionable Paris. Of fashionable homosexual Paris, need one specify? Writers, actors, dancers, couturiers, even politicians mingle there into the late hours of the night' (Angeli 1974: 158).

Many more bars and nightclubs soon sprang up in the neighborhood. Not all were as fashionable as Le Sept, but all were nearly as expensive, levying a hefty cover charge at the door and charging high prices for drinks. One of the busiest, Le Bronx, at 11 Rue Sainte-Anne, was only two doors down from Le Sept, but was otherwise, as an American journalist remarked, 'a far cry from the tight-assed atmosphere of its neighbor.'[35] Le Bronx was the city's first 'backroom bar,' so-called because it provided a dimly lit back area where customers packed together for mutual groping and semi-public sexual activity in the darkness.

David Girard (1959–90), who began a highly successful business career by selling his body on the Rue Sainte-Anne in the 1970s, later remembered it as:

> the first and the only gay street in Paris. During the day, the only people you met there were office workers and the neighborhood's little old ladies. But

once night fell, the little old ladies double-locked their doors, afraid of those boys who came looking for other boys, and who invaded the street.

(Girard 1986: 56–7)

A journalist writing in 1975 also noted the dramatic transformation: 'From 10 p.m., the street changed completely: it teemed with young men, clogged up with cars. By 1 a.m., it was nothing but chrome and blue jeans.'[36]

The heyday of the Rue Sainte-Anne coincided with an era of sexual liberation that began in France in May 1968, when strikes and riots almost toppled the conservative regime of Charles de Gaulle. The gay liberation movement came to the country with the foundation of FHAR (the Homosexual Front for Revolutionary Action) in 1971. The permissive mood of the 1970s meant increased social tolerance for homosexuals and a rapid expansion of commercial gay space. The first edition of the gay *Incognito Guide* in 1967 published the names and addresses of eleven bars, twelve restaurants and two cabarets in Paris. Its 1976 edition listed twenty-nine bars, nightclubs and discotheques and thirty-eight restaurants. The *Gai-Pied Guide* for 1986/7 carried entries for eighty-three restaurants and snack bars, thirty bars, eighteen discotheques and eighteen bath-houses.[37] This rapid proliferation brought diversification and specialization, so that by the 1980s there were gay venues for every taste: swanky discotheques, grungy leather clubs, convivial piano bars, sedate coffee shops, raunchy back-room bars, a wide choice of restaurants and a dozen or more bath-houses. This extensive network of establishments shaped and defined an emerging gay community.

In 1980 the pioneering gay activist Guy Hocquenghem (1946–88) told an American interviewer:

[W]e don't have a gay community in France. That is, we have a gay move-ment – with several organizations actively working for political rights, as in all the Western countries – but people do not feel part of a *community*, nor do they live together in certain parts of the city, as they do…in New York City or in San Francisco, for example. And this is the most important difference and the most significant aspect of gay life in the US: not only having a 'movement,' but having a sense of community – even if it takes the form of 'ghettos' – because it is the basis for anything else.[38]

Within only a few years, however, Hocquenghem's analysis was clearly out of date. A gay community was in the making in the 1980s and a so-called 'gay ghetto' had started to develop in the district of Le Marais.

Le Marais, once a wealthy neighborhood of aristocratic mansions, had decayed throughout the eighteenth and nineteenth centuries, gradually becoming a working-class district of small workshops and run-down housing. It was one of Paris's poorest and most decrepit quarters in 1965, when the Ministry of Culture stepped in to preserve its historic character by declaring it a 'protected district.' Restoration and gentrification could begin. 'The image of Le

Marais has profoundly changed in the space of a few years,' wrote a sociologist in 1980. 'Long forgotten, Le Marais...is tending to become an esthetic oasis reserved to the middle class.' Because 'its architecture reflects an order, [and] a more stable society,' Le Marais appealed to a bourgeoisie 'whose values are all being called into question.'[39] Ironically, the district's apparently ineluctable evolution into an stately bourgeois neighborhood was soon to be interrupted by an unexpected invasion.

Gay men found Le Marais attractive for a number of reasons: low rents that were still a bargain in the early 1980s (they later soared); old buildings and narrow streets of undeniable charm; and an exceptional location in the city center and in close proximity to Beaubourg and Les Halles. Beaubourg, a former slum, was enjoying new prestige after extensive urban renewal and the opening there of the Pompidou Center, a modern art museum, in early 1977. Les Halles, site of the city's immense wholesale food market since the Middle Ages, underwent major commercial development after the market transferred out to the suburbs in 1969 and also became a main hub of the regional public transportation system.

The first gay bar in Le Marais opened its doors in December 1978. This was Le Village, a tiny café on the Rue du Plâtre, a nondescript little street. The two new owners took over the lease mainly because they could afford the cheap rent and partly because of the proximity of the Pompidou Center just 150 metres to the west. Their gamble paid off and they were soon doing a roaring business. They sold out in 1980 and opened a larger bar nearby: Le Duplex on the Rue Michel-le-Comte.[40] Other gay bars were soon springing up in Le Marais (along with several bars and nightclubs close by in Les Halles). These quickly became (and have remained) some of the most popular gay venues in Paris: Le Bar Central in 1980, Le Piano Zinc and Le Coffee Shop in 1981, Le Swing (now l'Amnésia Café) in 1983, Le Quetzel in 1987 and so on.

The bars in Le Marais charged less than those on the Rue Sainte-Anne, they opened in the afternoon or early evening rather than at 10 or 11 p.m. and they did not screen their clients at the door: 'They valued visibility, which corresponded to the new public demand at a time of "coming out of the closet" (the bars were well lit and open to the street in Le Marais, whereas they were still equipped with reinforced doors, doorbells, peep-holes, and bouncers on the Rue Sainte-Anne)' (Martel 1996: 197–9). Maurice MacGrath, who still owns Le Bar Central today, explained in 1983:

> It was necessary to change the gay scene in France. Until [1980], it revolved principally around exclusive venues like Le Sept [on the Rue Sainte-Anne]. The idea of a daytime bar had been initiated with Le Village and I took the plunge....One of my goals in opening the Central was to integrate homosexual life into everyday life.[41]

Even Fabrice Emaer, who had launched the Rue Sainte-Anne in the 1960s, bestowed his blessing on Le Marais:

I am 100 per cent for these initiatives. The policy of low prices is the best, especially because we are in an economic crisis. I am, of course, in favor of the multiplication of places of [homosexual] expression....We are following in the footsteps of the Americans, the gay world is revealing itself.[42]

By the mid-1990s, at least forty gay businesses were operating in Le Marais. Mainly bars and restaurants, these also included the city's only gay bookstore, Les Mots à la Bouche (since 1983), and its only gay drugstore, La Pharmacie du Village (since 1995). One street in particular, the Rue Sainte-Croix-de-la-Bretonnerie, has become 'gay Paris's display window.' In 1996 its 100 meters boasted four bars, four restaurants, three clothing stores, a bookstore, a hotel and a sex shop, all serving a predominantly gay clientele.[43] While entirely new venues have opened in Le Marais every year, existing ones have changed in order to appeal to new customers. In 1995, for instance, when their regular business began to fall off, the owners of one traditional café at the strategic intersection of the Rue des Archives and the Rue Sainte-Croix-de-la-Bretonnerie modernized the decor and renamed it (in English!) l'Open Bar, 'to show that we are open to everyone: homos, lesbians, heteros, without distinction.' The bar is also open in the literal sense, because in good weather the waiters slide back glass panels to expose the interior and they line up tables and chairs along the sidewalk. Business booms every day through the afternoon and evening until 2 a.m.[44]

Initially at least, the commercial success of Le Marais appeared to signal the impending collapse of the gay liberation movement, as an English journalist living in France recognized in 1985:

On the one hand, the 'movement'...reminds us of our oppressed past and warns us (perhaps rightly) of a possible return of the pendulum. On the other hand, walk around the streets of Les Halles and you'll see hundreds of pretty young post-hunks who've never heard of Christopher Street (is he an American actor?) and who identify themselves much more with the subculture of Le Marais than with any gay movement. And why shouldn't they? It's surely the ultimate aim of all militant movements to become totally irrelevant.[45]

In fact, the fight against AIDS would rekindle political militancy in the late 1980s, but the new and stronger sense of gay identity that began to emerge in Le Marais in the first years of the decade owed more to capitalism and consumerism than to the gay liberation movement, as a French journalist has recently implied:

Le Marais...answered an urgent need: to bring gay men out of their anonymity and to free them of their shame. In creating establishments run by themselves and for themselves, gays set up prosperous businesses and have grouped interdependent activities in a single quarter for practical reasons...to bring together offer and demand [46]

David Girard, the former hustler whose business acumen and talent for self-promotion earned him a fortune as well as the contempt of most gay activists, responded to his many detractors by boasting that businessmen like himself had actually achieved more for the gay community than its political activists:

> The bar owner who, in the summer, opens a terrace where dozens of guys...meet openly, is at least as militant as they are. Even if he earns money from it. By creating two bath-houses, two magazines distributed in every city in France, a much-talked-about restaurant and a crowded night-club, I think that I have done more for gays than they ever have.
>
> (Girard 1986: 164)

Girard's self-serving argument has more than a germ of truth to it.

Of course, Le Marais did not at first entirely eclipse the older gay quarters. A guidebook published in August 1981 still divided gay Paris into four main districts: Montmartre (four bars, eleven restaurants), Saint-Germain-des-Prés (four bars, nine restaurants), the Rue Sainte-Anne (eleven bars, eight restaurants) and Le Marais/Les Halles (ten bars, seventeen restaurants).[47] By the late 1980s, however, the trend was evidently unstoppable. Today Saint-Germain-des-Prés has all but disappeared from the map of gay Paris, Montmartre and the streets around the Rue Saint-Anne count only a few bars and restaurants, while Le Marais and Les Halles have by far the heaviest concentration in the city. Even so, only a minority of Paris's many gay venues have actually located there. Le Marais does not possess a single bath-house (these are scattered across the city) and only one or two discotheques (most are located in Les Halles or the streets around the Palais-Royal or off the Grands Boulevards, while Le Queen, the newest and most fashionable, is on the Champs-Élysées). Even the city's Gay and Lesbian Center is elsewhere, 500 meters to the east of Le Marais on the Rue Keller.

Moreover, the inhabitants of Le Marais remain socially, ethnically and sexually a highly diverse group, including (among others) bourgeois families of Old French stock, orthodox Jews from eastern Europe or North Africa and much more recent immigrants from the Far East. Although many gay men have chosen to live in Le Marais and many more have installed themselves in the less expensive districts close by, generally speaking Parisian gays continue to live everywhere in the city. Le Marais nonetheless provides a clearly delineated gay space – a 'gay ghetto' – in the heart of Paris, where men can stroll hand in hand and kiss in the street without embarrassment. As one 20-year-old recently remarked: 'We feel more among family here than anywhere else in Paris. Perhaps that's what we mean by the [gay] community.'[48]

The ghetto in question

Some long-time residents of Le Marais are unhappy about what they see happening to their quarter. A neighborhood association protested in 1996 that '[t]he multiplication of homosexual businesses, with the special public that they attract, has provoked a major change in the atmosphere of [Le Marais] and growing irritation among the inhabitants, several of whom have already moved away or plan to do so.' The police responded to their complaints by harassing the gay bars – for example, by laying charges for making excessive noise or for blocking the sidewalk with their tables – and by forcing gay establishments to take down their rainbow flags (the international symbol of the 'gay nation'), which the district's mayor contemptuously dismissed as 'multi-colored rags.' The police justified their order by arguing that:

> [i]f a single flag in a quarter does not seem likely to provoke hostile reactions in the neighborhood, the grouped and systematic display of large emblems is likely to induce hostility. And, in these circumstances, it is not necessary to wait for trouble to occur before imposing a ban.[49]

The authorities soon called off their campaign of harassment, but French gays themselves have remained engaged in heated debate over the pros and cons of forming a 'gay community,' lobbying for 'gay rights' and constructing a 'gay ghetto' within Paris. Critics argue that such initiatives are quintessentially American and insist that any talk of a 'gay community' in France smacks of American-style 'identity politics.' They portray the United States as a mosaic of competing minorities, each affirming its own identity and lobbying for its own special interests to the detriment of the national community as a whole. This runs counter to France's so-called 'republican tradition' by which equal and autonomous citizens live harmoniously within a centralized and homogeneous nation-state. France has always sought to assimilate its minorities by imposing a monolithic culture and a single set of national values. Defenders of the republican tradition maintain that homosexuals are not and should not aspire to be one distinct minority among many others; they constitute no more than a broad group of varied individuals from all races and classes who happen to prefer their own sex.

Others condemn Le Marais as the embodiment of an insidious commercialism and consumerism that is no less objectionable simply because the capitalists who own the bars and restaurants are usually gay. One veteran gay militant has regretted bitterly that the social and political radicalism of the gay liberation movement of the 1970s has since given way to 'the management of the profits to be made from a very specific and captive public (nightclubs, specialized newspapers). This phenomenon is the *gay-ttoization* of the so-called "gay" movement and the Americanization of European homosexuality' (Dispot 1986: 310). Still others do not oppose Le Marais in principle, but do deplore the lifestyle that it promotes, which shows little tolerance for the poor, who cannot consume, or for the old, the homely, the flabby and the overly effeminate, who violate current canons of homosexual desire. Le Marais, one political activist has complained, 'has taken homosexuals hostage....A single look [predominates]: attractive, young, muscular, white, incidentally tanned and/or smooth-bodied, with alert eye and tight clothes. Without it, one earns a scornful glance....'[50]

This ongoing debate over the nature, significance and very meaning of Le Marais, by conflating issues of urban space and gay identity, takes us full circle back to the starting point of this chapter and reminds us that the two issues are inextricably intertwined. As a space that affirms and celebrates gay visibility, Le Marais shapes and sustains a nascent gay community. The quarter's venues are much more than highly profitable businesses to the men who frequent them. They facilitate sociability and reinforce solidarity among men who share a sexual orientation. But the dispute among gay men over the social utility of Le Marais is an important reminder that profound social, political and cultural divergences persist within the so-called gay community. And the fact that Le Marais is still at times sharply contested terrain, with gay men pitted against some heterosexual residents, highlights the limits of freedom even within a liberal and avowedly tolerant society.

A specifically gay ghetto in Paris is a recent phenomenon, but one that in hindsight has been centuries in the making. As the 'invisible city' – the hidden homosexual subculture that has existed in Paris since at least the eighteenth century – gradually emerged into the open, it required a geographical center to showcase its new visibility. It remains to be seen, however, whether a distinct and separate gay space will remain a permanent fixture of the urban landscape or whether, as some fear and others hope, the gay ghetto will ultimately disappear once gays, having attained full and equal rights, lose their sense of uniqueness and merge more completely into the larger society around them.

Notes

1   *Libération*, 28/9 June 1997, 1.
2   'La Tolérance des Français à l'égard des homosexuels tend à diminuer,' *Le Monde*, 22 June 1996, 11.
3   Harry Blake, 'Gay Paree,' *The Paris Metro*, 21 July 1976, 10.
4   'Dennis Altman's International Journal: Paris,' *Christopher Street*, July/Aug. 1980, 24.
5   Bibliothèque Nationale, Ms Clairambault 985, 'Extraits d'interrogatoires' (statistics provided by Jeffrey Merrick).
6   Thierry Vidal, 'Oiseaux de nuit,' *Gai Pied Hebdo* 309 (23 Feb./4 March 1987), 54–5.
7   *Gazette des Tribunaux*, 31 July 1845, 945–6.
8   Robert Justice, 'Le Scandale des Tuileries,' *France-Dimanche*, 16/22 Feb. 1966, 4.
9   APP [Arch. prefecture pol.], D/a 230, #140, letter to prefect of police, 27 Oct. 1845; D/a 223, #30, police report, 4 July 1868.
10 'Petit Guide de la Zone "Bleue",' in *Le Crapouillot*, Aug./Sept. 1970 (*Les Pédérastes*), 85.
11 APP, D/a 230, # 206, letter, 18 Nov. 1850.
12 Lever 1985: 299ff; Rey 1979–1980: 53–6, 1994: xii–xiv; Joly de Fleury, quoted by Cabanès, *La Vie aux bains*, 2nd edn (Paris, n.d.), 329–30; APP, D/a 230, # 343, police report, 19 May 1865.
13 *Gazette des Tribunaux*, 5 June 1847, 783.
14 *Le Temps*, 24 Dec. 1876, 2, 4.
15 Lucien Descaves, 'Invertis et pervertis,' *Le Journal*, 2 March 1910.
16 APP, BB6 (Pédérastes et divers). Arrests totaled 939.

17 Henri Fouquier, 'La Vie de Paris,' *Le XIXe siècle*, 25 April 1891, 2.

18 'Plus de vespasiennes de "papa" en 1963' and 'Une Nouvelle toilette pour les vespasiennes,' *France-Soir*, 18 March 1961, 26 Jan. 1980; M. Cazaux, 'La "Sanisette" renouvelle le mobilier urbain,' *L'Aurore*, 22 Feb. 1980; Frédéric Chaleil, 'Les derniers de la tasse,' *Télérama*, 11 May 1994.

19 *Weaver's 1984 Gay Guide: Paris* (London, 1984), 56; *Gai Pied hebdo: Guide France 83–84* (Paris, 1984), 124.

20 Catherine Alessandri, 'Tata-beach, la plage parisienne des homos,' *Libération*, 15 June 1981, 9; 'Tata Beach, mode d'emploi,' *Exit: Le Journal*, 4 Aug. 1995, 6–7.

21 Hervé Liffran, 'Fin des idylles nocturnes aux Tuileries' and Frédéric Bouelle, 'Dans les parcs, la baise pour la baise n'a plus la cote!,' *Gai Pied Hebdo* 218 (3/16 May 1986), 12–13, and 297 (5/11 Dec. 1987), 26–8.

22 AN, F7 9546, dossier 4339-A2, police reports, 8 July and 13 Sept. 1822.

23 Archives of the prefecture of police, BB6, 'Pédérastes et divers,' # 555, 1087–8.

24 'Les Homosexuels surpris par le commissaire,' *Le Journal*, 27 Jan. 1908, 1.

25 *Gazette des Tribunaux*, 18 June 1876, 1228; Archives de Paris, D1 U6/67, 17 June 1876.

26 For example, *Le Matin*, 25 April 1891, 3; *Le Siècle*, 25 April 1891, 3.

27 'L'Héresie sentimentale,' *Fantasio* 3 (1908–9): 647–8.

28 Marc-André Raffalovich, 'Les Groupes uranistes à Paris et à Berlin'; P. Naecke, 'Le Monde homo-sexuel de Paris' and *idem*, 'Quelques détails sur les homo-sexuels de Paris,' *Archives d'anthropologie criminelle* 19 (1904): 926–36, 20 (1905): 182–5, 411–14.

29 APP, D/a 230, # 89, letter to prefect of police, 4 Feb. 1840.

30 'Un Scandale à Montmartre,' *Le Journal*, 22 June 1909, 6.

31 Jean Laurent, 'Le Bal de Magic, un soir de Mi-Carême,' *La Rampe*, 1 April 1931, 35–8.

32 Henri Danjou, 'Les Pourvoyeurs,' *Détective* 181 (14 April 1932): 4–5.

33 Le Fiacre's advertisements appeared regularly in *Juventus*, 9 numbers (1959–60).

34 'Le 3e sèxe envahit St-Germain-des-Prés,' *France-Dimanche*, 21/27 Sept. 1961, 8.

35 Blake, 'Gay Paree,' 9.

36 Renaud Vincent, 'Les "nuits bleues" parisiennes: La rue aux hommes,' *France-Soir*, 25 Oct. 1975.

37 *Incognito Guide: Europe Méditerranée 1967* (Paris, 1967); *Incognito Guide: Europe 1976* (Paris, n.d.); *Gai-Pied Hebdo: Guide 86/87* (Paris, 1987).

38 Mark Blasius, 'Interview: Guy Hocquenghem,' *Christopher Street*, April 1980, 36.

39 Alain Prigent, *La Réhabilitation du Marais de Paris* (unpublished study for the École des Hautes Études en Sciences Sociales, Paris, Nov. 1980), 96.

40 Author's interview with Joël Leroux, owner of Le Village and Le Duplex, July 1997.

41 'Le Central,' *5 sur 5* 4 (Dec. 1983), 7.

42 Audrey Coz, 'Fabrice Emaer du 7 au Palace,' *Gai Pied*, Oct. 1980, 13.

43 Philippe Baverel, 'Le Drapeau gay flotte rue Sainte-Croix-de-la-Bretonnerie,' *Le Monde*, 22 June 1996, 11.

44 Claire Ulrich, 'Le Marais, quartier général du lobby homosexuel,' *L'Événement du jeudi*, 20/26 June 1996, 28–9.

45 Alex Taylor, 'A Gay's Gaze,' *5 sur 5* 20 (April 1985), 54–5.

46 Tim Madesclaire, 'Le Ghetto gay, en être ou pas?,' *Illico*, Aug. 1995, 48.

47 *Guide de Paris*, insert in *Gai Pied*, Aug. 1981.

48 'Micro-trottoir dans le Marais, rue Sainte-Croix de la Bretonnerie,' *Exit: Le Journal*, 21 July 1995, 8.

49 'Les policiers harcèlent les bars gays du Marais,' *Libération*, 18/19 June 1996.

50 Jean Le Bitoux, 'Marcher dans le gai Marais,' *La Revue h* 1 (Summer 1996), 50–1.

2 Moscow

Dan Healey

While going about her duties one summer evening in 1955, Tatiana Aleksandrova, a railway guard, noticed two males 'writhing' by the side of the tracks not far from Moscow's Kazan' Station. She sought a policeman and when they returned they found Mikhail Pokrovskii, 47, engaged in sexual intercourse with 16-year-old Sasha Borisov. Both men were found lying on their sides, with Sasha's back to Mikhail, their trousers round their knees. Tatiana testified she saw the older man's penis in the anus of the youth. That night in Moscow's police station No. 68, Pokrovskii and Borisov gave contradictory accounts of themselves.[1]

From the moment of arrest, the young man began loudly protesting his innocence, claiming he had been 'raped' by Pokrovskii. At the police station, he said he had met the older man at a beer kiosk near the railway, where Pokrovskii sexually propositioned him with an offer of 1 ruble. Borisov told police he walked with the older man along the tracks to a deserted spot. He admitted he allowed himself to be fellated, penetrated anally, and masturbated to orgasm, before being disturbed by Aleksandrova and the policeman. Pokrovskii meanwhile claimed he was merely sitting with the youth when they were arrested. A married man, he had been drinking vodka with two companions when the youth joined them. The lad allegedly offered the drinkers the use of a tumbler in exchange for the redeemable vodka bottle, once they had drained it. The transaction was agreed, the vodka drunk, and Pokrovskii's two drinking buddies then left. Pokrovskii denied any sexual act had been committed.[2]

Judging the 'truth' of these two conflicting claims from the handwritten, tattered file recording the criminal investigation, trial and appeal, all swiftly concluded within two months of the offense, is virtually impossible.[3] Yet in many details, this obscure case neatly encapsulates the experience of men who sought sexual contact with other males in Moscow from the seventeenth century to the present day. Men's sexual misconduct was frequently associated with the consumption of alcohol, and, indeed, vodka provided not only an opportunity to socialize, but an excuse for whatever misdeeds might ensue. Sexual relations between males were also inflected by social hierarchies. Age, relative strength, wealth or command of resources determined the forms of exchange which accompanied sexual intercourse (if not always who performed insertive or receptive roles). The vexed question of where Muscovites of all sexual proclivities were able to make love is also laconically evident in this sodomy trial. None of the authorities associated with the case was surprised by the commission of sexual acts out of doors, in an ostensibly public place. As we shall see, for a significant proportion of the city's population, heterosexual as well as homosexual, public sex was a familiar experience. In tsarist Moscow private space for the poor had always been at a premium, while in the Soviet era, domestic space for all was squeezed by unprecedented pressures. In such conditions, Muscovites were accustomed to appropriating public spaces, and constructing privacy in them through various devices. The city's gay male subculture today, characterized by alcohol abuse, great social and economic disparities, and a habit of discreet public contact, is not the result of a sudden change of regime in 1991, although this circumstance certainly has contributed much. (Excellent introductions to Russia's gay male culture in English are Tuller 1996 and Moss (ed.) 1996.) It is rather the product of several centuries of evolution and, as might be expected, it reflects the history of Moscow's society and culture at large.

Moscow 1600–1861: traditional masculinities and love between men

The relative paucity of sources on everyday life in early modern Moscow, the difficulties in gaining access to those held in the old USSR, and historians' conservatism, dictate that our knowledge of sexuality in Russia before this century is modest, compared to what we know about Western Europeans. A handful of Western works examine same-sex love in medieval and early modern Russia, using religious texts and foreigners' accounts of travels to Moscow. On all aspects of sexuality much is to be found in Levin (1989). Karlinsky (1976, 1989) wrote landmark articles on Russian homosexuality and culture. New American and Russian research on sanctified unions between persons of the same sex can also provide clues to the status of same-sex love in early Russia (Boswell 1994; Gromyko 1986). In the absence of more precise data about our subject from 1600 to 1861, a picture of masculine mentalities can at least be sketched as a means to understanding later developments and their differences from Western European experience.

Until some time into the nineteenth century, it appears that masculine norms for the majority of Russians (i.e. peasants and lower orders of townsmen) included permission for some forms of same-sex erotic contact. There was no 'homosexual identity' discernible among a subset of Muscovite men, much less a corresponding subculture. Instead, 'sin' with boys or men was celebrated in the general male culture through bawdy stories and praise for the sinner, and justified by the immoderate consumption of alcohol. Europeans in Muscovy in the sixteenth and seventeenth centuries commented on the prevalence and acceptance of sex between males they observed, noting that married men of many classes, under the all-forgiving influence of drink, might prefer other males to their wives as sexual partners. Karlinsky (1976: 1; 1989: 348 n. 3) discusses such reports as does Kozlovskii (1986: 20–1. Westerners' accounts of sexual disorder they encountered elsewhere in this period, in the Americas, Asia and Islamic societies, often noted critically the practice of 'sodomy' in native populations, and such reports must be treated cautiously as sources on actual customs (Bleys 1995: 18–22). Yet Moscow, on the fringe of Christendom, represented a border zone between supposed 'barbarity' and 'civilization,' and travellers' accounts of Muscovite 'sodomy' could resemble condemnations of the vice internal to European societies. Adam Olearius, a diplomatic secretary, visited Moscow four times from Holstein between 1633 and 1643, and his comments on 'sodomy' during these years are revealing:

> they speak of debauchery, of vile depravity, of lasciviousness, and of immoral conduct committed by themselves and others. They tell all sorts of shameless fables, and he who can relate the coarsest obscenities and inde-cencies, accompanied by the most wanton mimickry, is accounted the best companion and is the most sought after...
>
> So given are they to the lusts of the flesh and fornication that some are addicted to the vile depravity we call sodomy; and not only with boys...but also with men and horses. Such antics provide matter for conversation at their carouses. People caught in such obscene acts are not severely punished. Tavern musicians often sing of such loathsome things too, in the open streets, while some show them to young people in puppet shows.
>
> (Baron 1967: 142)

Olearius' description conveys accurate information about popular culture in seventeenth-century Muscovy. The introduction of 'sodomy' into the text is clearly a device to distinguish European readers from the Muscovites, yet it is integral to a description of a coherent popular culture. Sex between males in Muscovy appears to have been, at least on a plebeian level, scarcely a sin 'not to be named,' but an aspect of male sociability lightly proscribed and effectively protected by a double standard.

One of Russia's most cherished national institutions, the bath-house, which by the late nineteenth century had become a significant locus of male prostitu-tion in Russian cities, was a probable site for sexual indulgence between men at an earlier period. The first commercial baths appeared in Moscow in the seven-teenth century and the state mandated that the sexes should be scrupulously segregated (Biriukov 1991: 17; Rubinov 1990: 19). Authorities vary on how rigorously segregation was observed, and on whether the baths represented a desexualized space in Russian culture. Levin (1989: 195–7) concludes the Russian baths were desexualized space, although foreigners' accounts contradict this picture of decorum, suggesting that in peasant villages and disreputable establishments in towns the sexes mixed freely (Grève 1990: 948–54). Separate steam rooms for men and women created a homosocial environment which certainly contributed to the evolution of bath-house male prostitution in a later era. A seventeenth-century miniature illustrating a visit by bearded, mature males to the baths shows four beardless, youthful males serving them.[4] One youth, in trousers, removes an older man's boots; another trousered lad draws water from a well. A naked young man pours water on the stove to produce steam, as another, also unclothed, beats a bearded older visitor, lying nude on a bench, with a leafy switch. While there is no intimation of sexual acts in the illustration, the young men's subordinate social position in their roles as servitors is emphasized by their beardlessness. Clerics, for example the fifteenth-century Metropolitan Daniil, and later archpriest Avvakum, condemned men who shaved off their beards as inciting immorality, apparently because smooth faces were an invitation to sodomy (Kozlovskii 1986: 21). Russian men adopted shaving from the West in the seventeenth century. With the growth of commercial relations in the eighteenth century, youths appear to have sought out careers in Moscow's public bath-houses. A group of 16-year-old peasant males apprehended entering the city in 1745 claimed they came to seek work in commercial baths.[5] Moscow's spas, staffed by beardless youths, may have been sites of mutual male sexual relations long before the recorded instances of the nineteenth century, to which we will return.

The apparent indulgence of same-sex relations does not mean that there were no countervailing cultural norms. Religious prohibitions existed, but were never as harsh as Roman Catholic ones. Russian Orthodox authorities preserved a vague definition of 'sodomy' as any 'unnatural' sexual act, with man, woman or beast, well into the seventeenth century. Penances were lighter than those for rape and adultery (Levin 1989: 197–203). The intensification of contact with the West in that era brought new attitudes which altered some aspects of elite strictures on male same-sex relations.

John Boswell (1994) discussed the widespread observance of rites of bonding between persons of the same sex in early Christian liturgy. The 'same-sex union,' known in modern Russian as *pobratimstvo* ('making brothers' might accurately render the sense of this term), was part of the Christian heritage Russia shared with Europe. Such services of union were expunged from the Roman Catholic liturgy in a systematic fashion after the twelfth century, leaving only vestigial documentation. There were female ceremonies as well (Boswell 1994: 19–20, 264). Boswell said little about the later fate of *pobratimstvo* in Russia. These rituals survived as officially approved offices in Russian Orthodox liturgical texts until the mid-seventeenth century. Unions of two men or two women of this kind when solemnized by the Church were 'almost on the same level with blood relations (*rodstvo*) and served to some degree as a barrier to marriage' between families; and prayerbooks carried advice about mixing bloodlines created by *pobratimstvo*, marriage pledges, and godparenting.[6] Canon law revisions of the mid-1600s saw the first prohibitions of ceremonies of 'making brothers' under reformer Patriarch Nikon (Gromyko 1986: 81). But popular versions of the ceremony were observed around rural Russia until approximately the 1880s. The exchange of crosses worn on the body was very common; other rites included swearing vows in church before a revered icon, or in a field facing toward the east (Gromyko 1986: 81–2).

Any possible erotic element in these unions remains a subject of speculation

(Boswell 1994: 267–79). Gromyko wrote of the depth of emotional and material support offered by *pobratimstvo* but it would have been politically impossible for her 1986 monograph to address homosexuality directly (chapter 2, passim.); she noted one instance of denial of erotic content in these unions, from a female late-tsarist ethnographer (Gromyko 1986: 86). The two cultural traditions, an indulgence of male lust for boys or other men, and a religious and popular custom of male pair-bonding, *could* have overlapped to create a space for emotional and sexual relations between men. Yet the two cultural traditions were not identical. Male sexual adventuring reflected Moscow's hierarchical society; much of the mirth generated by tales of 'sodomy' was evoked by the inversions of popular and religious notions of order they retailed (Levin 1989: 199–203). Such inversions in Russian popular culture have been discussed by Peter Burke (1978: 214). Sexual relations between males reflected the forms of domination and submission prevalent in Muscovite society. *Pobratimstvo*, on the other hand, emphasized loyalty and particularly friendship, 'brotherly love and devotion.' The bond has frequently been presented as a matter of mutual aid and emotional intimacy. Nineteenth-century observers reported pairings between peasant males of the same occupation, especially where distance from home and the dangers of a livelihood made pacts of mutual assistance prudent (Gromyko 1986: 82, 86–7). The two traditions organized different elements of everyday life – lust on the one hand, and personal survival and mutual comfort on the other – and reading into them modern notions of companionate marriage distorts our understanding of their place in Muscovite mentalities. Boswell's 1994 monograph on 'same-sex unions,' because of its vast temporal and geographic sweep, obscures the differences between local practice and the continuity of a specific liturgical rite; his argument that these unions often had erotic content is a speculative hypothesis at best.

These traditions were disrupted by the cultural division which began with the westernizing rule of Peter the Great (1689–1725). As nobles adopted European dress and mores during the eighteenth century, peasants retained older folkways. Enlightenment ideas on relations between the sexes, and the Europeans who came to teach, practice technical professions and serve what became in Peter's reign the imperial court and state, infused new attitudes toward the erotic, including a novel stigmatization of 'sodomy' (Healey 1993: 28). Sex between men in the remodeled military was criminalized, and while indulgence of such relations beyond the army and navy doubtless continued, occasional attempts to impose 'civilized' norms by condemning sodomy in elite circles can be observed (Costlow *et al.* 1993). Sanctions for improprieties with imperial choirboys were enunciated (Maroger 1955: 193). Moscow ceased to be the capital of Russia, and the transfer of power to the 'window on the West,' St Petersburg (founded 1703), introduced another division in Russian culture, between the 'old,' Muscovite, capital, where traditional ways were thought to persist, and the 'new' city of Peter, a center of wealth and European influence. Moscow's eclipse as capital until 1917 rendered the forms of same-sex love observed there perhaps less Western, less 'modern,' than those found in its glittering rival.

Popular *pobratimstvo* declined during the eighteenth and nineteenth centuries among settled urban dwellers, while it probably persisted among peasants who migrated to Moscow for seasonal labor. Meanwhile, in elite culture, the adoption of Western codes of morality followed at an accelerating rate, and in 1835 'sodomy' between males was formally criminalized for all parts of Russian society, in legislation enacted by Nicholas I. Indulgence of male-to-male lust apparently continued, since few cases of sodomy were actually formally prosecuted (Healey, 1993: 28).

Moscow 1861–1917: the appearance of a homosexual subculture

The late tsarist decades were a period of rapid social transformation, and as might be expected, Moscow shared in that change. In 1861, when the Emancipation Edict freed the serfs, there were 350,000 inhabitants in the old capital. By the 1880s and 1890s, a national policy of industrialization had transformed Moscow into a major manufacturing center and transport hub. Meanwhile, much production continued in workshops, often extended households with apprentice boys. To be an apprentice, in the language of the day, was to be 'in the boys' (*v mal'chikakh*). Industrial districts began to develop beyond the city's traditional limits, while more peasants came from the countryside to stay and an urban working class emerged. By 1914, the population of Moscow had reached 1.4 million.

The character of same-sex erotic relations underwent associated transformations. We notice an increase in sources on same-sex love, logical given that eros in general was receiving greater attention. Diaries, criminal court records and medical texts now began to speak about love between men, and these are only beginning to be exploited by historians. The continuing inflection of sexual relations by social ones took on new forms as market relations mixed with traditional patterns. Finally, in Russia's cities, gathering places appeared where individuals who felt desire for their own sex began to recognize each other and create a subculture.

The transitional mentality characteristic of the era is illustrated in the attitudes of a Moscow merchant from the peasant estate, Pavel Vasil'evich Medved'ev, whose diary of the year 1861 describes his emotional and spiritual inner world.[7] Unhappily married, Medved'ev sought consolation alternately in church and at the tavern. When drunk, he indulged in 'lustfulness' with both male and female partners – and recorded these encounters in his diary. This document reveals a male homosocial culture, indulgent of sex between men, reminiscent of that witnessed by foreign visitors two centuries before. Yet at the same time, in the commercialization of Medved'ev's sexual encounters, and their location outside the home, we can also discern the seeds of a transition to a 'modern' homosexual subculture.

When aroused, Medved'ev and his companions were apparently indifferent to the sex of potential sexual partners. While walking one June day to Sokol'niki (a park beyond Moscow's Garden Ring) with his wife and a male friend, he quarreled with his wife and she abandoned them. Medved'ev wrote of his emotions:

> And so with annoyed vexation Sinitsyn and I continued walking along the railway line, and the desire to drink and give myself up to debauchery took shape in me, there appeared a disturbing desire to have a woman or a man for onanism, '*kulizm*,' anything...[8]

Eventually, Medved'ev got drunk with Sinitsyn, meanwhile trying to 'prepare' his companion for mutual masturbation or anal intercourse by encouraging him to talk about his own fantasies. Sinitsyn was at first unresponsive, and so they visited a 'den' of women prostitutes (referred to as 'camellias'). There, they discovered that all the women were 'busy' – and drunkenly, Sinitsyn agreed to Medved'ev's proposition, declaring spontaneously in the street 'Let's f—— each other!' They found a deserted spot in Sokol'niki and set about trying to 'produce lust' – falling asleep, dead drunk, in the mud before their tryst could be consummated.

Medved'ev and his companions habitually used subordinate males for sex when lust was unleashed by vodka. An account of an evening of theater, dining and drinking 'to excess' ended with Medved'ev's reflections on how to satisfy one's arousal on the journey homeward:

> For some time now my lust leads me to pick a younger cab-driver, who I make fun of along the way; with a little nonsense you can enjoy mutual masturbation. You can almost always succeed with a 50-kopek coin, or 30 kopeks, but there are also those who agree to it for pleasure. That's five times this month.[9]

Cab-drivers who supplemented their income (or simply took pleasure) in this fashion are not unusual characters in Russian legal and psychiatric literature of the era (Tarnovskii 1885: 69–71).[10] Coachmen were not alone among male servants willing to service male employers sexually. From medical reports we can observe that youths and young men profited in this fashion as waiters, household staff and as simple soldiers or officers' servants.[11] It is not always possible to gauge whether subordinates were motivated solely by incentives of money and advancement, but the easy willingness of Russia's urban serving classes to tolerate 'gentlemen's mischief' as they were said to call it (Tarnovskii 1885: 70) suggests continuities with an earlier indulgence of mutual male relations.

In workshops, apprentice boys were the object of sexual advances or assaults by older males, often in positions of authority over them. Medved'ev confessed to his diary that he repeatedly masturbated with a member of his large household, a 'boy' of 18 – an apprentice or servant – who 'satisfied me according to my desire with manual onanism, and I did the same for him.'[12] Medved'ev consoled his religious anxieties by writing that the youth enjoyed their encounters, arguing he was old enough to know what he wanted. Court records of male rapes in Moscow workshops demonstrate a similar if more violent pattern of relations. In one 1874 trial, the 17-year-old rapist was the son of the workshop's owner, and the court reacted sternly to his assault on an 11-year-old apprentice. In another case in 1892 a more indulgent attitude prevailed, because the alleged rapist was himself a subordinate within the workshop, and because the 13-year-old youth was perceived as nearly fully grown and capable of looking out for himself.[13]

Bath-house attendants, whose age and status probably made them objects of sexual commerce in an earlier era, appear in a range of sources from the late tsarist years as homosexual prostitutes. Pavel Medved'ev wrote of a visit with an old drinking buddy to an unnamed Moscow bath-house, where they found 'onanism and *kulizm*' awaiting them, in 1861.[14] Few references to this trade in Moscow appear in forensic texts or the city court records, but there are enough discussions of the phenomenon in St Petersburg baths to suggest that what Medved'ev encountered at the bath-house in Moscow persisted and flourished until the 1917 revolution. In one 1866 St Petersburg sodomy trial, a young peasant told of finding work in an upper-class bath with private rooms, where another lad from his village was already an attendant. The young man's testimony reveals a high degree of indulgence of clients' tastes without regard to sexual object choice:

> [the client] lies with me like with a woman, or orders me to do with him as with a woman, only in the anus, or else [he is] leaning forward and lying on his chest, and I [get] on top of him, all of which I did. Besides all this, other visitors to the baths demanded that we bring them a woman from a public house; they would first make me do the deed (copulate) with her, while they watched, then they would use the woman in front of me.
>
> (Merzheevskii 1878: 239)

These attendants earned about 1 ruble for each session of 'sodomy' they provided. Petersburg bath-houses were noted in professional and later popular texts as places where 'pederastic' prostitution flourished. Blackmailers exploited the bath as a site for shaking down victims (Merzheevskii 1878: 252; Koni 1912: 152–6); psychiatric patients reported discovering their sex inclinations with the help of bath-house attendants (Bekhterev 1898: 1–11); eventually, social critics bemoaned the existence of such male brothels (Matiushenskii 1908; Ruadze 1908), while foreign homosexual advocates sang their praises (Mayne ?1908: 431).

The records of a case against a Bishop Palladii in 1919 indicate that homosexual practices in spas, especially ones with private rooms, were notorious in Moscow as well. This cleric was accused of 'pederasty' with a monastic novice of 14 who served as his servant, Ivan Volkov. Twice the bishop testified that while they had indeed been to 'public' baths or the baths for the upper clergy in Moscow, he specifically insisted he had never taken the novice to baths with private rooms. He said 'it was the custom that two boys went with me, to allay the suspicions of bystanders.'[15] The allegation that he had been to different bath-houses with Volkov and other novices was perceived as damaging, and the notoriety of baths with private rooms in Moscow was sufficiently widespread to move Palladii to repeated denials.

A most significant development in the emergence of a homosexual subculture in Moscow was the arrival of patterns of street cruising, with the mutual recognition and communication beyond workplace and client–patron relations this implied. Also increasingly evident is the use of public space not merely for socializing, but for sex as well. Sources for these patterns are again more modest for Moscow than St Petersburg, and suggest a slower evolution toward 'modern' homosexual behaviors. Medved'ev's 1861 diary made no mention of cruising or male prostitution in the streets (as in European capitals); meanwhile public cruising, male prostitution and sex were already part of the St Petersburg streetscape. Well-to-do individuals such as the composer Peter Tchaikovsky found lower-class sexual contacts in Moscow among servants or through louche friends, rather than risk scandal through direct cruising. In 1878, Tchaikovsky wrote to his homosexual brother Modest, describing how a friend Nikolai Bochechkarov introduced him to a young butler. The three met on the boulevard, went to a pub, and an 'infatuated' Tchaikovsky took the butler to a private room (Poznansky 1996: 19).

An example of a Moscow street pick-up comes from an 1888 sodomy trial of 42-year-old Petr Mamaev. Mamaev was apprehended after a drunken scuffle with Nikolai Agapov, 28, on Prechistenskii Boulevard on the night of 29 July 1888. The older man claimed he had committed sodomy with Agapov on the boulevard and admitted that he had picked up strange men for this purpose on city boulevards for the previous eight years. Medical examinations of the men convinced investigators that Mamaev was a 'passive pederast,' while Agapov was released, since he bore none of the supposed signs of active pederasty. Married with two sons, but with his family living in distant Ekaterinburg, Mamaev described his sexual habits thus:

> For the past eight years I have been committing sodomy with different, unknown persons. I go out to the boulevard at night, strike up a conversation, and if I find a lover (*liubitel'*), then I do it with him. I cannot identify who I did it with…. I attempted to do just the same with Agapov, without money, without any exchange of money in mind, just to obtain pleasure for myself and for him.[16]

Mamaev was able to find 'lovers' on the boulevard who shared his aim of pleasure without necessarily requiring payment for a service, an indication that like-minded individuals might recognize each other and even use public space to consummate their desires.

Rather later, in 1912, the same Moscow boulevard was the scene of a formative encounter for Pavel, a 17-year-old peasant newly arrived from Smolensk province. The story of this youth's progress through the 'homosexual world' before and after the 1917 revolution was described by psychiatrist V.A. Belousov in 1927, as a case history of 'male prostitution' in a 'psychopathic' individual.

Forced to leave home after compromising sexual misadventures, Pavel found employment through a woman from his own village who was resident in Moscow. While working as an apprentice at the 'Nature and School' shop, he began to attend night courses for workers. Coming home in the evening after classes along Prechistenskii and Nikitskii Boulevards, he met 'his own people' and 'many acquaintances appeared.' He began to have sexual relations with these men, and found himself drawn to loiter on these boulevards every night – 'it was boring to stay at home.' Pavel soon met Prince Feliks Feliksovich Iusupov and they had a sexual liaison intermittently over the following two years. Pavel joined the prince's household service as a lackey 'in order to deflect the suspicions of the prince's wife.' Iusupov reportedly kept two other male servants, a cook and a coachman, as sexual partners.[17]

Pavel recalled the two years before the Great War as 'a marvellous time,' when first Iusupov then a second wealthy sponsor showered him with money and presents. Pavel also described to his psychiatrist aspects of the homosexual subculture of that time. He attended 'balls of women-haters' (*zhenonenavistniki*) in drag as an Ukrainian woman; to avert the attention of the suspicious, 'lesbian-prostitutes' were invited to come along, but 'we weren't bashful around them.' A beer-hall near Nikitskie Gates was run by an 'auntie' (*tetka*), an older homosexual man, and there was a special room there 'with an electric organ,' where only 'our kind' were admitted and where dancing was permitted.[18] When he wasn't staying with the prince, he would pick up a variety of men for sex, claiming to his psychiatrist (who did not believe him) that he did this without mercenary motives. He said he would take home beggars, give them a bath and

Figure 2.1 Nikitskie Gates, a square on the Boulevard Ring notorious as a haunt of homosexuals. Behind the monument were underground public facilities where men had sex together during the 1920s and 1930s.
Source: Photo undated, late 1920s; D. Healey collection.

Figure 2.2 Arbat Square on the Boulevard Ring, *c.* 1930. In the foreground of the photograph is the start of Prechistevskii Boulevard where the young peasant Pavel met his first homosexual contacts upon arrival in Moscow in 1912.
Source: D. Healey Collection.

make them stay the night; he also loved soldiers, and cruising public pissoirs and baths. When Pavel lived with Prince Iusupov, he was not permitted to 'loaf about' in the street, perhaps with good reason, for he had a sharp nose for finding Moscow's homosexual street life of the day.

Pavel's account of Moscow's male homosexual subculture on the eve of the Great War and the 1917 revolution catalogues the transformation of mutual male erotic relations and the social practices which grew up around them. The contrasts and continuities with Medved'ev's world are instructive. Instead of a sexual identity based on a sinful but unavoidable male lust to be satisfied with either woman or man, Pavel's world included men who identified themselves as exclusively attracted to their own sex (the so-called 'women-haters'). Others, like Prince Iusupov, indulged themselves with both men and women, and still others, perhaps from poverty, confined the homosexual element of their lives to a subculture of the streets (for example, the tramps and soldiers Pavel picked up, or the men he cruised in public toilets). Yet a new group of 'our people' also appeared in Pavel's account, and they had ways of recognizing each other on the boulevard (argot, gesture and dress were among the signs they used, to judge from criminological comments about male prostitutes). Moreover, they congregated in notorious public locations to socialize and have sex. New commercialized spaces for the subculture (balls organized by 'their own kind,' a beer-hall with music and dancing) reflected the growing intrusion of the market even into highly specialized leisure activities. Despite these changes, as in Medved'ev's time, same-sex relations continued to reflect social hierarchies, and the cash-for-sex exchange (and its non-monetary variations) remained a prominent part of everyday life for both the affluent and the indigent.

Moscow 1917–91: carving privacy from communal space

The World War, revolution and then civil war brought sweeping and devastating change to Moscow in the years between 1914 and 1921. Combat, epidemics, migration and starvation decimated the urban population, and from a 1917 high of 1.9 million, the city's inhabitants dropped to only 1 million in 1921. An important factor for the future of the city's homosexual subculture was the government's move from Petrograd to Moscow in 1918.[19] This shift brought diplomatic and administrative personnel to the Soviet capital and also contributed to its artistic life. The arts, as we shall see, were to become a refuge for male homosexuals in the Soviet era.

As would be expected, the social and political realignments of the first socialist state greatly affected the lives of Moscow's homosexuals. Revolution brought pluses and minuses for them. On the one hand, formal legalization of sodomy between consenting adults came with the first Bolshevik criminal code (1922), and this along with marriage, divorce and abortion legislation was heralded as the most radical sex reform in Europe (Healey 1993: 37). Yet the regime's instrumental view of law, and frank embrace of terror, meant political campaigns (especially in the 1930s, during the first Five Year Plans) could overwhelm mere legislation. More pervasive perhaps was the effect of the new government's economic policies on everyday life. A culture of shortages and exchange through informal and illegal networks evolved, re-casting human relationships in ways unintended by economic and social planners. Also unanticipated were the effects of socialized housing and the elimination of private space on the human need for intimacy.

Sources for Moscow's male homosexual subculture in the 1920s and early 1930s are scant. With sodomy legalized from 1922 until 1934, formal court records hold less information than in previous and subsequent periods of criminalization. The psychiatric literature of the 1920s presents a shift of interest away from male homosexuality toward lesbianism, leaving us with fewer sources on men's same-sex relations for the entire decade.[20] The male prostitute Pavel, described by Dr Belousov in 1927, remains our richest informant on Moscow's homosexual subculture for the 1920s. His testimony may be compared with data drawn from 1930s sodomy trial records held in Moscow's municipal archive.[21]

Pavel reported that in the post-revolutionary era, the Boulevard Ring remained the focal point for meeting and socializing between homosexual men. Apart from factors affecting housing opportunities, to which we shall return, the street setting in itself had considerable logic. This ring of connected boulevards (each with its own name) surrounded the heart of Moscow in a semi-circular band of greenery dotted with shrubs, benches and small kiosks selling newspapers and refreshments. There were also public pissoirs and toilets. Ideally situated to become the arena for a male homosexual subculture, boulevards provided pleasant places to sit, smoke and converse; there was a constant circulation of pedestrians; links with public transport made them accessible. The boulevards were but a few minutes' walk to Moscow's greater and lesser theaters, to the Conservatory, and to shops and department stores. Pavel quite accurately noted, 'You can find and meet men on any boulevard.'

Parts of the Boulevard Ring also had a seedy reputation as the main centers of female prostitution, and, as in European and American centers, there was often a sharing of urban territories between public women and male homosexuals. Tsvetnoi Boulevard and adjoining Trubnaia Square were dubbed by two 1923 critics 'the classic centers of Moscow prostitution.' In that year they observed how organized 'professional' women sold themselves on the boulevard and consummated their liaisons in private rooms, usually rented out by older women, in the side-streets off these thoroughfares.[22] Meanwhile the boulevards near Trubnaia Square were becoming homosexual haunts, as would the nearby Ermitazh Park and Trubnaia's public toilets by the mid-1930s.

The specific stretches of the Boulevard Ring which homosexuals frequented seem to have changed little during the 1920s and 1930s, to judge from Pavel's remarks and the 1930s court records. The stretches of Nikitskii Boulevard leading to Moscow's 'most important "den",' the square known as Nikitskie Gates, were singled out by the male prostitute; the memoirs of Yugoslavian communist Anton Ciliga, also name this square as the site of a 'secret market' of homosexual men in the late 1920s (Ciliga 1979: 67). In a trial of three young men in 1941, contacts were said to have been made on Nikitskii Boulevard and on Trubnaia Square and the adjoining boulevards. One of the three men explained during his interrogation: 'In 1936 in the apartment where I lived, Afanas'ev, an artist of the ballet, moved in…. He showed me the places where pederasts meet: Nikitskii Boulevard and Trubnaia Square.' Not long after this friendship began, the dancer was convicted for sodomy while on tour in Irkutsk in Siberia. During interrogation, another defendant in this case related how 'Sasha told me that the chief places for pederasts were Nikitskii Boulevard, Trubnaia [Square], a bar on Arbat [Street], and the Tsentral'nye Baths.' He was speaking of the early 1930s.[23]

Sretenskii and Chistoprudnyi Boulevards were also mentioned by the ex-prostitute Pavel as places where 'an especially important public' among Moscow's homosexuals gathered and made assignations.[24] In a 1935 sodomy trial, Sretenskii Boulevard was mentioned as a meeting place and as a possible trysting ground too. Thus in its sentence a municipal court noted that '[the accused] met by chance on Sretenskii and other boulevards of the city of Moscow with men-pederasts [*muzhshchiny-pederasty*], and entered into sexual intercourse with them in toilets, in apartments and on the boulevards….'[25] Other places mentioned in the trials include Manezh Square and nearby Sverdlov Square, located in front of the Bol'shoi Theater in the heart of the city.

Public toilets were noted by Russian psychiatrists as places of male homo-sexual contact from the late nineteenth century. In the early Soviet period, many venues for meeting, such as bath-houses or sympathetic bars, were nationalized and consequently grew less likely to function as homosexual gathering points or havens for same-sex prostitution. Locations for 'balls of women-haters,' or even homosexual poetry readings, hired in the past in private transactions, were now controlled by government functionaries hostile to displays of disorder. The public toilet thus took on a new significance for the male homosexual world. Dr Belousov reports that Pavel observed, 'Now, after the revolution meetings in toilets have become the most predominant [means of contact].' The male prosti-tute's description of the toilet in the cinema 'Maiak' in Khar'kov in the 1920s, as 'particularly convenient,' betrays an awareness of the perverse applications of such architectural accidents.[26] The revolution, by virtually eliminating commodi-fied indoor space available for private rental and enjoyment, relegated male homosexuals to a 'culture of the toilet.'

In the sodomy cases from the 1930s various toilets betray their reputations: the most important one in the decade, it seems, was on Trubnaia Square. This facility was constructed underground in the shape of a circle, with the stalls against the perimeter wall, facing inward. There were no doors on the stalls, which had simple holes in the floor.[27] All users were in a position to observe each other, and this perverse panopticism apparently enabled as many meetings as it prevented. One defendant investigated for sodomy in 1941 described his discovery of this facility:

> Once in autumn 1940 I left a restaurant on Tsvetnoi Boulevard and was walking toward my apartment on Neglinnaia Street. On the way I stopped in the toilet on Trubnaia Square and there, against my will, an act of sodomy was committed with me. A man came up to me and began to masturbate, touching my penis. I did not particularly object. A month and a half after this I once again went to the toilet on Trubnaia Square, but this time with the deliberate intention of committing an act of sodomy. In this manner I committed acts of sodomy about five or six times…[28]

Sometimes, this man invited partners home to sleep overnight with him; others he had sex with then and there. He claimed to police that his loneliness drove him to drink, and it was only the alcohol that was responsible for his cruising in the toilet – not his desire for company.

The public toilet remained a focal point for Muscovite gay lives after World War II, when more efficient enforcement of the sodomy statute raised the number of convictions from 130 in 1950 for the entire Russian Soviet Federated Socialist Republic to 464 in 1961 and 854 in 1971.[29] Facilities in the heart of the city, near major department stores, railway stations and in Aleksandrovskii Gardens by the Kremlin wall, were well known to homosexuals, police and the KGB, and entrapment was common.[30]

In the handful of post-1945 sodomy trials preserved in the open sector of

Moscow's municipal archive, one unveils something of the 'culture of the toilet' – and in an outrageous location. In 1955, two young men met and attempted to have sex in the very center of Moscow. Klimov, a 27-year-old stoker at a Moscow railway depot, who commuted to work from an outlying settlement, related in his interrogation:

> I came from the village to Moscow, and I was looking for food in GUM [Department Store on Red Square], when during that time I went to the men's toilet. In the toilet a young lad came up to me, shook my hand and said let's get acquainted. He was called Volodia, and he said to me 'Let's go over to the Lenin Museum....' I went with him to the Lenin Museum, he bought the entrance tickets with his money, and we went straight to the men's toilet. He began to grope me, he grabbed me by the penis, held it for some time, but just then some strangers came in and disturbed us and we left the Lenin Museum.[31]

The pair agreed to another rendezvous, but Klimov, apparently unnerved by city-dweller 'Volodia's' bold ways, did not keep the date. Nevertheless, some three weeks later in the GUM department store toilet, Klimov and 'Volodia' chanced to meet, and this time they took the metro to Sokol'niki Park, where they made love in a secluded wooded spot.[32]

The men's toilet in the Lenin Museum surfaces some twenty-five years later in a memoir written by a lawyer who defended the ringleader of a gang of Moscow queerbashers in the late 1970s or early 1980s. The ringleader claimed he had been raped in this particular toilet and believed himself to be a 'fag' (*gomik*) (Kozlovskii 1986: 196–9). It is probable that facilities such as this one, the GUM department store toilets, and those in nearby Sapunov Lane and the Aleksandrovskii Gardens, remained points of contact for Moscow homosexuals, because of architectural features exploited by homosexuals to construct a ration of privacy. Their proximity to Sverdlov Square in front of the Bol'shoi Theater, a cruising ground from at least the mid-1930s, guaranteed a steady circulation of men seeking contacts. Homosexuals made creative use not only of the 'convenient' layouts of toilets, but of entire streetscapes between them, and by the 1970s observers spoke of a periodically shifting 'route,' a kind of gay promenade between the Bol'shoi Theater and Nogin (now Old) Square (Kozlovskii 1986: 54; Gessen 1990: 46–7).

If the garden in front of Russia's most famous theater was a constant on the homosexual map of mid-to-late twentieth-century Moscow, then other gathering spots in the vicinity appeared and disappeared over time. Cafés located near the Bol'shoi such as the 'Sadko' and 'Artisticheskoe,' with an apparently indifferent management, were meeting places in the 1970s and 1980s. Of the two nearby bath-houses, the Sandunovskie and the Tsentral'nye, the latter most often appears as a place where contacts were made (though not consummated) in this period. An anonymous writer 'G' reported queues for entry to the Tsentral'nye lasting for up to an hour ('G' 1980: 16).[33] An American reported in 1973 that

Pushkin Square (a favorite gathering place for dissidents of all stripes) and the lanes off Gor'kii Street (also close to the Bol'shoi) offered cruising possibilities, as did the more distant embankments at Gor'kii Park. Moscow University's riverside embankment, a hangout for youthful non-conformists, was another place to meet the sexually adventurous (Reeves 1973: 5–6). The instability of such cruising grounds was the result of more intense but episodic police and KGB surveillance, especially as dissident subcultures blossomed in the Brezhnev era. Another factor peculiar to Soviet society, the state ownership of even the smallest café or refreshment kiosk, made control over such sites unlikely for stigmatized groups, putting homosexuals who frequented such spots at the mercy of managerial whims and periodic clampdowns.

The single most significant cause of the resort to marginal communal space such as toilets, parks and the boulevards were domestic arrangements, and their peculiarities in the command economy. Homosexuals were often forced to seek privacy in public spaces because of the state's total control over housing, and the relatively low priority in the national economy which apartment construction commanded. The capital's housing shortage, and the types of housing available, produced a situation where the divisions between households were blurred. Moreover, the paltry rations of space between family members within households drove individuals who sought illicit sexual release out of their homes and into the streets.

After the 1917 revolution, most urban housing was nationalized and the 'communal' apartment was born. A flat in which an entire family would inhabit each room, the *kommunal'ka* often brought together dozens to share a single kitchen, toilet, bath and telephone. Soviet planners discarded the bourgeois household as the basic unit of domestic space, and thought in terms of a per capita entitlement to square footage, more amenable to collective living arrangements. It was also cheaper to build (Kotkin 1995: 158ff). Many pre-revolutionary tenement blocks in Russia's towns were converted to communal flats, and demand for this housing remained high since most of these blocks were located in city centers. The pressure on urban housing space was always great, but it intensified during the rapid industrialization of the Five Year Plans in the 1930s. Factories constructed their own housing, and placed favored workers in these blocks, while newcomers resorted to distant barracks and flop-houses. In Soviet towns, the average number of dwellers *per room* rose from 2.71 in 1926 to 3.91 in 1940 (Hoffmann 1994: 131–3, 139).

Privacy was therefore a luxury many were unable to achieve. Those who had access to housing in the capital took advantage of this scarce resource. Many Moscow sodomy cases of the 1935–41 period mention an exchange of accommodation for sex, usually in terms found in one 1935 trial. The defendant Bezborodov is said to have initiated a sexual liaison with one Timofenko in 1927, and 'using his dependent position,' offered him a place to live in exchange.[34] The nature of Timofenko's 'dependent position' is not explained, but usually this condition was either youth or being a newcomer to Moscow. Murav'ev, another man accused of sodomy the same year, met an unnamed visitor from Turkmenia on the tram in Moscow, and spent a day off showing him the sights of the capital. Murav'ev was said to have displayed 'particular zeal' in trying to find the Turkmen a place to live; he introduced him to a homosexual Communist Party member, Venediktov, who testified that the Turkmen immediately offered him sex, apparently in hopes of obtaining accommodation.[35]

A 1950 Moscow sodomy case illustrates the vulnerability of the domestic sphere in the communal flat which was a constant of Soviet lives.[36] Ivanov, a 50-year-old professor of Marxism-Leninism in a Moscow technical institute, was arrested after his wife, with whom he shared one room in a *kommunal'ka*, became fed up with his drunken carousing with men half his age. She did not put up with his disruptive behavior for long. In one statement to the police, she described how she watched her drunk husband and a man of about 25 'commit sexual acts' together in their room:

> [The younger man] undressed my husband and laid him on the bed. Then he got undressed and lay down with my husband. I demanded that he not get into bed with my husband, but he didn't listen. They both began to shout at me to get rid of me, but I stayed. [The young man] embraced my husband. The light in the room was on. Then they began to commit sexual acts…. I was indignant at this and pulled the sheet off them…my husband fell from the bed, but then he got up and started to swear at me. I took fright and called for our neighbor, Vera. She arrived when my husband and [the young man] were already up out of bed.[37]

Ivanov's wife did not call the police this time, but a later episode exhausted her patience. Police were summoned and caught Ivanov in bed with a 17-year-old youth. The neighbor Vera, a trusted Communist Party member, provided sharp-eyed reports of gossip against Ivanov in the communal kitchen, and an eye-witness account of his unmasking in bed with this friend.[38] The crowded world of the communal flat was dangerous territory for all sexual non-conformity, and drove illicit relationships out of the domestic sphere. A 1946 survey of 5,000 male clients of the capital's central VD clinic revealed that 75 per cent had met female sexual partners (previously unknown to them) on the streets or in theaters and restaurants; fully 30 per cent had sex with these women not 'in domestic circumstances' but 'on the street, in entrance halls to blocks of flats, in parks or automobiles.'[39] Homosexuals were not alone in constructing privacy out of public spaces for sexual purposes.

Although Moscow's housing stock expanded after World War II, so too did its population, reaching 9 million by the 1980s. The domestic situation of Sasha, a young homosexual met by Tom Reeves on the streets of the capital in the early 1970s, was typical. A student in his twenties, Sasha shared a two-room flat with his mother and sister; all three slept in the same room (Reeves 1973: 5). Reeves and Russian observers also reported encountering pockets of privilege. Dormitories at Moscow State University – a top institution of higher learning – had been alienated by non-conformists, the children of high officials, and among these Reeves found 'two suites of gay men' living among a larger grouping of artists and musicians, in a congenial version of communal domesticity. Parental connections were instrumental in obtaining self-contained flats for other fortunate gay men described in 1980 ('G' 1980: 18–20). Widespread overcrowding affected innumerable groups in Soviet society. Yet pervasive surveillance, whether by family, neighbors and inquisitive superintendents, or more formally by the police and KGB, rendered the home a desexualized space for all but the most resourceful of Moscow homosexuals (Gessen 1990: 46–7).[40]

If physical space was difficult for homosexuals to control in Soviet conditions, then at least one social 'space' offered the hope of respectability and even prestige. This important locus of Moscow's male homosexual subculture was the art world. Homosexuals believed with some justification that they were tolerated there, and they gravitated toward music, drama, dance, the visual arts and allied professions. Homosexual figures at the summit of Russia's artistic life have been well documented in English (Karlinsky 1976, 1982, 1989; Poznansky 1991, 1996; Moss 1996). Little has been said, however, about ordinary homosexuals and their use of the arts as a cloak of respectability in a society which assigned great prestige to official culture.

'*Antinoï*' (Antinous), a private arts circle devoted to the appreciation of 'male beauty' in prose, verse, drama and music, functioned in Moscow during the early 1920s, staging readings of consciously homosexual poetry, recitals of music by 'their' composers, and even an all-male ballet. The group made plans to publish an anthology of homosexual verse from ancient to modern times. The collection went unpublished, and our knowledge of the Antinoi group's activity begins and ends with correspondence relating to the Leningrad poet Mikhail Kuzmin's May 1924 reading to the group in the Blue Bird Café just steps from Tverskoi Boulevard. The group appears to have disbanded as it became more difficult to rent meeting space, or publicize its activities even by word of mouth.[41]

If private artistic action was politically dangerous, then official culture provided opportunities for homosexual men, and indeed would have been the poorer without them. Great talents such as Sergei Eisenstein and Sviatoslav Richter married to make their peace with an economy offering only one patron: the state (Karlinsky 1989: 361–2). Others did not always fare as well. Of the thirty-six individuals named in the Moscow sodomy trial documents for 1935–41, fully one-third were employed, or getting training, in the arts. A further four out of ten homosexuals briefly mentioned in the 1941 sodomy trial of students at the Moscow Glazunov Musical Theater College were cultural employees. Most of these men were dramatic actors, but there were dancers, a film executive, a pianist and a humble ticket-collector from a branch of the Bol'shoi Theater. One man even claimed to be a stage designer when he met boulevard pick-ups, according to the man whose testimony led to his arrest.[42] A student of the Musical Theater College, examined in court by his defense lawyer, explained that he deliberately sought out actors 'and wanted to work in the theater, because I engaged in that [sodomy].'[43]

The cultural world remained a haven for male homosexuals after World War

II, although the authorities' increased awareness of homosexuality in general meant that periodic prosecutions, centered on elite institutions and sometimes involving the sons of high officials, took place. Mosfilm Studios, the Moscow Conservatory of Music and Moscow State University were scenes of at least one sodomy scandal each in the 1950s through 1970s. Such scandals were normally hushed up and archival access to criminal records on them remains blocked.[44] A 1959 sodomy case against an instructor in the Moscow Conservatory was perhaps typical of these scandals. The teacher was accused of requiring sex from his male students in exchange for serious instruction from 1950 to 1959. When the son of a high Party member complained, about two dozen students signed a petition to the procuracy praising their instructor and demanding his release, on the grounds that Khrushchev's newly enunciated principles of socialist humanism dictated that individuals should not be prosecuted for such offenses. Nevertheless the instructor received a five-year prison sentence.[45] Despite these setbacks, some homosexuals interviewed in 1973 recalled the Khrushchev years of political 'thaw' as a time when the invigorated culture of jazz clubs and literary cafés brought fresh opportunities for gay men to meet and forge social networks (Reeves 1973: 6). Khrushchev's successors tried to force all non-conformism back into the closet. High-profile sodomy prosecutions of cultural and sexual dissidents took place, such as that of poet Gennadii Trifonov in 1976. Other homosexuals sought to lead their lives discreetly in the hopes of escaping official persecution. Some wrote honestly but 'for the desk drawer' (Evgenii Kharitonov's then unpublishable stories of gay experience were written in the 1970s), adopted false marriages or relied on friendship networks in the arts world for mutual support (Kozlovskii 1986: 187–95; Gessen 1990: 47; Moss, 1996: 196, 226–32).

Driven from communal domestic space and forced by the command economy to retreat from the once commodified spaces of bars, meeting halls and hotel rooms, Moscow homosexuals along with others who had illicit sex sought contacts – and consummation – in public space. For men who had sex with men, certain boulevards, parks and toilets became the chief zones where sexual release was possible. At times during the communist era, bath-house contacts and café or bar pick-ups were possible; but the subculture was not able to gain stable purchase on these now nationalized establishments. Homosexual desire, unacknowledged by the planned economy, led some men to appropriate and redefine public space to satisfy their own needs. Others sought respectability and perhaps an escape from the 'culture of the toilet' in the arts as a means of making contact with like-minded men. And there were those who inhabited both territories, crossing the boundary between respectability and illicit acts, some paying with harsh prison sentences when they were unmasked.

In the 1990s, gay men in Russia are enjoying a social and political 'thaw.' The emergence since 1991 of a small network of bars, dance clubs, publications and campaigning groups owes much to the end of Communist Party rule, the decriminalization of sodomy in 1993, and the arrival of foreign activism and money. As so often in Russia's past, a number of Western models (of gay liberation, of AIDS activism, of commercialized identities) compete for influence – but they do not confront a blank slate. An indigenous homosexual subculture has been an element of Russia's urban heritage for the past century, a reflection of the simultaneous 'modernization' or westernization of social relations, character-ized by lunges and lags in diverse fields (Engelstein 1993: 338–53). Russia's gays and lesbians are faced with appeals to 'come out' and to adopt identities that may not always make sense in a culture which seems almost Mediterranean in its respect for family and in its extreme patriarchalism (Tuller 1996).

At the heart of the evolution of Moscow's homosexual subculture lie the priv-ileges of masculinity in Russian culture. Overwhelmingly, homosexuals formed a *male* subculture. Women who loved women rarely took on an open, public role as 'lesbians' (Healey 1997: 83–106). Men's mobility, their relative freedom to earn a living, the drinking culture and the permissiveness conferred by vodka, and the licensing of heterosexual brothels between 1843 and 1917, were all elements of a masculine culture increasingly inflected by market relations. Traditional hierar-chies of age and social position within the homosocial world of men reproduced themselves in new forms during the nineteenth century, as men with experience, status and resources exploited these advantages over apprentices, servants and newcomers to Moscow.

The tsarist bath-house, too, contributed to the evolution of a homosexual subculture, by sheltering and institutionalizing commercial sex between males, in a quintessentially homosocial and hygienic environment. Although bath-houses continued to operate and remained popular during the Soviet era, socialist disapproval of commercial sex, and modern forms of surveillance, drastically reduced the degree of male prostitution they sheltered. Nevertheless the national culture of the bath-house, in its elemental celebration of all bodies, lent itself to a perverse reinterpretation through homosexual eyes. If men were less able to consummate sexual relations in these spas, they were at least capable, through the rituals of bath-house sociability, to recognize like-minded men and begin the search for privacy.

Moscow's homosexuals still confront the problem of constructing privacy in a transitional economic order. In the past, they made astonishingly bold use of Moscow's most important central landscapes. They persistently exploited secluded and marginal spaces in the heart of the national capital, perhaps secure in the knowledge that their perverse appropriation of these sites was sufficiently unthinkable to call attention from the uninitiated. Such energetic resistance, given the frequency of official persecution, suggests that Russia's gay men have a heritage which we would do well to study before we offer them models they may not wish to assume.

Notes

1 The case of Pokrovskii and Borisov is located in Tsentral'nyi munitsipal'nyi arkhiv Moskvy (TsMAM), Moskovskii narodnyi sud, fond 1919, (Zheleznodorozhnyi raion), opis' 1, delo 238. All names in criminal cases cited from TsMAM have been altered.

2 Ibid., ll: 9–12, 45.

3 The people's court sentenced Pokrovskii to five years imprisonment for aggravated sodomy (i.e. with the use of force). On appeal, his defense lawyer had the crime requalified as consensual sodomy by convincing a higher court that no force had been proven, but the court refused a shorter penalty. No action was taken against Borisov despite the implied shift from victim to consenting partner; ibid., ll. 46, 53–4.

4 Akademiia nauk SSSR *Istoriia Moskvy*, 7 vols (Moscow: Akademiia nauk SSSR, 1952–9), vol. 1, p. 515.

5 *Istoriia Moskvy*, vol. 2, p. 553.

6 See article under '*pobratimstvo*' in Vladimir Dal, *Tolkovyi slovar' zhivogo velikorusskogo iazyka*. (St Petersburg-Moscow: 1903–9), t. 3, col. 348.

7 Jeffrey Burds, trans. and ed., *Dnevnik moskovskogo kuptsa Pavla Vasil'evicha Medved'eva, 1854–1864 gg.* [Diary of Moscow merchant Pavel Vasil'evich Medved'ev, 1854–1864] (forthcoming). I am very grateful to Prof. Burds for providing me with generous access to this text.

8 *Kulizm* (i.e. anal intercourse) was derived from French '*cul*' (ass); see entry for '*culiste*' in Courouve (1985).

9 Burds *Dnevnik moskovskogo kuptsa*, p. 152.

10 See e.g. V.G. Golenko, 'Pederastiia na sude,' *Arkhiv psikhiatrii, neirologii i sudebnoi psikhopatologii* (3 1887): 42–56.

11 N.A. Obolonskii, 'Izvrashchenie polovogo chuvstva.' *Russkii arkhiv patologii, klinicheskoi meditsiny i bakteriologii* (1898): 1–20, esp. 15; V.M. Bekhterev, 'O polovykh izvrashcheni-iakh, kak patologicheskikh sochetatel'nykh refleksakh,' *Obozrenie psikhiatrii* (7–9 1915): 1–26, esp. 9–13; V.A. Belousov, 'Sluchai gomoseksuala-muzhskoi prostitutki,' *Prestupnik i prestup' nost. Sbornik II* (1927): 309–17.

12 Burds, *Dnevnik moskovskogo kuptsa*, p. 144.

13 Tsentral'nyi gos. istoricheskii arkhiv g. Moskvy (TsGIAgM), f. 142, op. 3, d. 233; f. 142, op. 2, d. 433.

14 Burds, *Dnevnik moskovskogo kuptsa*, p. 157.

15 Gosudarstvennyi arkhiv rossisskoi federatsii (GARF), f. A353, op. 3, d. 745, ll. 39, 32 ob.

16 TsGIAgM, f. 142, op. 2, d. 142, l. 148.

17 On Pavel, see Belousov, 'Sluchai gomoseksuala-muzhskoi prostitutki'; on the prince's identity and family life, see V. Sheremet'evskii, 'Neobkhodimoe dopolnenie,' *Zerkalo: Informatsionnyi biulleten' 'GenderDok'* (2 1996): 14–15. The prince's son, himself a bisexual, was the famous murderer of Grigorii Rasputin.

18 The word '*tetka*' used to denote homosexuals, following from the French '*tante*,' dates at least from Merzheevskii's (1878: 205) use of the Russian word to render the Parisian argot for a male prostitute. *Tetka* soon acquired the meaning of 'middle-aged homosexual,' to judge from Tchaikovskii's use of the term in his diary (13 March 1888) to describe a gathering of such men: 'Russian *tetki* are repulsive' (Chaikovskii 1923/1993: 203) and Kozlovskii (1986: 69).

19 St Petersburg was redubbed Petrograd in 1914; from 1924 to 1991 it bore the name Leningrad.

20 On the shift of attention to lesbians, see Dan Healey, 'Unruly identities: Soviet psychiatry confronts the "female homosexual" of the 1920s,' in *Gender and Sexual Difference in Russian Culture and History*, ed. Linda Edmondson (London: Macmillan, forthcoming).

21 Part of the following discussion is based on a sample of fourteen sodomy trials (with forty-four named defendants) from Tsentral'nyi munitsipal'nyi arkhiv Moskvy (TsMAM), dating from 1935 through 1956. Eight of the trials, and thirty-six defendants, fall within the 1935–41 period; the remaining eight individuals were tried between 1949 and 1956. All names cited from these trials have been altered. It is not possible to determine from TsMAM inventories what proportion of Moscow sodomy offenses this sample represents. Uncatalogued and inaccessible sodomy files are known

to exist. I am grateful to Julie Hessler whose suggestions on this archive were invaluable.

22 L.M. Vasilevskii, and L.A. Vasilevskaia *Prostitutsiia i novaia Rossiia* (Tver': 'Oktiabr',' 1923).

23 TsMAM, f. 819, op. 2, d. 51, ll. 57, 106 ob.

24 Belousov, 'Sluchai gomoseksuala – muzhskoi prostitutki,' p. 312. Pavel also listed meeting places and trysting grounds in major cities of the USSR in the 1920s. All of these were on public terrain: embankments, boulevards, toilets in cinemas, public gardens.

25 TsMAM, f. 819, op. 2, d. 10, l. 297.

26 Belousov, 'Sluchai gomoseksuala – muzhskoi prostitutki,' p. 314.

27 Personal communication, Viktor Gulshinskii of the Russian Library of Lesbians and Gays (GenderDok), 4 Nov. 1995.

28 TsMAM, f. 819, op. 2, d. 51, l. 83. 'Sodomy' in Soviet-era police documents might mean any sexual contact between males.

29 Convictions for 1950: GARF, f. A353, op. 16s, d. 121, ll. 16 ob.–24. In this year, Moscow's share of convictions was just six persons, while Leningrad had nine, see l. 18 ob. Convictions for 1961, GARF f. 9492 sekretnaia chast',' op. 6s, d. 58, ll. 37, 99; for 1971, f. 9492 s.ch., op. 6s, d. 177, l. 45. Convictions remained stable at this approximate rate in the 1970s; 849 persons were sentenced in 1981 for sodomy, f. 9492 s.ch., op. 6s, d. 328, l. 30. These now declassified sources do not distinguish between convictions for consensual or aggravated sodomy.

30 Kozlovskii (1996); see also TsMAM, f. 1919, op. 1, d. 136 for a 1952 trial involving sex in public toilet near Leningrad railway station.

31 TsMAM, f. 1921, op. 1, d. 69, l. 10.

32 This is the same park where, ninety-four years earlier, Pavel Medved'ev sought to 'produce lust' with his male friend. Klimov and 'Volodia' had the misfortune to be discovered by a police dog while it was being walked by two Moscow policemen; both defendants received 3-year prison sentences. TsMAM f. 1921, op. 1, d. 69, ll. 6, 8, 43–4.

33 Both baths served approximately 2,000 customers a day in 1979, see P.A. Voronin *et al.* (eds) *Moskva: Entsiklopediia* (Moscow: Sovetskaia entsiklopediia, 1980), 126.

34 TsMAM, f. 819, op. 2, d. 11, ll. 238–45.

35 Ibid, l. 242.

36 On the communal flat's effects on heterosexual married couples, see Kotkin (1995: 195).

37 TsMAM, f. 901, op. 1, d. 1352, ll. 49ob.-50.

38 Ibid, l. 7.

39 GARF, f. A482, op. 47, d. 4868, ll. 40–40 ob. Soviet-era hotels officially only admitted out-of-towners or foreigners, eliminating another site for non-approved sexual encounters.

40 Pokrovskii, described in the introduction of this chapter, lived with his wife and stepson. The wife told police she slept in a bed with her son while Pokrovskii 'always slept apart, on the sofa' and refused sex with her, TsMAM, f. 1919, op. 1, d. 238, l. 27 ob.

41 Describing obstacles to holding the reading in a letter to Kuzmin, V.V. Ruslov blamed 'the generally awful mood reigning at the moment in Moscow, among Muscovites in general (the reason – mistrust and arrests) and also among "our own," who, as you doubtless know, are more timid than desert gazelles; as a result, frightened by the mood here, they are prostrate and at the thought of "our" evening immediately fall into hysterics and refuse to purchase tickets.' See A.G. Timofeev, 'Progulka bez Gulia? (K istorii organizatsii avtorskogo vechera M.A. Kuzmina v mae 1924 g.).' In *Mikhail Kuzmin i russkaia kul'tura XX veka: tezisy i materialy konferentsii 15–17 maia 1990g.*, ed. G. A. Morev. (Leningrad: Sovet po istorii mirovoi kul'tury AN SSSR, 1990), p. 187.

42 TsMAM, f. 819, op. 2, d. 51.
43 Ibid., l. 106 ob.
44 While conducting research in Moscow in 1995–6, employees at one archive advised me of the existence of a classified file on a 1955 sodomy scandal at Mosfilm; in another archive, employees allowed me limited informal access to a file on a similar scandal at the Moscow Conservatory of Music. 'G' described a psychiatrist who treated several gay Conservatory students, sons of powerful officials, for homosexuality in the 1970s, and described a similar scandal involving the University, ('G' 1980: 21–2)
45 1959 criminal case in RSFSR Supreme Court against music instructor at Moscow Conservatory of Music, personal communication from staff at one Moscow archive. Tolerance of 'amours of a different kind' at the Conservatory was the subject of journalistic attack in 1878, see Poznansky (1996: 18).

3 Amsterdam

Gert Hekma

Introduction

Amsterdam's gay world came into full blossom in the 1960s. The city afforded an example of tolerance and of pleasure for people all around the world. During the Golden Age of the seventeenth century the city was already famous for religious toleration when other religions were permitted alongside the Dutch Reformed Church. Many dissidents from other parts of Europe sought refuge in the city. By the eighteenth century Amsterdam was considered a center for the distribution of pornography, especially libertine writings in French. That tradition continued to the present for kiddy and bestial porn that elsewhere in the Western world is more strictly controlled. This reputation of tolerance is not always well deserved. During the eighteenth century the Dutch Republic, including Amsterdam, was the location of the largest persecutions of sodomy of the age with at least 800 men persecuted and 200 capital punishments. Even in the 1990s a majority of the urban population and of the municipal authorities would like to see an end to Amsterdam's reputation as a place where sex and drugs are easily available. The city government enforced stricter rules on activities that denote hedonism outside the bounds of the capitalist marketplace (van Naerssen 1987).

Prehistory

The earliest settlement of the site of Amsterdam dated from around 1225. Dams were required to hold back heavy flooding of the River Amstel which threatened the 'terp' or artificial mound on the bank where houses were built. By 1275 Amsterdam became a city and the settlement grew from one of landowners and fish dealers to a center for commerce. The beginnings of the city coincided with rising persecution of sodomy in Europe. The first recorded burnings of sodomites in the Flemish Netherlands took place in Ghent at the end of the thirteenth century. Around 1500 Amsterdam accommodated about 5,000 inhabitants. It was a center of Catholicism with many cloisters. In 1578 the city converted from Catholicism to Calvinism, some time after other Dutch cities. After the occupation of Portugal by Spain in 1580, the fall of Antwerp in 1585 and the repeal of the Edict of Nantes in France in 1685 large numbers of Portuguese Jews, Flemish Protestants and French Huguenots found refuge in the city. Most of them were wealthy or skillful exiles. By 1700 Amsterdam had an cosmopolitan population of some 200,000 including Germans and Jews, Norwegians and Armenians among many others. The city was the financial and commercial center of the world. Its sea connections made it the prime trading center of the globe. The East and West Indies Companies (founded in 1602 and 1621) made Amsterdam their home. During the eighteenth century the city gradually lost its pre-eminent position to Paris and London although it remained a financial center. Industries and markets declined and, while the rich continued to enjoy prosperity, it derived from their property rather than from trade or industry. The lower classes bore the burden of Amsterdam's commercial and industrial decay.

After Amsterdam joined the Calvinist insurrection against Catholic Spain in 1578 it became the principal city in the Dutch Republic of seven relatively autonomous provinces that forged its political identity during the eighty-year war against Spain (1568–1648). The city itself belonged to the province of Holland, by far the richest part of the country. Because of the intricate but weak organization of the Republic and because of the city's wealth and power, Amsterdam was very independent in its policies. The functions of the Republic, based in The Hague, were mainly restricted to foreign and military affairs. The city was a world to itself and has remained so. In 1806 it became the capital of the Kingdom of Holland under King Louis, brother to Napoleon. Nowadays Amsterdam is the capital as well as the financial and cultural center of the Netherlands while The Hague has remained the seat of government. As the saying goes, money is earned in Rotterdam, divided in The Hague and spoilt in Amsterdam.

The secret world of sodomy

The first recorded execution by fire for sodomy in the northern part of the Netherlands concerned two men in Egmont, not far from Amsterdam on Holland's coast, in 1321 (Noordam 1995: 22–4). The first known court case in Amsterdam for 'crimine pessimo,' probably sodomy, was in 1534 and involved a priest and a Franciscan monk, but the sentence is not known (Boomgaard 1992: 276). During the seventeenth century there were some convictions in 1632 and 1641 of women who married or had sex with one another. The latter concerned Hendrikje van der Schuur who had served as a soldier and had a passionate relation with a woman named Trijntje. The case attracted attention because the Amsterdam physician Nicolaas Tulp discussed their case in his *Observationes* (1641). He attributed the masculine sexuality of Hendrikje to her large clitoris.

An Italian was banned from the city in 1648 for buggering little girls and possibly also a boy; he was later punished for the same crime in Utrecht and The Hague. Persecution of men for sodomy remained rare in Amsterdam until the great persecutions of 1730–1. One legal treatise mentioned two men who were executed in Amsterdam in 1686 while in 1726 Pierre Pelaxi was sentenced to thirty-five years of solitary confinement. The first notorious cases dealt not with sodomites but with those who tried to blackmail them. In 1664 the court sentenced a blackmailer to flogging, branding and banishment from the city. Two other men received a similar punishment in 1689 while a third man was hanged. Another blackmailer was convicted in 1715. Their presence in the judicial records suggests that at least since the 1660s there was a twilight world of sodomites in the Dutch Republic (Van der Meer 1995).

In other places convictions were more common, especially in much smaller Rotterdam, where in the same period fifteen men were convicted for sodomy or 'tentamina sodomitica' of whom six received the death sentence. From the thirteenth century until 1730 some 100 convictions for sodomy have been recorded for the northern Netherlands. Most of these were for anal intercourse between men. About fifty men were executed for this crime. Very few cases of bestiality or heterosexual anal intercourse are known (Noordam 1995). It is possible that more cases will be identified in archives in future research; it is equally possible that judicial records have not survived. The suggestion that sodomy trial records were deliberately destroyed seems in general not to have been the case in the Netherlands because of the number that have survived and because legal treatises rarely specified such a requirement of records of the 'crimen nefandum' (the crime that should not be discussed).

If convictions for sodomy in Amsterdam before 1730 were so few the question can be asked whether the activity was rare. It appears that same-sex sexual acts were not as general in the Netherlands as in fifteenth-century Florence described by Rocke (1996) where such pleasures were part and parcel of male sociability. However research has been concentrated on judicial records and there is a lack of historical inquiries into the fields of art, literature and private life. A thorough investigation of Dutch art, from Maerten van Heemskerck and Hendrick Goltzius to Rembrandt van Rijn, Johannes Vermeer, Jan Steen and many others who painted mythology as daily life would provide more information on same-sex desires. Goltzius made drawings of heroic figures, van Heemskerck is famous for his *Lord of Sorrows* which serves as Leo Steinberg's (1983) main example of a Christ with pronounced genitals, while Rembrandt depicted a Ganymede and a masturbation scene. One of Vermeer's portraits may be of a male-to-female transvestite. Etchings of Sodom and sodomy were widespread from the start of printing culture and many tracts that appeared in the wake of the sodomy persecutions of the 1730s were illustrated (Schenk 1982).

Sources from private life and literature might also yield a harvest of information but in the present state of research we can only offer some hypotheses. Obviously official attitudes and those of the public at large were quite negative, especially when cases of sodomy became public. Sodomites themselves felt guilty about acts that were considered the epitome of sin, although since it should not be named perhaps many individuals did not know what was meant. A group of young orphans who had anal intercourse with each other continued to do so after one of them suggested sodomy was not what they did sexually but meant the cutting off of penises. Men arrested for sodomy in the village of Faan who

Figure 3.1 'Justice glorified by the discovery and punishment of rising sin'. The drawing
represents the unveiling of the underworld of sodomites, below left, by Justice,
in the middle. Some men run off to escape Justice. Above right, the fire that
extinguished the city of Sodom. Below right, four women who represent the
sins of folly [frolic], avarice, lewdness and voluptuousness. Above left, the angel
of revenge with the bible text 'men abandoning the use of women'. From 1730.
Source: Reprinted from: *Jahrbuch fuer sexuelle Zwischenstufen* 8 (1907).

might have heard their clergyman inveighing against sodomy seem to have made
no connection with their own behavior.

Research in the archives of the Amsterdam Reformed Church revealed that
Church Councils discussed sexual sins quite frequently, especially in remon-
strating with the faithful for frequenting prostitutes, but sodomy was never
mentioned (Roodenburg 1990). In provincial meetings the topic came up not in
Holland but in the northern district of Drenthe. Dutch Calvinists were little
exercised about sodomy until 1730 and even after that date the state was much
more active in combating it than the Reformed Church.

What about homoeroticism that was not sodomitical? Clearly men lived in
homosocial worlds in their workplaces, aboard ships, in army camps, and close
friendships were highly valued. Lower-class men of all ages often slept together
because of lack of space and money. In homes, hostels and on ships they shared
beds with nephews, uncles, apprentices, friends or strangers whom they perhaps
never saw again after a night of secret delights. However there is a dearth of
factual evidence about those practices.

Amsterdam was, relatively speaking, little affected by the 1730 persecutions.
The authorities in Utrecht accidentally uncovered a small network of sodomites.
After they arrested Zacharias Wilsma, a soldier and hustler who had sexual relations
with rich and poor men all over the Republic the prosecution became nation-

wide. Of ninety-four death penalties for sodomy during the period 1730–2 six were pronounced in Amsterdam. Thirty men were sentenced in their absence. They probably escaped because rumors of the persecutions reached Amsterdam before arrests took place. The authorities started the prosecution after they had asked the learned advice of three jurists on the lawfulness of arresting an individual on the basis of a single denunciation by an accomplice, and whether social class made a difference. On the first point the answer was negative and on the second positive. An allegation of a suspect had to be confirmed by other evidence certainly if he was of a higher social class.

The court was prudent. The first man accused of sodomy was a merchant who on 19 May 1730 firmly denied Wilsma's denunciations against him and he was released on bail. Five days later he had left his home for an unknown destination. The second man, lower class, also denied all allegations even when put to the torture and confronted by Wilsma, who was cooperating with the authorities. He finally confessed with two others only about a month later; all three were executed on the 24 of June. A fifth accused, a footman named Maurits Schuuring had confessed immediately and was executed with them. He said he had been introduced to sodomy by Jurriaan Bakbandt, the inn-keeper of the Serpent, which was the main meeting place of sodomites in Amsterdam. Bakbandt had already fled the city but his wife was arrested and banished from the city. The inn seems to have had two rooms where sodomites gathered in a semi-public arena. Bakbandt never permitted his wife to serve the clients in those rooms, doing so himself (Van der Meer 1984, 1995; Boon 1997).

One of the convicted men implicated another thirty-eight men four days before his execution but the Amsterdam court slowed down its proceedings. In September a fifth execution occurred; in 1731 an accused man committed suicide while in prison. The extent of the Amsterdam sodomitical subculture was small for a city of 200,000 inhabitants. There was another inn beside the Serpent where sodomites foregathered. They met in public spaces like privies, the walls of the city and the ground floor of the City Hall on the Dam Square (at present the Royal Palace). Ironically this was the very place where sodomites were imprisoned after arrest, where they were judged and finally executed on a wooden scaffold built in front of the first floor of the edifice.

All the executed men in Amsterdam were lower class. This was a clear trend towards a class-based justice. Although many patricians and aristocrats were implicated by their footmen none of them were arrested. Some went into exile although the principal noble of the province of Utrecht, in spite of many accusations, was not even indicted. Another 'Utrechtenaar' (since these persecutions, synonymous with sodomite) Jan van Lennep, a prebendary (bought title of honor) from a merchant family, was the highest placed sodomite to face the death penalty. William III, stadtholder of the Republic and King of Britain, was in 1730 already twenty-eight years dead. His fame as a male lover of Count Bentinck and Lord Keppel certainly lingered on much longer but was never evoked in the 1730s.

More prosecutions of sodomy in eighteenth-century Amsterdam: in 1741

Figure 3.2 A print representing 1. a meeting of sodomites, 2. who abandon their wives, 3. are arrested, 4. in prison 5. hung and burnt, and 6. drowned in a barrel. The last scene shows the scaffold placed in cases of corporal punishment before the Amsterdam City Hall, now the Royal Palace. Sodomites met for pleasure on the ground floor of the same building. From 1730.

Source: Reprinted from: *Jahrbuch fuer sexuelle Zwischenstufen* 8 (1907).

three orphans were sentenced to long prison terms; in 1743 another two received the death penalty. In 1762 the man who was the city executioner for many years, and who may have tortured imprisoned sodomites, was banished on grounds of sodomy. He told the court about the cruising at the City Hall and the authorities decided to install lamps there to prevent such activities. Subsequently they organized entrapments in well-known meeting places. The policies changed in enlightened times from reactive to active, from punishing to preventing.

Another wave of persecutions hit the city in 1764–5 with eight death penalties and sixty-four men exiled from the city. It began with the arrest of a soldier for theft who, condemned to death, confessed before his hanging 'to relieve his conscience' his 'terrible sins of sodomy, active as well as passive' with a variety of partners. The court proceeded cautiously. The soldier was hanged two weeks later for his theft and not strangled as was common in sodomy cases. The judges wanted to avoid giving the alarm as had happened in 1730 when suspected sodomites got away. Notwithstanding their caution, few Amsterdam men were arrested and sentenced.

In 1776–7 a more widespread network of sodomites originating from Amsterdam was revealed. Two individuals accused of fraud had in their luggage letters of an unmistakably sodomitical nature. The two men did not confess anal intercourse and received long prison sentences but not death. However their love letters led to persecutions throughout the Dutch Republic. Hermanus Kloek, leader of the Amsterdam soapboilers guild, had written one of the letters. He confessed to mutual masturbation but no more than that, but, more embarrassingly to the city elite, he implicated a reigning patrician of Amsterdam, George Clifford. The authorities now sought to hush up the case, did not prosecute Clifford and exiled Kloek. Other men had been sentenced to long prison terms for the same activities and the blatantly class-biased judgments were unpopular with the population. When warrants calling for the arrest of fugitive sodomites were posted they were painted black by unknown members of the public, probably as a gesture of protest.

The type of meeting places of sodomites revealed by the eighteenth-century trials continued to exist. Public toilets until the 1970s were favored cruising grounds. In the eighteenth-century these toilets were wooden structures under the city's many bridges. They offered an early-warning system of new arrivals since most lower-class people walked with wooden clogs so an individual descending the stairs was easily audible to persons in the latrines. In the mid nineteenth century street-level urinals were installed and these were heavily frequented by men wanting sex with other men. They had soon to be redesigned to make homosexual activity impossible but however clever the new design may have been, the new model has been employed by gay men until the 1970s. After the walls were pulled down, the parks that came in their place were another venue for same-sex encounters.

Inns and bars were a salient feature first of the sodomitical underworld and later of the gay upperworld. The inns mentioned in 1730 were not exclusively sodomitical. About bars mentioned in later court proceedings no details are given. Two bars in the Egelantierstraat (Jordaan) are designated in 1764 as places where '*lolders*' (sodomites) congregated and in the 1790s the Rondeel on the Heiligeweg is mentioned several times. Sodomites met also at private homes. Both in 1809 and 1881 houses were raided and 'wrong lovers' arrested. Nothing is known about bars or inns for most of the nineteenth century. At the end of the century a list of bordellos made by a reform society mentions half a dozen bars and houses as sodomitical meeting places.

The question has often been debated if these men who had sex with other men had a sense of homosexual identity. The historians Noordam (1995) and Van der Meer (1995) assume, following Trumbach, that such an identity existed since the late seventeenth century. Further questions arise from that assumption: what did that identity involve, how did it affect sodomites and their surroundings, and what place did the identity hold in the cultural context? A subculture of sodomites was developing in Amsterdam from the late seventeenth century. As a reaction to their persecution some sodomites started to defend their inclinations and to claim in the mid-eighteenth century that their desires were innate. These whispers became outspoken only in 1883 when the first self-conscious homosexual was published. The development of a homosexual identity should be seen as a process of stages where other same-sex practices existed concurrent with this identity such as romantic friendship, boy-love or males seeking sex with adult males in homosocial arrangements or on the streets. My view of the Dutch situation is that most men who had sex with other men did not self-consciously embrace a homosexual identity until the 1950s. Most homosexual acts till that time were perpetrated by men who sought sexual pleasure and did not care much about the gender of their partner (compare Everard 1994 and Van de Pol 1996 for female sexuality).

Modern times

In 1795 Dutch radicals, with the backing of French troops, chased out the patricians and the Stadtholder of the Oranges who held power in the Republic and founded the revolutionary Batavian Republic. After many political perturbations in 1806 Napoleon made his brother Louis King of Holland and, in 1810, included the kingdom in his empire. In 1813 the Netherlands again became independent, after Napoleon's Russian defeats. After the Congress of Vienna Belgium and the former Republic were united in the Kingdom of the Netherlands until 1830 when the two parts became separate kingdoms.

After the revolutionary changes of 1795 the persecutions of sodomy surprisingly increased. More men were arrested and also some women. The range of sexual acts considered criminal was extended. The 'tentamina sodomitica' included touching another male intimately. On the other hand the punishments were less severe. The net result was that little progress was made under the new regime. In Amsterdam two of the leading police chiefs seem to have been at odds, one being eager to prosecute sodomy while the other was alleged to be a sodomite in several cases. After the first officer left his position the persecutions abated but did not stop altogether.

Legal opinion about sodomy was evolving somewhat. In 1777 a lawyer close to the Stadtholder, Abraham Perrenot, wrote in the spirit of the Enlightenment a tract which called for prevention rather than harsh punishments of sodomy. He still expressed vehement repulsion for sodomites. In 1795 G.J. Gales, another lawyer, discussed whether the sin of sodomy should be decriminalized because of the separation of church and state in the Batavian Republic. His conclusion was that sodomy should remain a crime because the law was introduced by the state.

New criminal law proposals of the Batavian Republic did not propose to decriminalize sodomy although capital punishment was now reserved only for cases when it occurred under conditions of force, seduction or misuse of authority. These proposals were not enacted in law. When Holland was incorporated into Napoleon's Empire the French *Code Pénal* was introduced in 1811. This law had no provisions against sodomy, only against public indecency. After the defeat of the French the law remained in force and was replaced only in 1886. Some Dutch legal officials in the Kingdom of the Netherlands like the long-serving Minister of Justice C.F. van Maanen had wanted to reintroduce the crime of sodomy to the law. The 1840s saw a lively discussion among lawyers mostly in favor of recriminalizing sodomy. However, in 1880, the majority in parliament supported the idea of privacy and resisted the insertion of articles against sodomy. To prevent seduction of youngsters the legal age of consent was raised initially to 14, but after a case of homosexual seduction of somewhat older youths came to the public attention it was finally raised to 16 years of age in the law that replaced the Code Pénal in 1886.

The nineteenth century was a liberal age in the Netherlands but towards the end of the century, other political groups, especially Protestant and Catholic, gained in force. They made moral and sexual issues prominent in politics and campaigned for a stricter sex law that was discussed and accepted in parliament in 1911. This law outlawed same-sex acts between adults and minors under 21 years, as well as public exposure of pornography and contraceptives, abortion and pimping. This new sex law was the outcome of a long struggle focused mainly on medical regulation of prostitution. The ill-assorted coalition of Christian fundamentalists, feminists, progressive liberals and socialists that, for a variety of reasons, supported the struggle against prostitution, extended its field of interest in 1898 to other sexual topics like male homosexuality and pornography which were both widely held in disregard.

The political struggle around prostitution was a result of its medical regulation. Since Napoleon introduced this measure to police prostitutes more effectively, regulation had spread over Europe. The nineteenth century was the age of progress. Physicians believed in and struggled for a stronger medical hold in the state. They had deeply socialized medicine by introducing a specialization called 'medical police' or, more neutrally, 'public hygiene', that broadened the field of medical interest towards social issues such as the quality of food, labor circumstances, housing conditions, public festivities. The lewd and drunken behavior of the lower classes was curtailed and more healthy alternatives of sport and music were propagated.

Prostitutes were given a weekly medical inspection. Christians opposed this regulation because it legalized vice, feminists because it degraded women, socialists because capitalists could in that way legally and with impunity abuse working-class women. As the medical control was not effective even physicians started to oppose it. In the end this struggle was successful and most Dutch cities abrogated the regulation and forbade bordellos. After this victory abolitionists found other targets in the struggle against pornography, homosexuality, abortion, child abuse and other forms of immorality (de Vries 1997).

Amsterdam had never had medical regulation although an unofficial system existed. At the end of the century the city council appointed a committee to research the social conditions of prostitution. Its conclusions were straightforward. Bordellos were not so much used by young and unmarried men for whom they were intended but by older married men. Those men were less interested in normal copulation than in 'counternatural' sex. Among the prostitutes tribadism was common. Instead of damming dangerous desires of youngsters prostitution promoted perversions among everyone. The regulatory system was put into question and never recovered from this final blow. In its stead free clinics for the treatment of venereal diseases were introduced.

Wrong lovers

Discussion of prostitution made homosexuality visible. A strongly voiced opinion among doctors was the argument that if the state forbade prostitution worse vices would become general, like masturbation or seeking sexual relations with others of the same sex. One strong supporter of the system had been a naval surgeon and he confirmed that thousands of men succumbed to these vices in the absence of women. His Christian opponents sustained the possibility of chastity and found a captain of the merchant marine who said that sailors could live chastely during their long sailing trips. The discussion on prostitution brought homosexuality into the limelight of public discussion. Books and pamphlets on prostitution frequently had chapters devoted to same-sex behavior by men and women.

A new kind of yellow press with strong socialist or left-wing antecedents started around 1890. These journals railed against capitalism, the church and the aristocracy, whose main faults were of course sexual. *The Red Devil* attacked men of higher classes and of religious ranks for all kinds of social and sexual misbehavior. *The Amsterdam Lantern* edited by Abraham Cornelisse did so fervently. It opened its first issue in 1897 with a verbal assault on a sodomitical meeting place and produced a pamphlet against this bar of George Hermans. In the few copies of the journal that have survived, gay bashing is a regular feature. Cornelisse not only cried out in his paper against sodomites but went so far as to smash the windows of Hermans' bar. He was arrested and sentenced for this. He produced at least one more pamphlet against pederasts who were said to interfere with young patients in the city hospital.

His articles offer an interesting insight on the gay bars of those times. Hermans was a strong supporter of the royal family whose portraits decorated his bar. This infuriated the anti-royalist Cornelisse. Flowers, an uncommon feature of bars in those days, added to the atmosphere. Hermans was more than a bartender since his denouncer claimed he was a quack purporting to cure venereal diseases. He was also said to place young men for work as man-servants or as nurses in psychiatric asylums. This employment service gave him ample opportunity to give free rein to his debauched desires.

Similar information is not available on the other places that catered to sodomites. Those on the list of bordellos probably did not offer rent boys. One man who figured on the list was arrested for public indecency and apparently had pictures of nude males in his home. Perhaps the pictures were of male whores for inspection by potential clients, but it seems more likely that the man sold or collected male pornography. Probably the meetings places changed regularly because of harassments by the police, annoyed neighbors or Cornelisse and his like.

The main meeting places were not bars and bordellos, however, but parks, public toilets and streets. Judicial archives give abundant material on those places as public indecencies persecuted in Dutch courts generally concerned men involved in same-sex activities. The number of arrested men grew rapidly as Table 3.1 shows:

1. Vondelpark
2. Weteringplantsoen
3. J. D. Meyerplein
4. diverse plaatsen langs het Y, waar zich een 'zwemschool' en de af-
   vaart van stoomboten richting Zaandam, Purmerend etc. bevon-
   den
5. Nieuwe Brugsteeg 4 (koffyhuis en logement)
6. Prins Hendrikkade 57
7. Spuistraat 287
8. Singel 438

9. Egelantiersgracht 142
10. Nassaukade 114
11. bierhuis Wesseling, Utrechtsestraat 137
12. bierhuis Spits, Kerkstraat 212
13. bierkelder Catacombe Marnixstraat 398
14. restauratie N.Z. Kapelsteeg 10
15. café hoek Molsteeg/N.Z. Voorburgwal
16. bierhuis George Hermans, Smaksteeg (bij Nieuwendijk)
17. Monthaansteeg (verzamelplaats sodomieten)

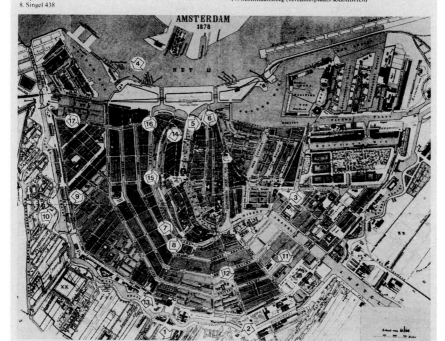

Figure 3.3 Map of Amsterdam, indicating the meeting places of 'wrong lovers' in the late nineteenth century, numbers 1–4 cruising places; 5–10 houses mentioned on a bordello list as sodomitical locations; 11–17 bars that operated around the turn of the century at some stage as meeting places for sodomites.

Source: From *Spiegel Historiael* 17: 10 (October 1982).

Table 3.1 Number of arrests and convictions for homosexual acts in the Amsterdam district (public indecency and seduction of minors)

Year	Arrests	Convictions
1830–9	12	10
1840–9	8	7
1850–9	14	7
1860–9	27	12
1870–9	51	27
1880–9	73	23
1890–9	97	48
1900–9	187	87

Source: From Hekma (1987).
Note: Most cases concern Amsterdam city; during the two last decades one and five of the arrested men respectively were sent to a psychiatric asylum without a conviction.

An obvious explanation for the rapid rise in numbers of arrests is the growth of the Amsterdam police force from 56 to 686 men between 1838 and 1878. The less effective system of night watchmen had been abolished. There were more prisons, asylums and public toilets; there were more efforts to discipline social behavior but also more possibilities to escape control.

Convicted men had practiced consensual sex in all kinds of places: in horse carriages, trains, hospitals, swimming pools, on boats, markets, in bars, bedrooms, the poorhouse and, most often, in parks and public toilets. Sometimes the police took a long time to arrest their victims. Two men who had once been observed kissing on a street corner were followed for a fortnight before they were caught having sex in the same public place. In another instance two men spent an hour and a half in an old-style public toilet under a bridge where they were fucking each other. A woman vendor of eggs and pickles testified that one of the pair had bought two eggs from her before going down to the toilet where he was joined by his partner a little later. She said the couple had been in that toilet before, and remained there until the night watch took up their post at 9:30 p.m. Their arrest was the work of a man who had staked out the toilet for hours. A volunteer constable in the Vondelpark was very zealous and made several

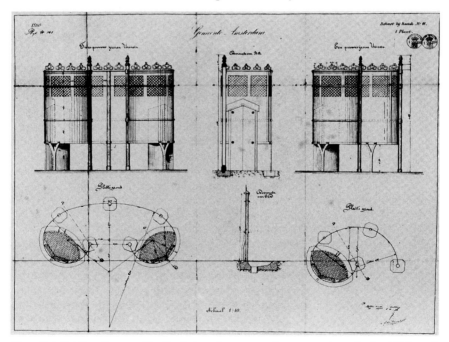

Figure 3.4 Public toilet, specifically designed to prevent homosexual acts in the 1880s and still present in contemporary Amsterdam. The two pissholes are spatially segregated to prevent indecent gazing, and the underside of the walls is open to make it possible for police officers to see from the outside what is happening inside.

Source: *Gemeente Archief Amsterdam.*

arrests there of men engaged in sexual acts. Some other citizens of Amsterdam were less vigilant, like the cabman who drove around while two men had sex in his carriage, until the policeman who had ascertained their behavior arrested them.

The arrested men were nearly without exception from the lower classes. Of course they had less access to private space for sexual activity than the well to do. The handful of upper middle-class men arrested for public indecencies took effective measures to escape condemnation by employing a lawyer to defend them or by appealing against an unfavorable sentence. They could also leave the country before the trial because there was no preventive imprisonment once the charge of public indecency had been laid.

The convicted men were of all ages, the youngest in Amsterdam being 15 years old. Convictions for having sex with boys were rare before 1886 when the new law set the age of consent at 16. Between 1886 and 1909 there were twenty-four convictions for this crime, whereas in the preceding period of 1830 to 1885 only five men were convicted of having forcible sexual relations with boys in that age group. In fact force was rarely an element in the cases researched, including those in the Haarlem Military Court which is astonishing because (sexual) violence was until recently widespread in the army.

Charges of public indecencies raised the question in court of what was to be considered public. In general, wards in hospitals, army barracks and places clearly visible from a public place were considered to be public. If men had sex in a bedroom without closing the curtains their activities could become a public indecency. A court in Appingedam near the German frontier acquitted two men who had sex behind a hedge, which meant they were not seen by the witness but heard. However the court ruled that the sounds of their love-making did not make their behavior public. A lawyer published a comment in a journal in which he argued that their acts should have been punished since the garden did not belong to either man. The 1886 law countered such problems by adding the proviso that there was public indecency if other persons were involuntary witnesses to such acts. Dutch law-makers never went as far as the British who regarded all sexual situations in which more than two persons were present as public indecencies.

Medical theories, emancipatory efforts

In the late nineteenth century, psychiatrists and uranians started to discuss the bio-medical aspects of homosexuality. The first author was the psychiatrist N.B. Donkersloot, editor of the weekly *Geneeskundige Courant* (Medical Journal). In 1852 he summarized J.L. Casper's findings on the signs of sodomy, but did not mention Casper's suggestion that pederasty might be innate. In a review of K.H. Ulrichs' work on uranism he concluded that it was better to talk the topic to death than to condemn its devotees to death. He did not succeed in banishing the topic into silence as an anonymous colleague wrote him a long letter in which he defended his desires. Donkersloot published this letter as the first

Dutch case study of man who wrote 'I am a uranian, not a pederast.' This fascinating first gay autobiography in Dutch was the apotheosis of a long article of Donkersloot on the 'Clinical-forensic significance of the perverse sexual drive' which appeared in several installments in 1883, the first major article on the topic in Dutch.

This first uranian claimed that there were 50,000 uranians like him in the Netherlands, with male genitals, body-hair, voice, build and habitus but female from the inside. From his earliest days he desired men and abhorred women. For him, having sex with uranians and dionings (heterosexual men) was natural, while sex with women was counternatural. His sexual activity was not anal as he was not a pederast, and neither, he went on, were 199 of each 200 of his ilk. This man claimed to be a well respected doctor who wanted to speak out about uranism like the courageous Ulrichs because he believed that already in the same century uranism would be accepted on an equal footing with dionism.

More ambivalent was the second apology for uranians by Schoondermark who spoke as if he held a professorate and a doctorate but who had neither. He had been a medical student and a collaborator on the *Geneeskundige Courant*. He made his living by writing tracts on medical subjects from dentistry and hygiene to sexology and birth control. Most of his very many works were simply translations of foreign books under his own name. In 1894 he published a small book *Van de verkeerde richting* (Of the wrong direction) which was mainly a translation of Norbert Grabowski's *Die verkehrte Geschlechtsempfindung* (1894). It ended with an emotional appeal: 'one should have strong compassion with, not contempt for homosexuals.' Later he would translate Nicolo Barucco's work on *Neurasthenia sexualis* (1901) which had a much more negative tone. Schoondermark did this work probably for financial rather than emotional reasons as he was not homosexual himself. Notwithstanding his active publishing he twice went bankrupt and was denounced in the *Geneeskundige Courant* as a quack.

Schoondermark's books appeared with Amsterdam-based publishers such as Van Klaveren, Moransard and Graauw who started to produce erotic and sexological books with great success in the late 1880s. Van Klaveren published the first full-length book on homosexuality, the aforementioned *Van de verkeerde richting*. After 1894 many other original and translated works would appear like Ambroise Tardieu's *Misdrijven tegen de zeden* (1896), Richard von Krafft-Ebing's *Leerboek der zielsziekten van het geslachtsleven* (1896), Edward Carpenter's *De homogene liefde* (1896), Magnus Hirschfeld's *Sapho en Socrates* (1902) and Havelock Ellis's *Het contraire geslachtsgevoel* (1901). It was a popular genre. Many translations were compilations of the originals, fabricated to satisfy the sexual curiosity of the public. Van Klaveren sold these books in series, for example the 'People's library for sexual life.' This sexological literature promulgated for the first time in Dutch history quite positive ideas of sexual variations. It offered models for homosexual and other sexual identities and stimulated their development. In a court case it was used against a man arrested for public indecencies that he had spoken approvingly about Schoondermark's work to his tobacconist.

The two main Dutch authors in the field were Arnold Aletrino and Lucien

S.A.M. von Römer. They were both medical doctors living in Amsterdam, Aletrino teaching criminal anthropology and Römer becoming a highly regarded collaborator of Hirschfeld and a productive contributor to his *Jahrbuch für sexuelle Zwischenstufen*. Aletrino was already famous as a realist author of somber novels about nurses when he published in 1897 his first article on uranism. It was a long and positive review of Marc-André Raffalovich's *Uranisme et unisexualité* (1896) whose thesis of the masculine and chaste uranian he supported. In his later publications he was more inclined to Hirschfeld's ideas on 'sexual intermediaries.' In 1901 Aletrino provoked a scandal when he defended the rights of uranians at the fifth conference of Criminal Anthropology in Amsterdam, facing an audience of staunch opponents, among them the Italian criminologist Cesare Lombroso. In 1904 the Calvinist Dutch Prime Minister attacked both Aletrino and the University of Amsterdam for teaching the sins of Sodom. Both Aletrino and Römer belonged to the Dutch section of Hirschfeld's 'Wissenschaftlich-humanitäre Komitee' (NWHK) founded in 1912 in The Hague.

Römer held already the post of '*Obmann*' (leader) in the German WHK. He wrote major essays on the persecution of sodomites in the eighteenth century, on androgyny and on the nature of homosexuality for the *Jahrbuch*. He carried out the first Dutch sex survey with 308 male student respondents in which he found that 2 per cent admitted homosexual and a further 4 per cent bisexual feelings. A total of 21 per cent reported sex with other males during puberty and 85 per cent had masturbated. He later helped Hirschfeld carry out a similar inquiry in Germany. In a lecture for the Christian-Socialist organization '*Rein-Leven*' (Pure Life) he defended not only the natural essence of homosexuality but also the right to gay sex within a loving relationship. Nobody else endorsed this position, not even Aletrino, who held the opinion that uranians should remain chaste. Römer took up polemical positions against professors of the Medical Faculty. This would have influenced his supervisor, professor of psychiatry Cees Winkler, to reject his dissertation. Official grounds were that the manuscript was written in German, contained lewd pictures of naked men and included genealogies of sexual perversions in royal families. Although he never got his degree, some of the material was published in his work 'The uranian family' which was published in both Dutch and German editions (1905 and 1906 respectively). Römer became a member of the NWHK but after the rejection of his outstanding work on homosexuality he withdrew from that area of investigation. He emigrated to the Dutch East Indies where he worked as a medical practitioner, married a woman and had two sons.

Aletrino, also a married man, helped his friend Jacob Israël de Haan to come to terms with homosexual feelings. The year 1904 saw the publication by De Haan of the first gay novel in Dutch, *Pijpelijntjes*. The title is derived from the then new Amsterdam neighborhood, De Pijp. The novel is a quite explicit description of the sadistic relationship between two students who lived in that district, who occasionally fought and who had other lovers on the side. The two principal characters had the nicknames of Sam and Joop – names also known to many as the nicknames of Aletrino and De Haan. In doing this, De Haan

implied a homosexual relationship with his friend, although Aletrino always maintained that writers like Hirschfeld or himself who wrote on uranism were not
necessarily themselves homosexual. The novel caused a major scandal. However
Aletrino and De Haan's fiancée together bought up all the copies of the book
soon after it was printed. De Haan was fired from his job as a journalist at the
Socialist daily newspaper as well as losing his post as a schoolteacher. The furore
underlined how ferocious was the opposition to homosexuality in the Netherlands
in the decade before World War I.

The novel described two men sharing a room in a boarding house and having
lovers' spats. At the same time they are portrayed going into the city looking for
sexual partners. Joop pursued working-class boys aged 13 years and over who
were ready to share sexual pleasures for a drink or for some money. The novel
contained graphic scenes of everyday life in De Pijp. De Haan's second novel
Pathologieën published in 1908 portrayed a sadomasochistic relationship between a
student and his cruel lover who was a painter. It contained sex scenes that were
quite explicit by the standards of the times. The Flemish writer George Eekhoud
wrote a complimentary introduction. This novel did not provoke the same
scandal as the first. Later De Haan became famous for his pederast and Jewish
poetry. After the Great War he emigrated to Palestine as a Zionist but then
joined forces with the Anti-Zionist Jews, defended their case in London and was
murdered by Zionists in 1924. A line in Dutch from one of his poems 'Such a
boundless desire for friendship' decorates the Homomonument in Amsterdam.

De Haan was not alone in his choice of topic. The Amsterdam-based artistic
circle of the 'Eighties' whose leader was the poet Willem Kloos and whose main
paragons were Baudelaire, Verlaine and Huysmans had done so earlier. Kloos
was a passionate person and a drunkard who fell in love with a succession of
artistic friends for whom he wrote thinly veiled love poetry. Albert Verwey,
himself a poet and later a professor of literary history, responded with a famous
cycle 'Of the love named friendship.' Lodewijk van Deyssel, another member of
this group, published in 1889 a novel on boarding school life *De kleine republiek*
(The little republic). The main character falls in love with another boy, has sex
with him and is subsequently sent away. The story followed quite closely Van
Deyssel's own experiences in the elite Catholic school of Rolduc. The male circle
once staged a tribunal that had to decide on the lesbianism of two female artists
on the margins of their clique who had rejected the advances of a male member.
The judges, advised by Aletrino, acquitted the two women who for sure had an
intimate relationship.

Before the sex law of 1911 was enacted, parliament had discussed the
declining sexual morality of the nation on several occasions. The rise of pornography and apologies for uranians awakened the rage of several Christian
politicians but they had to face some opposition. A lawyer of aristocratic descent,
squire Jacob Anton Schorer, and H.J. Schouten, who was from a family of clergymen and used the pseudonym of G. Helpman, wrote several leaflets against
the impending sex laws. Their voice was heard but had too little weight in a
parliament dominated by Christian parties. Article 248bis, that forbade sexual

relations between adults and minors under 21 years, was accepted after extensive discussion. The law remained in force till 1971 and has been used in about 5,000 cases against homosexual men and in forty-eight cases against lesbians. Half of the cases resulted in a sentence, most often a prison term.

Schorer founded the first homosexual rights' movement in the Netherlands in 1912. Schorer had been an Obmann in the German WHK, like Von Römer. The NWHK was, till the Great War, a chapter of the German organization and from the beginning of the war, in which the Netherlands remained neutral, an independent group. Although Aletrino, Von Römer and the gay novelists M.J.J. Exler and J.H. François were nominal members of this group, Schorer shouldered most of the work alone. He published a Dutch version of the WHK leaflet 'Wat iedereen behoort te weten omtrent uranisme' (1912) that included a petition against article 248bis. This was abundantly signed by luminaries of Dutch culture and left-wing parties. He edited annual reports for the NWHK in 1915–20 and 1933–40, established a major gay library, helped homosexual men and brought them into contact with each other. In the years between the wars he was the main spokesperson of the homosexual movement.

The two other members of the NWHK, Exler and François, both wrote gay novels. François' two novels had The Hague as a background, *Anders* (1918, Different) and *Het Masker* (1922, The Mask). Exler wrote *Levensleed* (1911, Life's Grief) on the homosexual awakening of an Amsterdam young man who was lectured by his brother on the theories of Hirschfeld (who contributed the preface). The youngster committed suicide when he learned of the agonies of the not so gay life of uranians. Several other mediocre gay novels and some more interesting books of poetry were published but they never described Amsterdam (Hekma 1987; Van Lieshout and Hafkamp 1988).

From twilight to floodlight

The homosexual movement was based in The Hague which was also the site of the major gay scandals in those years: a police raid on a male bordello visited by men from the upper classes in 1919 and the arrest because of article 248bis of the chief treasurer of the government Mr L.A. Ries in 1936. The subculture in both The Hague and Amsterdam was of the same small size. Apart from some bars, circles of friends who met in private homes formed a mainstay of gay life. For same-sex contacts men chiefly depended on a public circuit of toilets and parks. At least forty of these all over the city were sites of gay activity till the 1960s. The Vondelpark, toilets on the Rembrandtplein and under the Mint Tower, on the square in front of the Central Station, around the Rijksmuseum, and also news centers in the Kalverstraat where one could read the latest newspapers and rub up against other clients attracted men. Both male and female prostitutes were found on Kalverstraat (Duyves 1992).

Bars and houses were irregularly raided by the police. In 1922 the bar of a certain Krakebeen (crack-leg) on the Singel was raided and, in 1932, the Empire in the Nes near Dam Square. This was the most long-standing homosexual bar of the period between the wars, in existence from 1911 to 1935 with some intervals. A group of homosexual men had produced from this bar the first gay journal *Wij* (We) and intended to found a 'Dutch Society for Human Rights' following earlier German examples. Just a week before the founding meeting the police raided the bar and arrested sixty-one persons. Because no one had committed a legal offense the arrests had few immediate consequences. But the journal and the society evaporated as many men felt threatened by this kind of harassment.

The Amsterdam vice squad, founded in 1931, soon numbered twenty-five officers who regularly visited bars where they expected to find depravity. As soon as the police officers saw too many homosexuals or lesbians, they obliged bar-owners to remove them. Managers always protested their earnest intention to be rid of such customers although the police did not believe their sincerity. One subversive gay barman asked once why he should not allow homosexuals in his bar. This made him only more suspect in the eyes of the police officers who then kept track of all his activities. The policemen faced two problems. They could not determine who was homosexual and there were no legal provisions against the existence of a gay bar. But they could always withdraw drinking or music licenses or simply harass the pub by raiding it to make the owners bend to their wishes. Based on arrests and other information, the Amsterdam vice squad had in the late 1930s a list of about 4,800 homosexuals, an amazing 1.7 per cent of Amsterdam males over 18 years of age (Koenders 1996; Tielman 1982).

Before World War II there were several homosexual bars that mostly existed for short periods of time. Some of them were quite successful like the Empire or the Volendam better known as 'Aunt Annie' in the Watersteeg. Those cafés took preventive measures against unwanted visitors like officers of the vice-squad. Often they had a doorman who warned the public in the bar with a signal that 'owls' (straights) or 'Russians' (officers) were entering. This signal could be a electric bell or a light bulb. Those measures were only necessary in the more homosexual places while mixed bars did not need them. Especially in the red light district there existed pubs tended by lesbians, often former prostitutes, for a public of whores, sailors, johns and fairies. The most famous example was Bet van Beeren's 't Mandje (The Basket) on the Zeedijk that opened in 1927 and closed fifty years later. It got its gay reputation because the gin-drinking, cigar-smoking and motorbike-driving dyke Bet allowed same-sex couples to dance on the Queen's birthday, an occasion for festive transgressions (van Kooten Niekerk and Wijmer 1985).

The bars that existed before 1940 were replaced during the war by others. Amazingly, given the Nazi persecution of homosexuals in Germany, several cafés started up during the war: the Rigo and the Thorbecke near the Rembrandtplein and the Monico or 'Blonde Saar' in the red light district that opened in 1941. This last bar still exists and is nowadays the bar with the longest uninterrupted tradition, with Blonde Saar still the owner in 1998. During the war it was raided by the police at least once and also denounced in a Nazi weekly as a meeting place of the weaklings of society that should have been exterminated long since. Notwithstanding the introduction of the harsher German legislation regarding 'unnatural lewdness' in the Netherlands there was less persecution of homosexuals than before the war because the police had other priorities.

Until the 1950s the red light district was an ideal cruising area for homosexual men and lesbian women. Straight men came there for sex and prostitutes made themselves available. But the men did not always succeed in bedding a woman because of lack of money or drunkenness. These lonely, horny men were easy prey for '*nichten*' (queens) hunting for sex with 'normal' men whom they called '*tule.*' In exchange for a bed, a drink, a dinner or a guilder *tules* were often willing to fuck queens. Effeminate homosexuals were the passive sex partners of masculine, active 'heterosexuals.' Cruising *tules* posed dangers but offered great pleasures for '*nichten.*' Of course not everybody lived the idea of being '*nicht*' to the point of being a caricature of the feminine male but it was commonplace in shaping a social structure of desires. The sexual pattern closely reflected the relation between whore and john, although the financial exchange went mostly in the opposite direction. The ideal place for such contacts was of course a place where all groups mixed and not an exclusively gay bar. Gay and lesbian sexual life was integrated with straight sexual life in a way that has become unthinkable in contemporary queer communities.

The sexual ideal of homosexuals was often a 'normal' man and their object choice was reflected in medical theories on homosexuality that emphasized that sexual desire needed opposites of male and female to get going. Thus the feminine homosexual needed a masculine heterosexual, although some experts like Von Römer had the feeling that homosexual men could also ignite in passion for each other. The same was true for lesbians where dykes fell in love with femmes. Both *tules* and femmes were of course unfaithful to their homosexual lovers as they always returned to their 'real' passion. Dykes and queens had a homosexual identity, while their partners did not. Of course, some lesbian femmes and homosexual *tules* will have used the charms of 'normalcy' to seduce same-sex partners.

This system of opposites floundered after World War II. There were four changes that went hand in hand. In the first place, *tules* had more options to get straight sex because they had more money and because virginity became less important for girls due to the easy availability and the quality of contraceptive methods. Second, gay men redefined their gender identity and could be masculine as well as feminine. A new leather culture even stressed the virility of its habitués. This was closely related to the third change: that gay men no longer looked for sex among 'normal' men, but mostly among themselves. Their relational model was no longer a copy of transactions in prostitution but aspired to the marriage-model. Steady friendships ('*vaste vriendschap*') became the ideal, with interchangeable sexual positions no longer fixed along lines of gender opposition. To find such friends one went to a gay bar or dance-hall where no heterosexuals would be welcome nor would they dare to go there. The fourth change was the development of an exclusively gay subculture that replaced the older mixed places like the urinals and the pubs of the red light district.

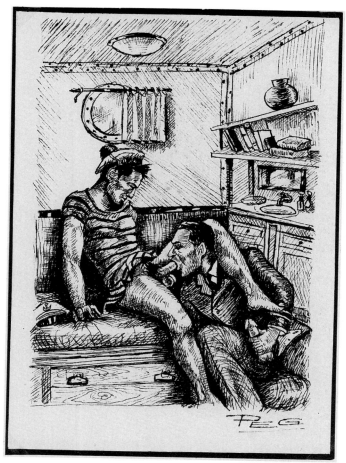

Figure 3.5 American drawing by 'Peg', seized by Dutch police. The image represents very nicely the unequal relation between 'tule' and 'nicht', trade and queen, the queen serving both the sailor and himself.

Source: Gert Hekma collection.

Only in the 1950s did Amsterdam become a gay capital. It offered bars with male prostitutes for the affluent. In 1952 the first leather bar, forerunner of the still famous Argos, started in a hotel. Two large dance-halls established Amsterdam's reputation beyond doubt. The gay movement COC (Center for Culture and Recreation) that was founded on 7 December 1946 in Amsterdam had organized lectures and weekly parties from the beginning. In 1952 it opened its first dance-hall, the DOK, on the Singel near the flower market, and also near the place on this canal where male hustlers offered their services. It was four times as large as the normal bar in Amsterdam. Being one of the very few dance-halls with a night license it could stay open during the week until 2 and at the weekend until 4. The financial administrator of the local COC succeeded in

Figure 3.6 The first leathermen on Amsterdam's streets, *c.*1955.
Source: Collectie Hartland, Nederlands Foto Archief, Rotterdam.

getting the license in his name in 1955 and the COC was forced to find another place. It opened in 1955 'De Schakel' (The Link) just off the Leidseplein. Both dance-halls were hugely successful and because homosexuals visited both places the Leidsestraat that connected them became in the late hours a major cruising street known as 'rue de Vaseline.' Soon, the Kerkstraat, halfway in between, also acquired its gay bars and, another innovation, gay hotels. In 1962 the first sauna 'The Athletic' opened.

The police developed in the 1950s the policy that queens could be better left among themselves in their bars and dance-halls than on the streets cruising normal men and boys and creating nuisances for the public. Bars were left alone but public toilets were controlled more strictly. The police patrolled toilets about twice a week and picked up often more than 100 men each year for public indecencies. The range of their anti-gay activities was broadened in 1955 when the city council of Amsterdam, following the example of other cities and on the request of the police, introduced a regulation that forbade men to be in urinals

Figure 3.7 Party in the dancing DOK, *c.*1955. The presence of a person in Dutch army
uniform is remarkable. Very few pictures have been made in gay venues with
the obvious aim of protecting the anonymity of clients.
Source: Collection Album Amsterdam.

more than 5 minutes. It was already forbidden to solicit for sexual purposes in
public. This article was primarily aimed against prostitutes but was also used
against homosexual cruising. The year 1955 marked a change in the anti-gay
policies in the city. Before, all homosexual meeting places had been repressed but
from 1955 on semi-public locations like bars and dance-halls were left alone,
while public indecencies were more strictly combated. This hampered the sexual
border traffic between gay and straight men. A separate gay world came into
existence that now started to integrate on a political level. The homosexual
movement, the COC, became a major force in this battle (Hekma 1992).

Before the war the NWHK had been bearing the flag of homosexual emancipation with little success and in 1932 there was the ill-fated effort to start a gay
magazine and movement that was raided away. But in 1940 some courageous
men started a new monthly *Levensrecht* (Right to Life). Its publication was interrupted after the German invasion of the Netherlands. After the war the same men
started their journal again and the COC that began as 'Shakespeare-club.' The
monthly soon got the new name *Vriendschap*. The movement was based in the
ground-floor apartment at the Keizersgracht of its chairperson Bob Angelo,
pseudonym of Nico Engelschman. It collaborated with the Amsterdam vice squad
which was ready to grant licenses for lectures and parties. Earnest discussions
with clergymen and psychiatrists of all denominations led to a growing acceptance of homosexuals. Opinions of highly regarded mental health-specialists in
the polarized Dutch environment did indeed change. Catholic and Calvinist
psychiatrists and clergymen who had in some cases compared homosexuality

with 'dunge' (shit) and irresponsibility in the early 1950s a decade later began to accept homosexuals as normal human beings whose steady friendships were an important contribution to their social well-being (Oosterhuis 1992). The COC was also the initiator of the 'International Committee for Sexual Equality,' the first postwar worldwide homosexual association. Its main activity was organizing conferences, the first in Amsterdam in 1951.

Engelschman had always worked behind the scenes using a pseudonym. Under the new chair Benno Premsela the COC went public and from 1965 on published a novel journal *Dialoog* (between homo- and heterosexuals clearly). Premsela made the first 'out' television appearance in 1964. Although the COC made much money from bar revenues it was disapproving of the subculture till the late 1970s, as, instead of helping homosexuals to integrate, it only strengthened the distinct queeny habits that were the object of social opprobrium. The COC wanted integration at the cost of a normalization of homosexuals and lesbians. Although the COC had earlier endorsed Hirschfeld's theories of a third sex, from the 1960s it argued for the normal homosexual who was no different from others apart from his sexual preference (Warmerdam and Koenders 1987).

Also, thanks to the continuous scandals provoked by the novelist Gerard Reve, social integration succeeded quite well. Reve, from a communist family, joined the Catholic Church in the late 1960s but not after many scandals, the most famous being the so-called donkey case. Reve published in the *Dialoog* a letter in which he described his relation to God. He himself fucked, as an expression of his divine love, the Lord who had taken the mundane form of a donkey. A right-wing Calvinist member of parliament took offense and requested a formal prosecution on grounds of blasphemy. All three times that the case went to court were major media events. Ultimately the case was reviewed by the Supreme Court of the Netherlands and, in the end, Reve was acquitted because the text was considered to be his private expression of religion and so could not be blasphemous.

Reve's novels were openly homosexual and expressed his favorite sexual scheme, the so-called 'revism': he himself being the adoring helper of a beloved young man who tortured an adolescent. This sadomasochistic triangle that is nearly always a fantasy scene ending up in (mutual) masturbation is repeated over and over in Reve's novels from the 1960s on. Other themes are his alcoholism, his hatred of communism and the working class, and his love for Catholicism, especially for the Madonna. In 1968 Reve won the major Dutch literary prize. To celebrate this prize, a kind of festive mock marriage of Reve with his lover 'Tiger' was celebrated in a Catholic church and broadcast on television. Early on in his career a Catholic minister had refused him a literary grant because of a masturbation scene in one of his novels. Sweet was Reve's revenge when he became in the 1970s the lover of this minister's son, the painter Joseph Cals (Hekma 1989).

In the 1960s Amsterdam became one of the magic cities of the sexual revolution. In 1967 the chair of the Dutch Society for Sexual Reformation (NVSH), Mary Zeldenrust-Noordanus, set a series of goals for sexual politics. Among them were the decriminalization of abortion, pornography, prostitution, homosexuality, and the legalization of contraceptives and divorce. The NVSH was at that moment a mass movement with 200,000 members, many of whom had become adherents because of the fact that the NVSH was allowed to distribute contraceptives. Amazingly most points the NVSH's program had been realized ten years later. In 1971 homosexuality was decriminalized and in 1973 gays and lesbians were allowed into the army while the COC won legal status. COC and NVSH joined forces in the 1960s to propagate civil sexual liberties and helped establish in 1967 an institute that offered help to gays and lesbians, the Schorer Foundation (Hekma 1990a).

To the left of the COC other gay and lesbian movements began, first of all homosexual students' action groups like the AJAH in Amsterdam. They danced in straight discos with same-sex couples and organized 'integrated parties' specifically for homosexual minors who were not allowed to enter gay dance-halls. They staged the first demonstrations, in 1969 in The Hague, against anti-homosexual legislation and, in 1971, at the official 4 May commemoration of the dead of World War II for the inclusion of the homosexual victims of the Nazis. In the 1960s the general feeling had been that homosexuals should learn to accept themselves, while the student groups were more political and requested that society should also change and make integration of homosexuality possible.

A new vibrant gay world

The AJAH disappeared into the COC in the early 1970s inducing a name change from Dutch Society of Homophiles (since 1964) to Dutch Society for the Integration of Homosexuality in 1971. Separatist groups would contest this policy of integration from 1973 on. 'Paarse (purple) September,' the first independent lesbian group in Holland, criticized the homophobia of feminism and the sexism of homosexual movements. In 1977, its successor Lesbian Nation came up with the first demonstration copied from the New York Christopher Street Day Parade. From 1975 radical faggot groups inspired by French activist Guy Hocquenghem began to criticize the COC for its normalizing policy asking the question what difference homosexuality made and answering that it made not only a difference in bed. These groups defended and practiced gay pleasures from gender-fuck and sadomasochism to pedophilia. They paved the way for separate gay and lesbian organizations within political parties, trade unions, health institutes and education. The COC, which had always wanted to be the mother-church and representative of all homosexuals, lost its central position. The Gay Krant took its place as the unofficial mouthpiece of the gay movement.

The development of gay groups in different institutions meant a major breakthrough, especially in politics. In 1978 the first openly gay member was elected to the city council. He resisted with some success the destruction of gay cruising places and with more success police raids on those places. He came up with the idea of the Homomonument (Koenders 1987). Amsterdam was the first city to have a report on the state and aims of gay and lesbian emancipation. This has now become a permanent part of city politics and the responsibility of one of the city's aldermen. Many more gay and lesbian council members have come out of the closet or were elected. Their number was in 1998 around the 10 per cent that is also the number of gays in the male population according to the city's only sex survey.

The gay and lesbian movement has seen many successes in the 1980s and 1990s. The growing acceptance of homosexuality has materialized in the development of local and national programs to combat discrimination, an anti-discrimination law, parliamentary support for same-sex marriages, inclusion of gays and lesbians in the ranks of army and police, subventions for gay and lesbian initiatives, support for gay and lesbian street parties on Queen's Day and around Amsterdam Pride during the first weekend of August and on other occasions. These successes are at the same time sapping the foundations of the movement because it has no attractive aims left. Many gays and lesbians and even more straight people have the feeling that homosexual emancipation is entering its end-phase because its goals have been reached. Often, people say emancipation may be needed among disadvantaged groups in far-away countries or among Christian and Muslim fundamentalist groups but no longer in Amsterdam, city of sexual tolerance.

Meanwhile the gay world of Amsterdam has only expanded further. Halfway through the 1960s the city authorities responded angrily to reports that planeloads of gay men came from England and Germany to Amsterdam and considered restraining the expansion of the gay world. But the sexual revolution overtook them and this world only swelled further. Liberation might mean to the COC that gays should dissolve into a tolerant society, for gay men it offered the possibility to embrace the gay world and to find there sexual partners and lovers. The on-going growth of the gay world and the increasing acceptance of homosexuality made Amsterdam into a very attractive city for gay men from everywhere.

When AIDS hit the world, Amsterdam had the distinct advantage that the epidemic struck the city with a certain delay, that gay health groups were active, and that health and gay authorities made a cooperative effort to combat the disease and prevent its spread. Measures were not repressive and no discos or saunas were closed but it was hoped that information would induce gay men to change their sexual behavior. This strategy was as elsewhere largely effective. A clear mistake was that gay campaigns tried to dissuade men from anal sex rather than promoting the use of condoms. AIDS has struck Amsterdam harshly. Half of all Dutch cases have been reported from the city although it harbors some 5 per cent of the country's population. Health care was offered to all patients often under conditions of social security, and a buddy system was set up immediately. Notwithstanding all measures, AIDS became a disaster for the gay world as many of its outstanding figures died of the disease, especially those from the leather scene and cultural life.

Since the start of the AIDS epidemic the size of the gay world has remained more or less stable. The leather bars that opened in the late 1970s in the vicinity of the famous Argos and the red light district did not disappear although many of their clients died. The leather parties that started in the 1970s withered away before AIDS but were taken up again in the 1990s as kinky parties were held in abandoned warehouses, attracting gay men in their thousands for wild dancing and sleazy sex. The old dance-hall of the COC closed in the 1970s and the DOK in the 1980s but other discos replaced them. Great fame has been bestowed upon Trut, Roxy and It, the trendy discos of the 1990s for their outrageous parties of drag extravaganza and other niceties.

Nowadays the city hosts at least 150 different gay and lesbian institutions: bars, discos, restaurants, hotels, health centers, book shops, sports clubs, archives, gay and lesbian studies, sex cinemas, shops for leather, rubber and underwear. Clubs have been founded for dancing, s/m, safe sex, 'horsemen and knights,' the affluent, for men interested in gardens, sailing, literature or old cars. Anglo-Saxons, Arabs, Surinamese and Turks have their own special events. Travel, legal, medical and many other services are offered to a gay public. Two or three free monthlies are available in the bar scene. The city is a vibrant spot for gays also because many 'general' public places have become highly homosexualized.

Since the late 1970s, other cities in Europe have seen a similar expansion and opening up of the gay scene that Amsterdam had experienced earlier. The progress Amsterdam had made in the 1960s can nowadays also be witnessed in other major European cities. The number and sometimes also the quality of gay institutions is higher nowadays in Paris, London or Berlin. The advantages the center of Amsterdam still has are its compact urban structure, its architectural beauty and its cosmopolitan, tolerant and easy-going atmosphere that has no equivalent elsewhere.

Around 1985, instead of raiding gay cruising places, the police began protecting them. Important incentives were the fag- and dyke-bashing at the national gay and lesbian demonstration in Amersfoort in 1982, and the murder of a gay man at a urinal in Amsterdam in 1985. Amersfoort was a watershed as both the gay and lesbian movement and the authorities started to develop policies to combat or prevent discrimination and violence. After Amersfoort self-defense groups were founded that developed into gay and lesbian sports organizations such as Tijgertje (small tiger) in Amsterdam. After the murder of a married and closeted gay man at a pissoir the mayor of Amsterdam came to the COC to express his outrage. Since that time, the Amsterdam police have, with some ups and downs, enacted a pro-gay and lesbian policy protecting gay meeting places and encouraging gays and lesbians to join the police force.

But not all violence was combated in the same spirit. During the 1980s two men were killed each year in the twilight world of male prostitution. The police always defined these murders as cases of robbery although their homophobic content was quite clear because of the excessive violence used. Neither the police nor the gay and lesbian movement paid much attention to these regular killings of mostly older gay men by hustlers who were highly unsure of their sexual preference and behavior. While in straight prostitution clients sometimes murder whores, in the gay scene hustlers murder their patrons, indicating the lack of self-consciousness regarding homosexuality in Holland both among hustlers and clients (van Gemert 1994).

Queer were the demands the police made for the Europride held in Amsterdam in 1995. This largest gay and lesbian demonstration ever in the Netherlands with about 50,000 participants was ordered by the police not to show sexual acts or representations of such acts, particularly forbidding images of pedophilia and bestiality. This outrageously formulated demand showed the police's lack of familiarity with gays and lesbians, and the persistence of theories of perversion which equate all sexual variations.

In recent years the Amsterdam vice squad has staged several raids on sex shops because of the alleged presence of kiddy porn and has succeeded, after active campaigning, in broadening the definition of forbidden material and raising the penalties. Erotic postcards that were for a long time a major tourist trap were removed from the streets on the orders of the police and mayor, using an outdated criminal provision against 'offensive images,' because they feared for the reputation of the city. Both gay and straight bordellos and hustler bars have been raided because of the alleged presence of illegal prostitutes while 'violent' transgender hustlers from Latin America working for a 'straight' clientele were removed by the police with unnecessary harshness. City officials showed little enthusiasm for the evident economic input of gay tourism in their city, instead deploring the negative reputation of Amsterdam as being a city of sex and drugs.

Most straightforward discrimination may have disappeared, but acceptance is no more than skin-deep. General culture, in Amsterdam as elsewhere, is hetero-sexual, with few visible signs of homosexuality. Expectations of someone's sexual preference will always be in a heterosexual, rarely homosexual direction. Explicit manifestations of gays and lesbians are always frowned upon and so the main question with regard to the Gay Games in Amsterdam in 1998 was whether it was not unnecessary to have such an event. Few people would dare to ask such a ques-tion about similar events for Chinese, Turks or Jews. Gay and lesbian groups are deemed to be past it, left without essential goals in contemporary society. The most clear example of this unsatisfactory situation is the difficulty young men and women who are on the verge of coming out face in finding safe places for homo-sexual pleasure and information because Amsterdam and the Netherlands are generally speaking still a straight ghetto. An amazing half of male adolescents say in surveys without hesitation that they disapprove of gay sex.

Since the sexual revolution gay men have developed a rich culture of erotic and social pleasures. Their culture has remained marginal, however, because straights and lesbians on the other hand have not succeeded in putting into prac-tice the expectations of the sexual revolution. The main changes in the straight world between 1965 and 1995 are the development from monogamy to serial monogamy and the rise of self-stimulation. No free-floating sexual culture emerged like that developed among gay men. A sexual breakthrough has failed among straights and lesbians. The most significant reasons for this in my view derive from the differentiation of male and female sexuality in culture and education which inhibits easy sexual communication between men and women. The pressure to combine sex and love thwarts both loving and sexual relations, as does the idea that sexuality belongs to nature and needs little cultivation, or the belief in sexual privacy while repudiating the public forms of sexuality like the coming out of gays and lesbians. These views still hinder the emergence of a rich and free sexual culture in Amsterdam and block the development of erotic pleasures beyond homo- and heterosexuality. Amsterdam has long been a vestige of the 1960s but it seems to refuse to become a vibrant herald of the next millennium.

4 London

Randolph Trumbach

By 1700 the City of London, urban Middlesex and Westminster had grown together
into a single city of 500,000, and by 1800 London's population had nearly
doubled to 1 million, making it the largest city in Europe. Culturally the city was
divided between a fashionable West End and a commercial East End. There were
pockets of poor to be found in the West End, many of whom were tied to the
service economy that catered to gentlemen and their families, but most of the
laboring poor lived and worked in the East End in industries like weaving or in
various activities connected with the port. London's population had to be
sustained by immigration from the countryside, especially in the early eighteenth
century when the level of mortality in the city was quite high. The steady flow of
people in and out of the city meant that at any one moment at least one person in
six in the country as a whole had spent some part of life in London. London's
influence therefore permeated the rest of the country but not simply because it
was the seat of the national government to which the gentry and the aristocracy
regularly came each year for several months. This yearly visitation by the elite
facilitated the flow of common fashions among them, not only in their clothes but
also in their deepest feelings, so that over the course of a single generation in the
middle of the century, they gave up the arranged marriage and the wet-nurse that
for centuries had set the tone of life in their families, and began instead to marry
for love and to nurse their infants themselves.

In the first generation after 1700 London also became the site of a profound
revolution in gender relations and sexual behavior. It affected all social classes
and was to be found not only in England but in all the modernizing societies of
north-western Europe. By 1730 all men were divided into what by the late nineteenth century came to be called a homosexual minority and a heterosexual
majority, but the male majority enacted their new sexual identity with women
who did not yet share their ideal of an exclusive heterosexuality. Among women
a homosexual minority only appeared in the generation after 1770. This sapphist
minority did not have the impact on women that the sodomite minority had had
on men two generations earlier, for the majority of women continued to define
their sexual identities through their relations with men. Male heterosexual desire
in eighteenth-century London sought its fulfillment whether men were married
or not, and it is in fact easiest to document and to locate physically this desire in

illicit sexual relations outside of marriage. In these relations a majority of men pursued various minorities of women. Some of these women were streetwalking prostitutes; some were seduced either at home or at work or in the street, and occasionally with promises of marriage; and some women (both married and single) were raped either at home or in the streets. Prostitution and seduction were to be found in different locations, but violence could occur anywhere. Prostitution was organized around the great thoroughfare that ran through the town and joined East End to West End. Seduction had a distinctive local pattern and varied according to the economy of the parish. Illicit heterosexual desire in the majority of men therefore reflected the spatial differentiation throughout the city between its fashionable center and the local neighborhoods, a differentiation which endured through the nineteenth and twentieth centuries as London grew to 4 million people by 1900 and 6 million by 1940. But illicit sexual desire in the majority of women (instead of being regulated by the standard of heterosexuality) came to be organized through the romantic love that was inculcated after 1750 in women living in London. This was the case for the women of the upper and middle classes in the second half of the eighteenth century, and by the early nineteenth century it was true for all women. A married woman was most likely to fall in love with a man she met at home or in her domestic circle. She justified herself by appealing to a higher standard of love and was not likely to think herself driven by the inexorable desire that heterosexual men supposed themselves to feel as an essential part of their masculine identity (Trumbach 1978, 1994a, 1994b, 1998).[1]

The effeminate homosexual minority of sodomites who made their appearance in the first generation of the eighteenth century have to be located in the city in the same alternations between center and neighborhood, and between driving desire and domestic romance, that contained the sexual lives of the majority of men and women. The coming into existence of this effeminate male minority produced in the rest of the century a revolutionary new system of three genders composed of men, women and sodomites. Modern European society had shifted from a system in which sexual relations between males were regulated by differences in age to one in which a third gender of biological males combined aspects of both male and female behavior. In traditional European society all adult males had desired both women and adolescent males. This is now best documented for Renaissance Florence. By the age of 40 two-thirds of all Florentine men had been legally implicated in sodomy. But their passive sexual partners were all adolescents between the ages of 15, when puberty began, and 19, when secondary male characteristics appeared. Between the ages of 19 and 23, boys could be either passive with someone older or active with someone younger. After this men were always active. They also went to female prostitutes and at 30 the majority married and had children. Statistical evidence of this kind cannot be produced for England before 1700, but the anecdotal evidence fits entirely into this pattern. Every example given in Alan Bray's book, for example, is of relations between an adult and an adolescent, and I have published a number of examples of the gentlemanly rake who was attracted to both adolescent boys and women. In that world all boys passed through a period of sexual passivity when they were objects of men's desire before they made the transition in their early twenties from the passive to the active role. But whether in ancient Greece or Rome, or in medieval Christian society, there was always a minority of males who found it difficult or impossible to make this transition and were mocked consequently for their adult effeminate passivity (Bray, 1995; Rocke 1996; Trumbach 1989a, 1989b, 1990).

After 1700 under the new system, the majority of males were supposed to be sexually active at every stage of life from adolescence to old age. But a minority of males were socialized as children into a role that was both male and female. Some of these males were effeminate as children, and played with girls and with dolls. As men they displayed varying degrees of effeminacy. A few lived an openly transvestite life and were usually referred to as *she* and *her*. Others were unable to conceal an effeminate manner in speech or movement. And a third group seemed to display no obvious effeminacy at all. But in the enclosed space of the molly-house or their private rooms many men used female names and were occasionally transvestite. These men found their sexual partners among men like themselves (and in this they differed from third-gender males outside the European world), but they also had relations with both adolescent and adult males who were not sodomites. It was even the case that for some sodomites (or homosexuals) their preferred sexual partners were males who were not sodomites, and this was true until at least the 1950s. Some other men who sought heterosexual partners preferred adolescents and wished to dominate them; they were likely to deny effeminacy in themselves. But other more effeminate men sought partners who would dominate them and whom they wished to believe were really attracted only to women. In some sexual venues a sodomite was likely to find only other sodomites, but in others he would also encounter men who were not sodomites. In the latter places a sodomite risked violence, blackmail and arrest, but this may have added an erotic charge to such encounters. In all places, however, the sodomite's sexual behavior was likely to approximate that of the female prostitute since if a sodomite were like a woman, he was taken by himself and others to be the most abandoned kind of a woman. The domesticated contexts in which heterosexual men seduced unmarried girls and other men's wives was therefore less likely to overlap with the sodomite's world than those places in which a man pursued a streetwalking whore (Trumbach 1988, 1997).

In the first generation of the new system of three genders, sodomites met each other either in the relatively safe enclosed spaces of their own rooms or of a molly-house that catered only to them, or they picked up in the streets, the public gardens or the arcades of shops in Covent Garden, London Bridge or the Exchange, men and boys who were often not sodomites, and invited them to the more enclosed space of a public toilet or private room in a tavern. There are descriptions of molly-houses in 1709, 1714 and 1729. In 1709 a soldier called Skelthorp, who was executed for sodomy, confessed the location of some of the houses. A footboy to a duke revealed another meeting place which led to arrests. A brandy shop in Jermyn Street was one location, 'the person who kept the shop being one of the gang.' The evidence for what occurred inside these houses in 1709 comes from Ned Ward. Ward wrote that men in these houses called themselves mollies. 'Molly' was a term originally used for female prostitutes. Its application to adult effeminate male sodomites began a linguistic practice that has been maintained for three centuries in which many of the popular terms once used for female prostitutes were subsequently used to categorize effeminate men. (Some later examples in English language usage: queen, punk, gay, faggot, fairy, and fruit.) According to Ward the men 'speak, walk, tattle, curtsy, cry, and scold' to mimic women, and their manners were 'the indecencies of lewd women.' The mollies entertained themselves with an enactment 'of a groaning woman' (or a woman in labor) who was delivered of a 'jointed baby' or a wooden doll. The man who played the mother was dressed in a 'woman's night-gown, sarsnet-hood, and nightrale'; the man who was the country midwife wore a 'high crowned hat and an old beldam's pinner'; and there was a nurse in a 'hussife's coif.' When the labor was done, the child was dressed, presented to its father and christened. A feast was laid and the women sat and talked about their husbands and children. But when the play was over, all these men had sex with one another. Ward protested that they profaned a holy sacrament as a diversion for profligates. Their sexual acts were those of men 'sunk into a state of devilism' and their club was a 'diabolical society.' These libertines mocked true religion and worshipped the devil. It is a description that intriguingly ties them to the devil clubs of the male libertines who went with women (*Full* 1709; Ward, 1709: 284–98).

The mollies were certainly irreverent, but it seems unlikely that they were self-consciously libertine. Their mock groaning and christening were probably based on popular traditions that used such public enactments to express disapproval of sexual irregularities. An incident seven years later, in 1716, in a rural Gloucestershire village of eighty inhabitants, helps to make the point. George Andrews, a tenant farmer, met a young farm laborer, Walter Lingsey, as he lay at midnight on a bridge. Andrews took Lingsey's hand, fondled it, complimented the softness of his skin, and put his hand into Lingsey's breeches. Andrews then said they would be more comfortable in his house. Once there, they got into bed, and Andrews sodomized the young man. The story came out when Lingsey explained to another laborer where he had spent the night. Andrews was an overbearing and unpopular man. He had also been 'infamous for these practices formerly.' But no one had ever denounced him, and in this case, no one at first brought him to the magistrate. Instead, a group of local men planned 'a mock groaning.' One of them was a tenant farmer; another was a blacksmith who had helped organize a groaning in another village; a third was a churchwarden, who was probably encouraged by his wife. A fiddler was hired, food and drink were prepared, and a hundred people from neighboring villages came to see the show (Rollison 1981: 70–97).

Lingsey was dressed in a 'mantua petticoat, white apron, and headclothes' to look like a woman. Another man played the midwife who delivered Lingsey of a child in the form of a wad of straw dressed in baby's clothes. Another man was appointed the parson. He christened the child saying as much of the Prayerbook ritual as he could remember. The two godfathers gave the child the name of George, since his father was George Andrews. They then feasted and sent for some women to 'wait with the lying-in woman as they termed Lingsey.' This groaning was a scandal to some. It was reported to the absentee landlord who was a Chancery master in London. He was shocked that the sacrament had been profaned and that a riot had been tolerated. Andrews was eventually charged with sodomy, brought to trial and found not guilty.

It is apparent that both the villagers in Gloucestershire and the mollies in London saw sodomy as an inversion of sexual relations between men and women. When one male sodomized another, he treated him as man was supposed to treat a woman. The passive male indeed became a woman. But the purpose of the sexual act between men and women was to create children and by baptism make them Christians and heirs to heaven. This sodomy could not do, and it was the intention of the villagers to make that point. It is doubtful that they meant to mock religion. They much more likely saw themselves as its upholders, though perhaps in not so reverent a way as the gentry. But what did the London sodomites mean by their ceremony? It differed in a number of significant details from the rural one. In London there were, of course, no female participants. The men played all the roles. In Gloucestershire, one man acted the midwife, but they sent for actual women to sit with the lying-in woman and talk with him as his gossips. In London, the men were the gossips. They enjoyed the sociability of women's lives. In Gloucestershire the man who played the midwife could see his role not as social but as sexual. Midwives fingered women's sexual parts and men read midwifery books for sexual stimulation. But to be a gossip was to be interested in the things women spoke about, and with all that the Gloucester men wished to have nothing to do.

There is in the Gloucester story not much evidence or interest in male effeminacy. For the sodomites in London, it was the center of their world. This makes it unlikely that the Gloucester story shows that concern about the molly's role had already made its way into this rural backwater. It was instead that both groups of men drew on the satirical tradition of the charivari to make their points. The men in Gloucestershire wished to disapprove of a sexuality which was unnatural because it was not reproductive. It is more difficult to say what the mollies meant to satirize. Ward was certain that they wished to express their hatred for women. There was no doubt some of that. But the mollies also liked women's ways, and that to them was the rub. Men were not supposed to like women's ways. They tolerated them. As Ward said, these were 'all the little vanities that custom has reconciled to the female sex.' The molly, therefore, could express his fondness for what he in part desired to be only by mocking it. He both loved and hated the female part of his role. He could indulge it in the privacy of the molly-house. But if his taste was exposed in public, his shame could be so intense that he might take his life.

The molly-house from 1714 was documented by Jonathan Wild, the leader of the thieves' underground. He did not describe anything like the mock groaning but he confirmed the effeminacy of speech and gesture and provided the first clear description of group transvestism. It was part of his controversy with Charles Hitchen, the corrupt Under Marshall of the City. Hitchen was a sodomite who seems to have preferred the streets and a room in a public house for himself, but he was familiar with the group activity of the molly-house. In 1727 the Societies for the Reformation of Manners who had long tried to prosecute Hitchen, successfully brought a case for attempted sodomy against him. Hitchen had frequently picked up soldiers and taken them to a public house. There he would call for a private room and this made one of the servants suspect that he was a sodomite. But Hitchen for years had been confident that no one would move against him. Accordingly on a night in 1714 he told Wild that he 'would intro-duce him to a company of he-whores.' Wild did not understand the word, and 'asked if they were hermaphrodites: No ye fool, said the M[arsh]l, they are sodomites, such as deal with their sex instead of females.' The two men then went to a public house where Wild found that the men addressed Hitchen as 'Madam' and 'Ladyship.' The men called one another 'my dear,' hugged and kissed, 'tickling and feeling each other as if they were a mixture of wanton males and females,' that is, some took the male role and some the female. Their voices and their manner were effeminate. They were witty, 'some telling others that they ought to be whipped for not coming to school more frequently' (Wild, 1718: 30–2, reprinted in Lyons 1936: 278–81).[2]

Hitchen, however, had not received the attention from some of the younger men that he expected and so he decided to be revenged. He would arrest them when they held a ball. Hitchen explained that there was 'a noted house in Holborn to which [they] used to repair and dress themselves in women's apparel for the entertainment of others of the same inclinations in dancing and the like in imitation of the fair sex.' When the ball broke up, Hitchen arrested the men and took them to jail in their finery. The next day they appeared before the Lord Mayor still in their women's clothes. The Mayor ordered them to be taken through the streets in these clothes as part of their punishment. They were also sentenced to the work-house and stayed there until one of them threatened to reveal some of Hitchen's own adventures. There were similar balls in the next decade. The keeper of an inn in 1723 was arrested with several other men 'dressed in women's apparel very indecent and unseemly, accompanied with lewd actions and behavior.' Two years later, twenty-five men 'in masquerade habits' were arrested in a house near Covent Garden. These displays, however, were not for the public eye, and some men could not easily deal with the public exposure. One of the young men in 1714 found the public trial, parade and imprisonment 'so mortifying that he died a few days after his release.'[3]

The best evidence in the entire century for life in the molly-house comes from the arrests and trials that the Societies for the Reformation of Manners inspired in 1726. In the last few months of 1725, a group of at least four agents of the Societies (Samuel Stevens, William Davison, Thomas Willis and Joseph Sellers) began to visit the molly-houses in order to gather evidence. They were led by a young sodomite named Mark (or Martin) Partridge who in the end did not appear in any of the actual trials, perhaps because his fellow sodomites had become suspicious of him before the investigation was completed. Partridge had quarreled with another sodomite named William Harrington. In revenge he began to inform against the entire world of his fellows. On one occasion Partridge was nearly mobbed in a molly-house when some men called him a 'treacherous, blowing-up, mollying bitch, and swore they'd massacre anybody that should betray them.' Partridge was saved by the unsuspecting man who kept the molly-house who six months later was hanged for sodomy. In February 1726, Partridge bound himself to give evidence against eleven men and one woman for keeping molly-houses and against sixteen other men (including Charles Hitchen) for going to these houses and for 'acting sodomitical practices' there and elsewhere. The government intervened at some point early in 1726, and the prosecutions were directed by the Treasury Solicitor's deputy. The evidence of actual sodomy for which four men were condemned and three executed was in the end given by two young sodomites, Thomas Newton and Edward Courtney. They had been the passive partners and because of their evidence, presumably, they were not tried themselves. But a much larger number of men than the four condemned to death were arrested in 1726. There were at least (one of the quarter-sessions rolls is decayed) twenty-one in the City and twenty-three in Westminster. A further twelve men whom Partridge accused seem not to have been arrested. This makes a total of fifty-six men charged or arrested for sodomy or sodomitical practices. Partridge accused twelve people of keeping molly-houses in Westminster, and one more man was arrested on that charge. Three married couples and two men were also charged in the City with keeping molly-houses. Since two of the Westminster men kept a house together, this makes a total of seventeen houses.[4]

The *London Journal* was therefore not much off when it reported in May 1726 that 'twenty houses have been discovered which entertained sodomitical clubs.' The paper added that 'these monsters' also met each other 'at what they call the markets'; they were the Royal Exchange and the piazzas of Covent Garden, the Lincoln's Inn bog-houses, and Moorfields and the south side of St James's Park. The first two were arcades of shops, the last two were public parks, in all of which one might saunter, catch an interested party's eye, and consummate the act nearby. In these markets, unlike the molly-houses, a sodomite could meet men who were not sodomites. But these venues were used as much by female whores and their male customers as by sodomites. This must have confirmed the public identification of sodomites with whores. Women were not likely, on the other hand, to be found lingering in men's toilets, but even there the occasional whore was found with her man. The Societies, with the aid of disaffected sodomites, had laid open the topography of London's Sodom.[5]

The specific location was given for a dozen molly-houses: nine in 1726 and three more in 1727 and 1728. They spread themselves across all of London, but were concentrated in three areas, going from east to west. Three of them were close to Moorfields, which was itself the site of one of the sexual markets. There was a second concentration of three houses in Holborn. Two of them were near each other in Field Lane and Pye Corner near Smithfield Market. Between these two houses and the third in Drury Lane were the Lincoln's Inn bog-houses and Snow Hill, both used for making pick-ups. The third concentration of houses radiated in a circle from the hub of Charing Cross. There was one at Charing Cross and two in the courts at the top of Hedge Lane, where they must have mingled with Soho bawdy-houses. There was a house in St James's Square and one down Whitehall in King Street, Westminster. All but one of these were discovered in 1726. The two remaining houses were found in Whitechapel and Marylebone in 1727 and 1728, at the opposite ends of the thoroughfare that the female prostitutes used, and on either side of the three main concentrations of houses. It apparently had taken longer to reach them because of their relative isolation.[6]

The molly-house came in different kinds. Most of them were alehouses. Some of them may have been open to the general public with a more private room or two at the back for mollies. This seems to have been the case with the houses kept by Thomas Orme and George Whitle. But Whitle and his servants denied that his back rooms were used by mollies. He said that what Drake Stoneman had seen (Stoneman had been arrested for being in Margaret Clap's molly-house) were surgeons examining their patients. Margaret Clap and her husband kept a coffeehouse. In the manuscript records the house is described a number of times as being John Clap's coffeehouse. But only Margaret was arrested, tried and sentenced to the pillory where she was treated severely by the mob. She protested at her trial that since she was a woman 'it cannot be thought that I would ever be concerned in such practices.' But Samuel Stevens, one of the undercover agents, said that she had appeared 'to be wonderfully pleased with' the obscene conversation of the men. On Sunday nights (the busiest night of the week for the molly-houses) there usually had been from twelve to forty men in her house. At least two other houses were run by married couples. One of the husbands, Samuel Roper, was clearly a molly. He was charged with sodomy as well as with keeping a disorderly house and was known as Plump Nelly. He died in prison awaiting trial. Two men, Robert Whale and York Horner, were mollies who together kept a house in King Street, Westminster. Whale was known as Margaret or Peggy and Horner was Pru. John Towleton who was Mary Magdalen and Thomas Mugg who was Judith also kept houses. But a molly-house could be a very modest affair. Thomas Wright kept two different rooms around Moorfields. He went out to fetch drink from alehouses, and the men 'allowed him a profit out of it.'[7]

The life inside five of the molly-houses was described in 1726. There was, however, no mock birth or groaning like those in Edward Ward's description or the Gloucestershire case. It may simply have been that the agents of the Societies were not present on the night that this occurred in 1725. It certainly continued to occur throughout the century. Robert Holloway claimed that around 1790 in a house in Clement's Lane near the Strand, a group of men were arrested 'in the very act of giving caudle to their lying-in women [with] the new-born infants personated by large dolls.' What was described in 1726 were the effeminacy, the sexual flirtations and their consummations. Three of the trials described

Margaret Clap's house. It may have drawn the largest crowd. Thomas Newton, the 30-year-old sodomite who led the agents to the house, said that she had beds in every room of the house for 'the more convenient entertainment of her customers.' Samuel Stevens saw men in a group of twenty or thirty, hugging and kissing and sitting in each other's laps in one room, 'and making love (as they called it) in a very indecent manner.' Couples then went into another room, and when they returned, they 'would tell what they had been doing, which, in their dialect, they called *marrying*.' Stevens said that William Griffin had kissed everyone around, and had then thrown his arms around Stevens' neck, hugged and squeezed him, and tried to put his hands into his breeches. Men got up to dance and made curtsies. They mimicked women's voices: 'O fie, sir! – Pray, sir – Dear, sir – Lord, how can you serve me so? – I swear I'll cry out – You're a wicked devil – and you're a bold face – Eh, ye little dear Toad! Come buss!'[8]

When Mark Partridge agreed to take Joseph Sellers to the house in Drury Lane, it was arranged that Sellers should pass as Partridge's 'husband,' to 'prevent my being too far attacked by any of the company.' Martin Mackintosh – who like many of the men took a 'maiden' or woman's name: his was Orange Deb – came up to Sellers nonetheless and 'thrust his hand into my breeches and his tongue into my mouth.' He swore he would go 40 miles to enjoy him and begged him 'to go backwards and let him.' When Sellers refused, Mackintosh offered to be passive himself and pulled down his own breeches and tried to sit naked in Sellers' lap. Partridge chased him off with a hot poker from the fire and 'threatened to run it into his arse.' (Samuel Stevens who was also present confirmed this story.) Mackintosh, like most of the men in the house, had adopted some feminine characteristics, but in the sexual act he was prepared to be either active or passive. This sexual versatility, according to *The Wandering Whore* in 1660, had once been a characteristic only of a minority of adult sodomites in the days when desire between males was organized by differences in age. It is likely that by 1726 it was widespread among all sodomites. Joseph Sellers and William Davison gave similar descriptions of the men in Thomas Wright's room for mollies near Moorfields after they were taken there by Mark Partridge. There was a fiddler for music and dancing and bawdy songs were sung ('Come let us [fuck] finely') accompanied with sexual gestures. There was a second smaller room with a bed where some of the eight men went. They sometimes closed the door, but they sometimes left it open so that part of what occurred could be seen.[9]

The evidence for the remaining two houses came from an 18-year-old boy called Ned Courtney who, when things were hard, seems to have sold himself to his fellow sodomites. In his actual prostitution, he was probably exceptional, since although the molly copied the mannerisms of the female whore, most of the sexual acts in the molly-houses seem to have occurred without one man's paying the other. Courtney ordinarily worked as a servant in public houses: the Yorkshire Grey in Bloomsbury Market, the Cardigan's Head in Charing Cross, a cook's shop in St Martin's Lane, and finally at Tom Orme's Red Lyon in Crown Court, Knaves Acre, which was a molly-house. He was something of an upstart and had been put three times in Bridewell for insolence towards his betters. He abused one master's mother when he came home drunk. He was saucy to a constable who stopped him in the night as he helped Tom Orme to carry off his goods to avoid the creditors of the molly-house. On the third occasion, Courtney was arrested because he was making a scene in Covent Garden over a 'mollying-cull,' that is one of his male sodomite customers. Courtney could be threatening. George Kedger, who was convicted for sodomy with Courtney, said that once when Courtney met him he told him that all he had to live on was what he got from prostitution, that he wanted money, and that if Kedger would not help him, 'he would swear my life away.' Kedger was found guilty of sodomy but later reprieved, probably because Courtney made a poor witness. More certainly, the jury did not believe what he had to say about the molly-house that he claimed George Whitle kept at the Royal Oak at the corner of St James's Square since the jury acquitted Whitle.[10]

The description of Whitle's supposed house is nonetheless interesting. It is possible that the house had in fact harbored mollies, for men could argue their way out of real evidence. John Derwin, for instance, was accused of sodomy with a link-boy (link-boys carried torches at night). But he was heard boasting in Margaret Clap's molly-house that he had 'baffled' the boy's evidence before the magistrate, and that the testimonial that Clap gave as to his good character had gone a long way in 'bringing him off.' It therefore may have been that the two women servants that Whitle brought to court to swear that they had seen neither mollies nor Ned Courtney in his house were being as helpful as Clap had been to Derwin. Whitle was married and had children like some of the other men accused of sodomy. He said that the story of the molly-house was spread by a neighbor who owed him rent and whose wife used to call him a sodomite dog. (It was common for women to call other women whore as a result of such disputes.) Some of his neighbors agreed that it was from this couple that they had heard the rumors of sodomy in Whitle's house. But a male neighbor did say that Edward Courtney had frequented Whitle's house and had told him that he quarreled with Whitle when he would not let Courtney have a pint of beer when it was time to close. Whitle was a peace-maker and reminded his customers to go home to their wives. On the other hand, at least one man believed the story and said that his fellow neighbors had stopped going to Whitle's when they heard that he kept a molly-house. Finally, Drake Stoneman, one of the men who was arrested and charged for being in Margaret Clap's molly-house, supported Courtney's statement as to what had occurred in Whitle's house.[11]

Courtney testified that behind the regular room for his neighborhood customers, Whitle kept a back room for mollies to drink in. Between this room and the kitchen, there was still another 'private room.' There was a bed in the middle of this last room for men to go in couples and be married, and for this reason they called it the chapel. Courtney said that Whitle had helped him to find two or three husbands there. Whitle had once asked him to 'give… a wedding night' to a 'country gentleman' who would pay handsomely. Courtney stayed till midnight, but the gentleman never came. Since it was too late to go home, he shared Whitle's bed who promised him 'a great deal of money' if he would let Whitle have him. Courtney agreed, but the next morning he got 'no more than six-pence.' Whitle, Courtney said, had 'put the bite upon me.' If it was true, it was probably to revenge this rather than the pint of beer he had been refused, that Courtney gave his evidence. Drake Stoneman added to Courtney's story that he had known Whitle's house for two or three years. He had seen men expose themselves to each other (Whitle said it was surgeons examining venereal patients) and had heard them say 'Mine is best. Yours has been battersead.' He also knew of a room called the Chapel, but he claimed not to know what the men did who went into it.[12]

Sodomites socialized and had sex with fellow sodomites not only in the molly houses. They sometimes did so as well in their lodgings, though they had to be careful of the neighbors. Thomas Baker in his play, *Tunbridge-Walks or the Yeoman of Kent*, (1703), has Maiden meet his friends in his chambers in the Temple, where they 'play with fans and mimick the women, scream, "hold up your tails," make curtsies, and call one another Madame.' Thomas Wright, one of the men tried in 1726 admitted at his execution that he had followed 'these abominable courses,' but when he attempted at his trial to save his life, the two women who lived above his room swore that while they had heard music and merry-making from below, they had never known of any sodomitical practices and that Wright himself behaved 'like a sober man and was a very good Churchman.' Wright and his friends were aware that their effeminate mannerisms could be displayed only once their doors were safely shut (Senelick 1990: 33–67).[13]

Sodomites also met each other in two kinds of public or semi-public environments. There were the arcades and the gardens or parks like the Exchange, London Bridge and Moorfields, and there were the bog-houses in the Temple and the Savoy, in which one lingered to show interest. There was a standard sexual opening. One man displayed his penis and tried to put it in the other's hand. After this he would reach into the other's breeches for his penis. If this opening was accepted, they then proceeded to negotiate the act to be performed. The sexual acts themselves (usually either masturbation or sodomy with fellatio a poor third) were then consummated on the spot or in a nearby lane or tavern. But these places were especially dangerous since many of the men encountered in them were not sodomites. The likelihood of being arrested or blackmailed was much higher than if one used a molly-house. For those men, however, who wished to have sex with men who were not sodomites, these dangers had to be risked.

Thomas Vaughan who was accused of blackmailing Edward Barker, said in 1706 that he had met Barker (an apothecary in the Strand) in the piazzas of Covent Garden, a place where it was common enough for men to meet female prostitutes and for sodomites to saunter. Barker asked Vaughan to go with him to the Savoy bog-house and when they were there, Barker asked Vaughan to bugger him. Vaughan did not say whether he did. A few months later Vaughan saw Barker going down to the bog-house in the Temple. (Vaughan clearly spent a lot of his time in or near the bog-houses.) He followed him in and sat on the seat

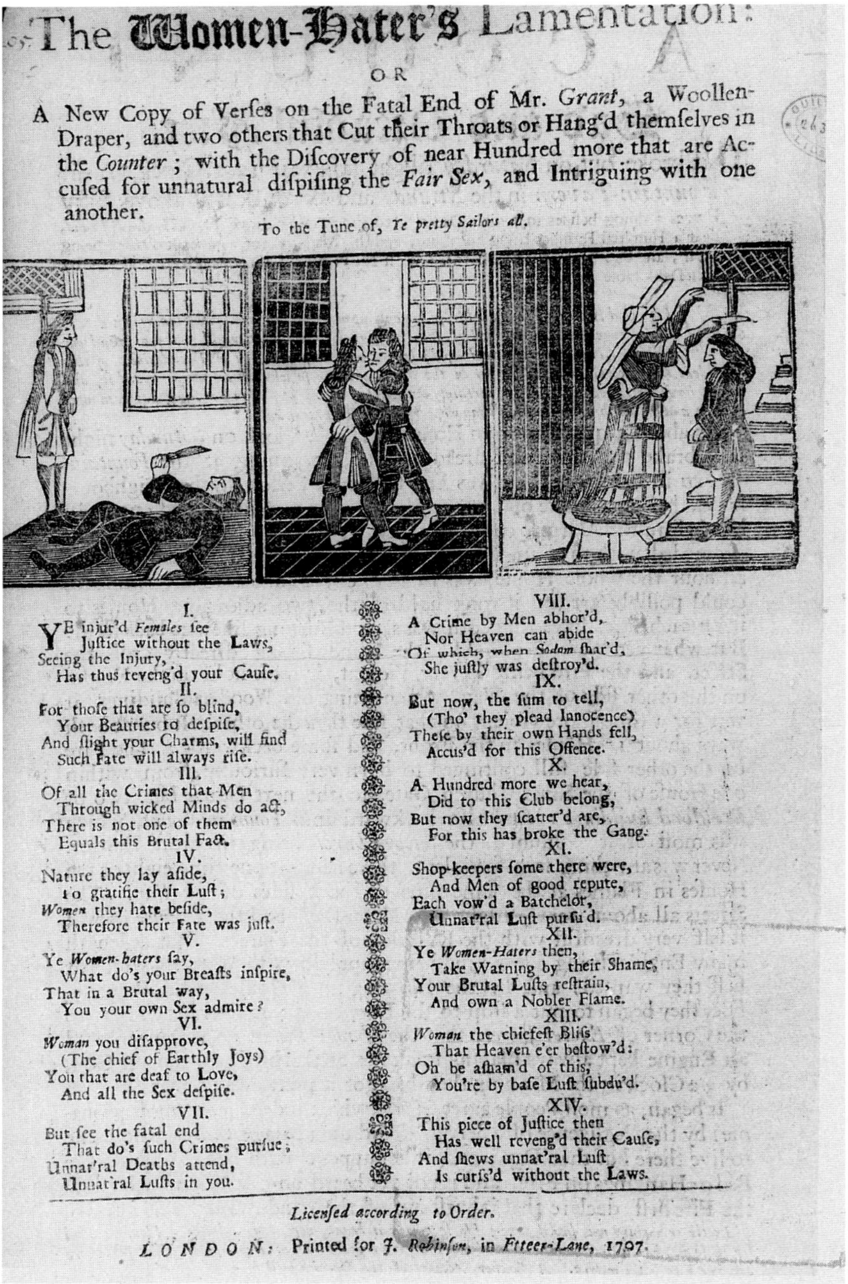

The Women-Hater's Lamentation:

OR

A New Copy of Verſes on the Fatal End of Mr. *Grant*, a Woollen-Draper, and two others that Cut their Throats or Hang'd themſelves in the *Counter*; with the Diſcovery of near Hundred more that are Accuſed for unnatural diſpiſing the *Fair Sex*, and Intriguing with one another.

To the Tune of, *Ye pretty Sailors all.*

I.
YE injur'd *Females* ſee
Juſtice without the Laws,
Seeing the Injury,
Has thus reveng'd your Cauſe.

II.
For thoſe that are ſo blind,
Your Beauties to deſpiſe,
And ſlight your Charms, will find
Such Fate will always riſe.

III.
Of all the Crimes that Men
Through wicked Minds do act,
There is not one of them
Equals this Brutal Fact.

IV.
Nature they lay aſide,
To gratifie their Luſt;
Women they hate beſide,
Therefore their Fate was juſt.

V.
Ye *Women-haters* ſay,
What do's your Breaſts inſpire,
That in a Brutal way,
You your own Sex admire?

VI.
Woman you diſapprove,
(The chief of Earthly Joys)
You that are deaf to Love,
And all the Sex deſpiſe.

VII.
But ſee the fatal end
That do's ſuch Crimes purſue;
Unnat'ral Deaths attend,
Unnat'ral Luſts in you.

VIII.
A Crime by Men abhor'd,
Nor Heaven can abide
Of which, when *Sodom* ſhar'd,
She juſtly was deſtroy'd.

IX.
But now, the ſum to tell,
(Tho' they plead Innocence)
Theſe by their own Hands fell,
Accus'd for this Offence.

X.
A Hundred more we hear,
Did to this Club belong,
But now they ſcatter'd are,
For this has broke the Gang.

XI.
Shop-keepers ſome there were,
And Men of good repute,
Each vow'd a Batchelor,
Unnat'ral Luſt purſu'd.

XII.
Ye *Women-Haters* then,
Take Warning by their Shame,
Your Brutal Luſts reſtrain,
And own a Nobler Flame.

XIII.
Woman the chiefeſt Bliſs
That Heaven e'er beſtow'd:
Oh be aſham'd of this,
You're by baſe Luſt ſubdu'd.

XIV.
This piece of Juſtice then
Has well reveng'd their Cauſe,
And ſhews unnat'ral Luſt
Is curs'd without the Laws.

Licenſed according to Order.

LONDON: Printed for *J. Robinſon*, in *Fetter-Lane*, 1707.

Figure 4.1 A 1707 London broadsheet of verse mocking suicides of men 'accused for unnatural dispising the Fair Sex' and set to the tune 'Ye pretty sailors all.'
Source: Guildhall Library, Corporation of London.

next to Barker. There were partitions between the seats, and this one had a hole in it which probably had been made deliberately. Barker put his penis through the hole into the other man's side where Vaughan caught hold of it. Vaughan claimed that he then ran out to get help to seize Barker, but Barker was gone when Vaughan returned.

Vaughan was also accused of blackmailing William Guilham who had chambers in the Temple. Vaughan had been told that Guilham 'committed frigging' or masturbation. His preference was evidently for boys since when Vaughan saw him enter the Temple bog-house he told a boy named Edward Knight to follow him in. Vaughan remained at a distance, presumably to allow time for something to happen. When he heard the boy cry out, he went in to seize Guilham who escaped. But Vaughan knew where to find his man. At the Anchor Tavern in Butcher Row, Guilham admitted to Vaughan what he had done. He asked him not to prosecute and to arrange that the two others involved, namely Edward Knight and Thomas Davis (who was probably a second boy), should not reveal to the senior lawyers or Benchers of the Temple what had occurred. He offered Vaughan money. Vaughan said he refused, and told him instead that if he made him a loan of 40 shillings, he would speak to the others. Guilham agreed and gave him 20 shillings in money and a promissory note to pay 20 more in three months' time. Vaughan must have thought he had covered his tracks. But Guilham decided on another course of action. He knew Edward Barker whom Vaughan and his gang were also blackmailing. Together Guilham and Barker brought a case against Vaughan, Knight, Davis and a fourth member of the gang, Thomas Penny. They, of course, charged the gang with intending to swear sodomy falsely. But the circumstantial detail of Vaughan's statement argues against Guilham and Barker.[14]

In 1709 in Moorfields, a public garden full of people, Hyems Harte, a Jew, came up to John Sanders and asked him how many women he had 'knocked.' Harte said he himself had knocked several a few nights before. He invited Sanders to drink with him. When they were seated Harte asked Sanders 'to show his prick.' Sanders would not, so Harte took out his own and reaching for Sanders' hand made him touch his. Harte now thrust his hand into Sanders' breeches and tore them as he pulled out Sanders' penis. At this point Sanders 'rescued himself from him' and ran away. But Harte was persistent. He came up to Sanders the very next day in Moorfields. He started the same conversation and tried to put his hand into Sanders' breeches. Sanders took him by the collar, but Harte shook free and ran, only to be stopped by another man.[15]

The locations of those places where sodomites met heterosexual men were intermingled with those where sodomites met each other. But the molly-houses were able to guard themselves against the unsuspecting visitor, and it is clear that one could enter them only if guided by a sodomite. Groups of men seem to have met occasionally in each other's lodgings, but since very few cases show up, this either did not happen very frequently or these meetings were even more protected from the outsider's gaze, which seems unlikely given the inquisitiveness of London neighbors. Heterosexual men very seldom took prostitutes home and were much more likely to have sex with them in a public house or out of doors. It is likely that sodomitical encounters operated by the same rule. This reinforces the point that the sodomite's sexual life was not very domesticated and in both its promiscuous behavior and location overlapped with the world of female prostitution. By contrast when heterosexual men seduced unmarried women they did so in the context of the local economy of their parishes rather than in the city-wide organization of prostitution. Male servants seduced their fellow workers in their masters' houses in affluent Chelsea. Soldiers picked up women in the streets of St Margaret's where they were stationed. Weavers seduced the maids of all work in the industrial parishes north of the City wall, and sailors, poor Irishmen and common labourers lived with their long-term mates in the poor parishes east of the City.

But sodomites do not seem to have clustered in any neighborhood or occupation. It is true that early in the eighteenth century it was suggested that sodomites congregated in the various trades that dealt with women's hair and clothes because they could there display an interest in such things and be licensed to behave with an elegance that verged on effeminacy. Thomas Baker in *The Female Tatler* in 1709 described the assistants in the millinery shops on Ludgate Hill as the 'sweetest, fairest, nicest, dished out creatures; and by their elegant address and soft speeches, you would guess them to be Italians' – when Italian could be synonymous with sodomite. But from the printed trials and the manuscript criminal records (the bonds and the recognizances, not the indictments which are unreliable), it is possible to recover the occupations of thirty-one men in the four years from 1726 to 1729. These were two perriwig makers, a tailor and a wire-drawer: these might have worked on women's clothes. But among the rest there were servants (3), yeomen (3) and gentlemen (4) (both of these were vague categories); carpenters (2) and a cabinetmaker; two cloth-workers; a milkman, a grocer and a coal-seller. Men who ran public houses and were classified variously as a cook, a fruiterer, an alehouse keeper, a vintner, or as victuallers, were the largest category (7). At least three of these certainly kept molly-houses, and the other four may have also. It may be that molly-house keepers (many of whom used women's names and were sodomites) were the most publicly known mollies and therefore very likely to become the targets of denunciations. But most mollies passed their lives as husbands and fathers or as single men who liked women. They were usually employed in jobs where they could show nothing of their sexual tastes. It was only in the molly-house that they came alive.

The kinds of meeting places used by sodomites and the nature of the relations displayed in them remained relatively constant over the next 250 years. This can be demonstrated by looking at three generations of men over that span of time. There were, however, three important changes. First, executions for sodomy ceased after 1835. Men convicted of actual (as opposed to attempted) sodomy were still condemned to death, but the sentences were no longer carried out, and in 1861 the penalty was reduced to life imprisonment (Harvey 1978; Crompton 1983). In the second half of the nineteenth century middle-class men began the long slow process of publicly justifying their sodomitical desires. They often did this by appealing to a historical tradition that ran from ancient Greece and Rome and continued through the Renaissance in men like Michelangelo and Shakespeare. But there were also less happy attempts by medical men (and sometimes by sodomites themselves) to explain their desires in terms of physical or psychological debility (Weeks 1977; Dowling 1994). Finally, in the early twentieth century it becomes possible to document long-term domestic relations between two men (Porter and Weeks 1991). These may have existed before, but they cannot be found easily in the legal sources. But it may be that it had taken that length of time (as well as changes in housing patterns) for the mid-eighteenth-century ideal of a happy romantic domesticity to be become a reality among some homosexual men. It certainly took a second revolution in gender relations after 1950 to produce in the second half of the twentieth century a gay liberation movement with its demands for the legalization of homosexual relations and the legitimation of marriage and families among gays and lesbians.

The arrests of sodomites in the early nineteenth century document the subculture of that generation and establish the real continuities with the men of the first generation of the modern homosexual identity in the early eighteenth century. In 1810 a number of public houses that catered to sodomites were raided. Thirty men were arrested on a Sunday evening at the Swan in Vere Street. In this house one room had four beds in it. Another was arranged as a ladies' dressing-room with pots of rouge and all the rest of a toilette. A third room was called the Chapel, and here marriages with bridesmaids and bridesmen in attendance were solemnized and consummated by two or more couples in the same room and in sight of each other. Upstairs there were rooms for male prostitutes and their more casual partners. Here it was safer to consummate an affair than in a man's lodgings as a 16-year-old drummer boy from a Guards Regiment explained to the Ensign who had recklessly proposed dinner and sex at his place in St Martin's Churchyard. Many of the men, even those with large athletic bodies, were effeminate and called themselves Miss Selina, or Pretty Harriet, or the Duchess of Devonshire. Some of the men had wives at home. There were other houses in the Strand; in Blackman Street in Southwark; near the Obelisk in St George's Fields; in Bishopsgate Street; in Eagle Street, Red Lion Square; at White Hart Yard, Drury Lane; and at the Star and Crown in the Broadway, Westminster. Men were also arrested for using the arcade of shops on London Bridge, and for picking up each other in the parks: in Moorfields, St James's Park, and Hyde Park. The parks were such a well-known rendezvous that two years before the Home Secretary had proposed locking them at night. But the parks and places like the Strand and Drury Lane and the Broadway were also used by female prostitutes who in a familiar pattern must have mingled with the sodomites (Holloway 1813 (with the newspaper clipping attached); Harvey 1978: 942).

The policing of sodomy seems to have grown more severe in this first generation of the nineteenth century. Only three men, for example, had been hanged for sodomy in the second half of the eighteenth century, but there were ten such hangings between 1804 and 1816. In all of England and Wales, fifty-four men were executed between 1806 and the last executions in 1835. And many more were sentenced to death than were executed: forty-two as opposed to twenty-eight between 1805 and 1815. The arrests for attempted sodomy in London by 1830 came to at least one in a week, but most arrests did not lead to convictions. Between 1810 and 1818, out of 102 men committed for sodomy in England, only 58 were brought to trial, and only 30 of these were convicted. In most of the arrests there were usually only two men involved. The raid on the Barley Mow in the Strand in 1825 is the only public house that has so far surfaced in the twenty years after the raids on the houses in 1810. There were attempts in the early 1830s to remove the death penalty for sodomy, but they failed (Harvey 1978; Clark 1987: 186–96; Crompton 1983). This early nineteenth-century severity may be accounted for by the appearance of the first explanations of sodomitical desire as a form of mental disease. Certainly Robert Holloway in his account of the trials in 1810 thought sodomy to be the 'effect of a dreadful malignant malady that assumes such an irresistible dominion over the faculties that neither religion, philosophy, or the fear of death can resist.' He knew of a man who ended in a mad-house after frequently spending periods of several days at the Vere Street house when he had from eight to a dozen different men and boys. This 'temporary insanity' needed to be restrained by 'castration or some other cogent preventative' (Holloway 1813: 16–17).

The historiography of sodomy in the last three decades of the nineteenth century has been dominated by the four scandals in 1870, 1884, 1889 and 1895 that were extensively reported in the newspapers (Montgomery Hyde 1962, 1970, 1976). But those trials unfortunately only document the interaction between men from the professional and landed classes (who were less than a quarter of London's population) and the upper reaches of the city's male prostitution. The sexual lives of the majority of sodomites in the city's streets, parks, lavatories, public houses, theaters and churches, and in their private lodgings, have not been considered because the more quotidian trials that are the principal source for the history of the subculture in the early eighteenth or the early nineteenth century remain to be studied. The sexual consciousness of these ordinary men was certainly influenced by the more sophisticated who figure in the famous trials. The young, effeminate shop-boys of 19 or 20 (the lineal descendants of the previous century's male milliners) who flocked to the ritual and aesthetic extravagances of the Anglo-Catholic churches in Holborn or Stoke Newington were following in the footsteps of Walter Pater and Oscar Wilde (Hilliard 1982: 188–9).

The male prostitution that surfaces in the great scandals shows a homosexual world that was organized by differences in gender, age and class, and in which domesticity and license coexisted. Elements of this system were already present in the eighteenth century and the system as a whole probably survived through World War II. The male prostitute was often an adolescent. The Post Office messenger boys whom Charles Hammond provided for his clients in Cleveland Street in 1889 were usually 15 or 16 years old (Simpson *et al.* 1976). The boys

Alfred Taylor provided for Oscar Wilde, or whom Wilde picked up for himself, were usually aged between 16 and 20. Wilde liked these boys to be pretty and effeminate. Charles Parker said that Wilde had asked him 'to imagine that I was a woman and that he was my lover...I used to sit on his knees and he used to play with my privates as a man might amuse himself with a girl.' The prosecutors in Wilde's trials repeatedly noticed that it was extraordinary that Wilde should take such young men to dinner and suggested that this kind of socializing across the age divide could only have had a sexual purpose. The prosecutors also made the same point about the differences in social class between Wilde and the boys. But the differences in age were not treated as any more startling that those in class (Montgomery Hyde 1962). There was, in short, no suggestion made (as there might well have been after World War II that Wilde or Lord Arthur Somerset were pedophiles even though a boy of 15 in the late nineteenth century would probably just have entered puberty. But it was also true that the majority of female prostitutes whom heterosexual men picked up in the streets were between 15 and 20 and that many of them would have experienced menarche very recently. The desire to separate rigidly men from boys in homosexual relations did not become prominent until after World War II.

The boys who walked the street in Piccadilly were notably effeminate, and the effeminate prostitute sometimes entered into a male marriage and domesticity with his lover. Alfred Taylor pointed out the Piccadilly boys to Charles Parker when he recruited him for his house in Little College Street, remarking that he did not 'understand sensible men wasting their money on painted trash like that. Many do though.' But when Taylor and Parker were arrested with sixteen other men in a raid on a house in Fitzroy Street in the year before Wilde's trials, two of the men were dressed as women. Taylor also had in his rooms women's clothes which he claimed were for masquerades. Parker even said that Taylor had told him that he had gone through a form of marriage with a youth named Charles Mason. Mason had dressed as a woman and the ceremony was followed by a wedding breakfast. Taylor denied the marriage; but Wilde himself wrote to Mason that 'I hope marriage had not made you too serious? It has never had that effect on me;' and Mason asked Taylor to 'come home soon, dear, and let us go out sometimes together' (Montgomery Hyde 1962: 131, 170, 173, 205, 228–9). Ernest Boulton and Frederick Park in the 1860s dressed as women to go to the theater or to mingle with the female prostitutes in the shopping arcades where the two forms of prostitution overlapped as they had since the eighteenth century and continued to do until the legalization of female prostitution after World War II removed the streetwalkers from public view. Boulton married his lover Lord Arthur Clinton and had calling cards printed that styled him as Lady Arthur Clinton. But poor Boulton after his arrest in 1870 was caught up in the new medicalization of the homosexual identity and had the folds of his anus examined by a doctor who was convinced that sodomy produced unmistakable physical evidence. Lord Arthur ended his role in the scandal by committing suicide (Upchurch 1996). These late nineteenth-century scandals do not provide much evidence for a male homosexual identity that was not tied to prostitution.

But the evidence for homosexual marriages in the 1920s and 1930s, and their certain presence in the Paris of the 1870s (Peniston 1997) makes it likely that they can be found in London for the generation after 1870.

From the middle of the nineteenth century and for another hundred years thereafter, sex between men was probably regulated less by either marriage or prostitution than by the public, free, and voluntary sexual relations that occurred in the public toilet or cottage. Cottaging brought together men across the divides of age, class and effeminacy, and it facilitated sex between homosexual and heterosexual men. A certain amount of sex had occurred in the eighteenth century in the few bog-houses where one sat to defecate. But men otherwise pissed against the wall where they could be approached by sodomites and by female prostitutes. The sight of public urination became increasingly shocking to respectable women, and by 1850 there were seventy-four urinals in the City of London, forty erected by the keepers of public houses and most of the rest by the City government. Most urinals were for one, but the largest held six men. By the 1870s the City had rebuilt its urinals to accommodate four men on average and had located them away from residences and in the center of roadways or in disused churchyards. In 1885 the City opened its first underground lavatory in which 6,000 men used the urinals in a day. The size and location of the urinals must have increased their sexual use since the City made room for two attendants to see that no 'improper conduct' occurred and to call a policeman if necessary (Andrews 1995: 5). In such a urinal the 33-year-old painter Simeon Solomon was arrested in 1873 for having sex with a 61-year-old laborer. This scandal his family managed to keep out of the newspapers and they saved Solomon from jail as well; but the same network through which Solomon met his patrons now spread the word, ostracized him and destroyed his career for the remainder of his life. Solomon must have gone to Paris in the next year in the hope that the scandal would abate, but there instead he was arrested in a *pissoir* with a young Parisian who had a subsequent career blackmailing and robbing older, richer homosexual men (Seymour 1985 and a personal communication; Peniston 1997: 127–31). This was a constantly recurring tale until the cottages were shut down a hundred years later.

In the first half of the twentieth century, the public male sociability and sexual promiscuity of homosexual men in London continued to appear in very much the forms they had taken in the subculture since the early eighteenth century. But it also becomes easier to document from interviews enduring domestic relations among men of all social classes. A young man like Norman, who at 19 came to London from Yorkshire during World War I, learned to pick up men in theaters, at the ballet and in the parks. Some men used the terrace below the National Gallery in Trafalgar Square which was called the meat rack. Others went to the cinema where in the dark they could lie on top of each other with their trousers down or go home together. A poor native Londoner like Roy started out in the local cinemas and then moved on to pubs and cottages and the back of the theater galleries where men milled about together, sometimes having sex. But men could dance with each other only at private parties or in private clubs, either of which might occasionally be raided by the police even though no sexual acts had occurred. The clubs cost half a crown a year to be a member and were mostly in Soho. Some pubs drew a mainly gay clientele, but in the East End 'mums and dads' mixed with homosexual men whom they called by their camp names (Porter and Weeks 1991: 24–6, 31–2, 134, 11, 73–7, 138, 140, 129–30).

Public effeminacy was taken furthest by the young male prostitutes who strolled up and down Piccadilly, with dyed hair, walking like women, and calling themselves Lucy or Annette. But some men were occasionally transvestite at private drag parties or at public annual events like Lady Malcolm's servant's ball in the Albert Hall, or at the Chelsea Arts Ball. But drag could be in the wearer's mind since a middle-class man who wore a camel hair coat and suede shoes might feel that he was publicly declaring his homosexuality. Drag could bless domesticity when one man at a party dressed as a bride and was married to another (Porter and Weeks 1991: 140, 148, 111, 139).

Male prostitutes were arranged in a hierarchy according to the places or the means by which they met their customers. They usually entered the life at 15 or 16, shortly after they had escaped to London. The street boys in Piccadilly were the most effeminate, the least educated, and the most likely to be arrested and taken off the streets in a Black Maria. More educated boys, some of whom danced in the theatrical choruses, used bars in Piccadilly and in Leicester Square as well as the bar in the Ritz. There were boys who worked through a pimp like Tommy who invited gentlemen to tea to meet the boys whose photographs he kept in an album. The men paid Tommy and he paid the boys. (These tea parties sound rather like those Oscar Wilde attended.) Some boys eventually lived with an older man in a relationship very much like marriage and constructed a social circle of similar boys who visited but did not sleep with each other – a circle somewhat like the traditional demi-monde of fashionable female prostitutes. Some very striking boys simply ran into men in the street and passed from one keeper to another. As they aged this life came to an end and the kept boy became suburban or respectable, going to an office in Waterloo or serving in the civil service (Porter and Weeks 1991: 117–24, 137–50).

The domesticity of the prostitute could only exist when there was enough money to finance it and tended to last only as long as the more youthful partner kept his beauty. But enduring relationships that were regarded as marriages existed between men of the same age and social class. Partners might be faithful or not. The union might last several years or be lifelong, and might be acknowledged by families or by fellow workers. Working-class men like Gerald and Phil lived together for seven years in the 1920s. They shared the cooking and the household tasks. They were sexually 'faithful to each other' but though one of them was 'the butch' and the other was 'the bitch,' Gerald detested drag because it was not 'natural.' Gerald also disapproved of sex in public places like cottages or cinemas. But the lovers did not reveal their relationship to their families who probably realized the nature of their friendship. The marriage ended when Phil met a former boyfriend. A marriage between two men could receive parental approval as Gregory's did when his lover's father suggested that Gregory should live with his son. At family dinners Gregory was treated as a son-in-law. But Gregory's own father was horrified when his son revealed his homosexuality, and he asked him not to tell his mother. There was room in this relationship for sex with others. Gregory disliked clubs and bars because he did not drink, but he did meet men in galleries and cottages. His sexual life was carefully separated, however, from his work as a consulting engineer. After World War II it may have become easier to live openly as a couple. Stephen and Bob met in 1946. Before this Stephen had had wide experience in the subculture in the 1930s going to clubs, pubs and private parties. For the first ten years the lovers kept separate residences, but for twenty years after they lived together. They never openly spoke to their parents about their relationship, but they were always given a room together when they stayed with Stephen's parents. In his work as a civil servant Stephen found it prudent to be less reserved. He carefully informed his superiors about his homosexuality and avoided any scandal, but as a result he was never promoted to the highest rank. His colleagues, however, always invited the two men to dinner as a couple. And as they aged, their social circle came to be composed of other men who were 'married couples' (Porter and Weeks 1991: 6–11, 36–9, 110–16).

Most gay men used cottages or public toilets at some point in their lives, though a few studiously avoided them. For most men cottaging was integrated into the rest of their homosexual world whether they had steady lovers or not. But a man could use cottages because of a psychological isolation that prevented him from becoming part of a homosexual network. One such man tried psycho-analysis to control his desires but went cottaging whenever he became depressed. Another man who tended not to know men who lived together, and who could not imagine doing so himself, found men in many locales but really always hoped to find men who were heterosexual. Some men eventually could have sex only with men who were married, or bisexual, or 'had gone out with girls and done them.' But it may be that for many the lure of the cottage was that it might be possible there to satisfy their desire for sex with a heterosexual man. The cottages however were the places most likely to be patrolled by the police. And an arrest in one of them could wreck the most successful of careers (Porter and Weeks 1991: 49–54, 22–34, 97–108, 65–71).

The spatial arrangements produced in the first generation of the eighteenth century by the revolution in gender and sexual relations that occurred in north-western Europe around 1700 probably endured through the next 250 years. They were intensified by the fourfold growth of London in the nineteenth century and by the emergence at the end of that century of the concepts of homosexuality and heterosexuality. After 1950 there was another marked shift in gender and sexual relations which was not so great as that around 1700, but it is likely that it significantly modified the spatial arrangements of London's homo-sexual world. By way of a conclusion I therefore wish to suggest the nature of the changes in gender and sexuality after 1950 (which like those around 1700 occurred throughout the Western world) and to ask how they produced the patterns of homosexual life that I observed in London over thirteen months of residence from 1977 to 1982 when in the summers and sometimes in January I collected my eighteenth-century material in the archives during the day and observed gay London at night and on the weekends.

The majority of women after 1950 acquired a heterosexual identity more nearly like that which men had had for the previous two and a half centuries. Women in greater numbers began to masturbate before marriage. Their sexual relations with men became easier as the taboo against pre-marital sexuality was eased and birth control became entirely acceptable and widespread. They were more likely consciously to separate themselves from lesbian women and consequently the feminine partner in a lesbian relationship was more likely to consider herself as much a lesbian as her more masculine companion. But it is probable that masturbation and homosexuality did not become as important in defining female heterosexuality as they were for male heterosexuality. Sexual experience was for women (more than for men) still tied to social interaction and less a matter of individual self-consciousness. Among men at the same time the sexual interaction of the heterosexual majority and the homosexual minority became more limited. Most gay men no longer desired sex with a straight man, and straight men were less inclined to accept the sexual attention of gay men. But straight men were also less likely to go to female prostitutes and sexual relations with their girlfriends became easier because pregnancy could be prevented more easily and marriage was not necessarily the goal of these relations.

As a consequence of these reformulated identities the geography and nature of male homosexual relations by the late 1970s had changed dramatically in three respects from the patterns established in the first generation of the eighteenth century. First there was no longer any overlap between the gay world and the world of streetwalking prostitution since prostitutes had finally been removed from London's streets by changes in the law that were certainly the result of a modified male heterosexual identity. Streetwalking prostitution had shocked opinion since the eighteenth century because it violated the ideals of romance and domesticity. But the fear that men would turn to sodomy if it was entirely eliminated was always stronger, and as a consequence the streetwalkers remained until the heterosexual male majority felt that they were no longer needed to establish their own sexual identity. The reform in prostitution also produced the legalization of homosexual relations between consenting adults in private. But this was accompanied by a determined effort to separate homosexual men from sexual interactions with heterosexual men and adolescent boys. Whereas in 1900 only 10 per cent of prosecutions had been for sexual relations between men and boys under 16, this grew to 75 per cent of all cases by the 1950s. And the bars and toilets where gay men met heterosexual ones, especially those in the army or the navy, were prosecuted vigorously or simply closed (Higgins 1996: 45–8, 61–80, 153–4, 161–5). A particularly famous north London cottage that Joe Orton had described vividly in his diary was shown to me in 1978 by the men whose flat I had rented as a relic from a former world that no longer existed. Gay men still in those days before AIDS had promiscuous sex. They met each other in saunas though they were not allowed to have sex on the premises as they did in those which I knew in New York. They met each other late at night in central London in places like Russell Square where they sometimes had sex in the bushes but from which more usually they went home together. The owner of another flat I used one summer guided me by the footpaths to the place on Hampstead Heath where late at night men had orgiastic sex under the trees. But all these acts occurred between men who were all gay. The gay man was still promiscuous but he was no longer a 'he-whore' as the early eighteenth century had classified him. He did not service straight men or mingle with female prostitutes. Instead he lived in various north London neighborhoods, sometimes alone, sometimes with a lover, sometimes with a group of friends. These neighborhoods did not have the density of gay inhabitants that could be found in some American neighborhoods like the Castro or the West Village. But those more integrated London neighborhoods produced sooner than the American ones the demand that children be taught in school that gay men and lesbian women could form families. Sodomites no longer gave birth to wooden dolls in mollyhouses. The domestication of gay sex had begun, though there was far more public resistance to it among both the general public and the parliamentary elite than there had been to the legalization of sexual relations between consenting adults in private (Jeffrey-Poulter 1991).

Notes

1 Donoghue (1993) puts all affection between women into the lesbian category, rejects all comparisons with the history of sodomites, and denies any chronological change, even though she admits that women who exclusively desired women were classified as hermaphrodites early in the century but described as sapphists after 1770.

2 *Select Trials at the Old Bailey*, London, *1742*, III, 74–5 (or *Proceedings...at the Old Bailey*, hereafter SP (12–15 April 1727), pp. 5–6; *St James's Evening Post* (15–18 April 1727); for Wild and Hitchen, see Howson (1970).

3 Wild, *An Answer*; CLRO (Corporation of London Record Office): SR (February 1722/3), R. 37; *The British Journal*, 2 and 23 January 1725.

4 For Partridge: SP (13–16 July 1726), p. 6; GLRO (or London Metropolitan Archive): MJ/SR/2458, Bond 82. The *Select Trials* do not print Partridge's name, giving only P-. The cases brought to trial may be found conveniently in *Select Trials*, II, 362–72, III, 36–40. The sessions rolls, with material for 1726, are in GLRO: MJ/SR/2458–2475 (2473 is too decayed to consult); CLRO: SR (April 1726 to January 1726/7). Norton (1992 chs 3–5) used some of the printed materials for 1726 and 1727 but did not consult the quarter-sessions rolls from which a more systematic picture can be constructed than from the printed trials and newspapers alone. Our interpretations vary considerably, however, because he believes in the existence across time of a continuous homosexual minority. He claims that a subculture was brought into existence by the attacks of the Societies for the Reformation of Manners, and does not consider the possibility of a revolution in gender and sexual relations. But the emergence in France and the Netherlands at the same time of similar patterns of behavior makes the purely English phenomenon of the Societies an unlikely cause, and urban reforming societies had been part of English Protestantism since the late sixteenth century. Norton (1992) also tries to downplay the crucial role of effeminacy (it is not acceptable to his gay liberationist perspective) and does not raise systematically the

issue of sex between sodomites and the heterosexual majority. His geography does not distinguish between places for sodomites alone, and places where sodomites and the male majority intermingled. In addition he uses the cases of men who seduced adolescents to establish a gay geography despite the fact that these men were usually operating outside the world of the molly-house. I discuss these cases in Trumbach, 'Sodomitical Assaults'; and review Norton's book in the *Journal of the History of Sexuality* 5 (1995): 637–40.

5 *The London Journal* (7 May 1726), p. 2.

6 Royal Oak alehouse, corner St James's Square (*Select Trials*, III, 369; *London Journal* (30 April 1726); King Street, Westminster (*London Journal* of July 1726); Beech Lane (GLRO: MJ/SR/2461: New Prison List; *Select Trials*, II, 367); Christopher Alley, Moorfields (*Select Trials*, II, 367); Charing Cross (MJ/SR/2464, Recog. of John Torelton); Marylebone Fields (*London Journal*, 5 August 1727; GLRO: MJ/SR/2488, Recog. 433, 120, 108, MJ/SR/2490, R. 181); Hay Court (GLRO: MJ/SR/2502, R. 135); Whitechapel (GLRO: MJ/SRT/2509A, R. 144); the King's Head, St Peter le Poor, Broad Street (CLRO: SR (July 1726), R. 36); Pye Corner, St Sepulchre (CLRO: SR (July 1726), Bond 9, SR (December 1726), R. 21); Drury Lane (*Select Trials*, III, 36); Field Lane (*Select Trials*, II, 363, II, 37; CLRO: SR (April 1726): Poultry Compter list, # 3); Red Lion, Crown Court, Knaves Acre (*Select Trials*, II, 366).

7 *Select Trials*, II, 366–7, 370–2: Orme and Wright; Stoneham 'for boasting of his having committed sodomitical practices in the house of John Clapp': CLRO: SR (April 1726), R. 17; 'in the house of Margaret Clap': CLRO: SR (May 1726), Bonds 5, 8; Clap's coffeehouse: CLRO: SR (December 1726): April Poultry Compter: #3, May Poultry Compter, #1; Margaret Clap's arrest, trial, and pillorying: CLRO: SR (April 1726), R. 40, R. 19, R. 8, SR (July 1726) calendar of Wood Street Compter, 28 February, SR (December 1726), April, Wood Street Compter, *Select Trials*, III, 37–8, *London Journal* (23, 30 July 1726); Plump Nelly Roper: *London Journal* (17 December 1726), CLRO: SR (July 1726), bond #9, SR (December 1726), R. 21; Robert Whale and York Horner: *London Journal* (23 April, 9 July, 3 December 1726), GLRO: MJ/SR/2458, bond 82, MJ/SR/2459, Newgate calendar, #57; Towleton and Mugg: GLRO: MJ/SR/2459, Newgate calendar, #'s 58, 59; Wright: *Select Trials*, II, 367.

8 [Holloway] (1813: 28); *Select Trials*, II, 362–3, 365, III, 37. Newton's age: GLRO: MJ/SR/2462, indictment 53. Newton also accused Gregory Turner, Thomas Turner and John Howard of having sodomized him, but they do not seem to have been brought to trial (GLRO: MJ/SR/2462, indictments 52, 53, 49). Newton was described as a wire-drawer by trade who lived in Grub Street (GLRO: MJ/SR/2464, Newton's bond). A wire-drawer worked in the gold lace trade (Campbell 1747: 148). Another man, John Grace, was probably also a sodomite who accused two men, Richard Gardner and Samuel Edmonds. His evidence does not seem to have been used (GLRO: MJ/SR/2463, bond #25, MJ/SR/2464, indictments 49, 50).

9 *Select Trials*, III, 36, II, 368. *The Wandering Whore* (London, 1660), part 4, p. 5. Mark Partridge was identified as a coal-seller who lived in Creed Lane, St Martin within Ludgate (CLRO: SR (April 1726), Recog. 19).

10 *Select Trials*, II, 366–7, 369–72.

11 *Ibid.*, III, 37, II, 370–72.

12 *Ibid.*, II, 370. Courtney also accused William Goldsmith of sodomy with himself (GLRO: MJ/SR/2464, Recog. of Goldsmith). Courtney's age is given in GLRO: MJ/SR/2462, indictment #50. Drake Stoneman was a groom who gave two different addresses in Stroop's Court in April and Union Court in May (CLRO: SR (May 1726), bonds 5, 8).

13 *Select Trials*, III, 36–40.

14 GLRO: MJ/SP/17 (September 1707), Thomas Vaughan; MJ/SR/2096, Recog. 88, 89; CLRO: SR (September 1707), Newgate calendar: 3 September 1707.

15 GLRO: MJ/SP/58 (July 1709).

5   Lisbon

David Higgs

Approached from the south by ferry at night across the Tagus River, Lisbon appears as mounds of lights festooned over seven hills that are reflected in the waters that lap around the jetties. The sheltered waters of the 'Straw Sea' (so-called for the windmills that ground wheat on the southern shore) make one of the finest natural harbors in the world. Although most foreign visitors now reach Lisbon by air or car the city for millennia was a bride of the Atlantic, and thence linked to the oceans of the globe. The oldest human habitation of the site dates back almost 3,000 years in legend to the Phoenicians, *c.* 1200 BCE.

Before the 1755 earthquake the royal palace stood at the side of the River Tagus and the ships that brought the riches of empire to Portugal could be seen by the kings and courtiers from its windows. The palace overlooked a big open space, shallower than the Commerce Square constructed after the devastation of 1755, but longer in extent. That rectangle, with one side open to the Tagus and the estuary, was also a market, a meeting place and the site of important public rituals. The Acts of Faith (*Autos-da-Fê*) ceremonies of the Inquisition which existed from 1536 to 1821 were frequently held there.

After the 1755 earthquake the core of the city lying on lower ground between hills was rebuilt on a rectilinear plan with the main streets running north from the waterfront. This was a shift of emphasis towards the hinterland. The royal palace was not rebuilt at water's edge but inland at Queluz, and in the French style. Future development in the nineteenth century progressed inland, particularly after the opening of Liberty Avenue in imitation of the Grands Boulevards of Paris. The focus of new suburban growth and installations was more often at right-angles to the river, rather than like the medieval city which hugged the river bank. In a sense the modern city with its new avenues constructed during the fascist era turned its back on the Tagus (Fernandes 1989).

The Inquisition and the sodomites

The most informative documents on male homosexual behaviors in Early Modern Portugal are those in the archives of the Portuguese Inquisition preserved in the National Archives in Lisbon. The Inquisition trials for the 'abominable' sin ('*nefando pecado*') resulting from denunciations were focused on anal intercourse: sodomy. As a result the discussion of other male same-sex sexual practices figures in the documentation primarily as an evasive strategy: the accused sometimes admitted to masturbation or frottage and much more rarely to oral sex as they tried to downplay any suggestion that they had been receptive or worse still had permitted a partner to ejaculate in their anus. The Inquisition Bye-laws and Edicts of the Faith specified sinful activities by those under religious vows and the laity that concerned the Church including sodomy. In the Inquisition Bye-laws of 1774 punishments for sodomy were less severe than those enunciated in 1613. The Inquisition was to seek out these sinners and to correct or eradicate them. The archives of the Portuguese Inquisition are the most complete of any in Europe, having survived both the Lisbon Earthquake of 1755 and Liberal disapproval that led to the suppression of the institution at the start of the nineteenth century.[1] They are open for consultation in the National Archives of Portugal in Lisbon (Farinha 1990).

In theory any person accused of sodomy, including prisoners already in a secular jail, should be transferred to the cells of the Holy Office. All Inquisition documentation was theoretically secret. Every individual interrogated by the Inquisition was bound to swear to keep secret all aspects of the trial or inquiry upon its conclusion. All documentation about investigations was to be sent to Lisbon so that it could be preserved in the archives. The obsessive secrecy of the Inquisition on the one hand and the precise nature of the interrogations on the other mean that a richly detailed archive about male homosexual behaviors has been preserved. Unlike individual love letters or recollections of sexual partners, which were almost always destroyed by relatives if discovered after the death of the owner, the Inquisition documents were numbered and cared for. Only a part of the inquisitorial records dealt with sex matters; by far the largest category in Portugal were those which dealt with Judaizing by baptized Christians usually of Jewish ancestry. These and other sins to be denounced like slippages into Islam or Protestantism, or freemasonry, blasphemy, witchcraft and so forth were enumerated annually at the reading in each parish church of the Edict of the Faith.

In some of the macabre public daylight ceremonies of the Inquisition sodomites processed among the victims. The numbers of male sodomites who appeared per decade in these rituals of punishment during the seventeenth century is shown in Table 5.1.

Thirty sodomites were burned by the riverside during the existence of the Portuguese Inquisition (1536–1821). As the numbers of convictions show, repression of the abominable sin was much sharper in the twenty years 1640 to 1660, years at the heart of what has been called the General Crisis of the Seventeenth Century, than before or afterwards. The number of full trials leading to lesser punishments for sodomites, like whippings, confiscations of property, exile from the kingdom for periods of time or life was approximately 400 over the existence of the tribunals responsible for continental Portugal, the Atlantic islands and Brazil.

The grand total number of names listed in the registers of denunciations of sodomites, the *Cadernos do Nefando*, was over 5,000. The majority of them were

Table 5.1 Numbers of male sodomites per decade in Autos-da-Fé in seventeenth-century Lisbon

1600–10	3
1611–20	15
1621–30	4 (1 woman sodomite also)
1631–40	7
1641–50	66
1651–60	34
1661–70	3
1671–80	0
1681–90	10
1691–1700	24

Source: Codices 197–200 National Library, Lisbon (note suspension of Inquisition activities 1674–82 by papal decision).

not acted upon. What emerged in the trials and other documentation was the high incidence of priests as participants and as observers. What is of interest is rather the degree of detail in the documentation that enables us to reconstruct the outlines of past sexual lives in Lisbon. There are examples of the *nefando* from all regions of Portugal but it can be deduced from the documentation that sodomy was overwhelmingly an urban offense rather than a rural one. It was most frequently denounced in the bigger cities, and especially in Lisbon. In short the micro-historical approach is much more informative than the laborious, and ultimately flawed efforts to establish a statistical profile from respondents seeking to evade punishment.

One individual whose homosexuality linked Lisbon and Rio, two of the cities in this volume, was Antonio Soares from a prosperous family who at age 14 was a postulant to enter the Dominican order at their Lisbon convent in Benfica. He went to the Carmelites after his rejection as an unsuitable candidate for the Dominicans because of homosexual behavior. Soares lived his sexuality in a religious setting. However his confessions in Portugal before his exile to Brazil were unusual in his insistence in his confession that he was both insertive and receptive in anal sexual activity with the same individuals. Many of his partners were novices or inside the plus or minus range of five years of his own age. One witness used the interesting turn of phrase that Soares' most frequent sex partner in Lisbon among the novices was so dear to him that it was said in the convent that the two were 'amancebados' – a word meaning in heterosexual usage cohabiting with a paramour or concubine, and that when the partner had a skin rash it was because of the 'seed' that Soares left in his backside. Soares was exiled to Brazil.[2]

As Lisbon expanded after 1600 it remained always the capital (until the independence of Brazil in 1822) and the largest city of the Portuguese-speaking world. It had perhaps 150,000 residents in 1600 and grew slowly to some 200,000 in 1800. Lisbon always attracted migrants from the hinterland many of whom went elsewhere in due course. Ambitious peasant youths and younger sons from families too large for their country resources constantly arrived in the city with the hope of bettering themselves. Many of them arrived from the rural zones that were a day's walk from the city, but others came from the more distant north of the country, Minho and Trás-os-Montes. The city was the interface between the World on the Move and the ambitious youths and men of inland Portugal.

The city council was aware of 'many lazy youths' as a problem in July 1642 when it petitioned the king that those who were usually hanging around the quay-side, the slaughter-house and the [Palace] Square and pilfering should be shipped out to serve in the navy and in the overseas possessions (Freire de Oliveira 1889 IV: 468). One distinctive group in this street youth culture was unmarried male migrants from Galicia in Spain who often worked in Lisbon as water-carriers or porters. They sought work in the urban economy as apprentices or errand boys, as stone breakers or baker's help, or servants and dock workers. Foreigners often noted that there was a glut of servants in Lisbon who were poorly paid but also under-employed.

If they were well recommended, youths might find a job as a lackey or page to a member of the nobility. Sometimes they provided sexual gratification. A saying of 1651 was that 'There is no hen that doesn't lay eggs nor lackey that won't participate in sodomy: this is the service that is wanted of them' (Mott 1988: 125). Some youths might be fortunate enough to have family members to provide lodgings; many more were in a bachelor subculture of the economy of makeshifts. One currency in that economy was male prostitution.

Girls and women in early modern Portugal were closely controlled and kept at home. There were many nunneries although not all of their inhabitants felt a strong vocation for the religious life. Relations between the sexes throughout Iberia were perhaps less free than in Europe beyond the Pyrenees, at least in the opinion of many foreign travelers prior to the twentieth century. Unmarried sexually mature females were strictly chaperoned in the urban upper classes. Among the working class girls were exhorted not to lose their 'honor' for if they did so they would be much less likely to find a worthy husband than a virgin. Lower-class males, particularly adolescents without money or power, who could not afford the services of a prostitute found scant opportunity to enjoy heterosexual sex.

Adults who had taken a vow of chastity however were presumably of a different nature. It has been calculated that there was a big increase in the number of Portuguese monasteries from the fifteenth to the seventeenth centuries. Around 1650 there were more than 25,000 regulars and nuns and more than 30,000 secular priests. For every thirty-six Portuguese one was under vows. Lisbon was the biggest center of clergy in Portugal, both seculars and regulars. The medieval cathedral was built along a military design so that it could be defended against sudden raids by enemies sailing up the Tagus. The city landscape was punctuated with the spires and roofs of churches and convents. The cassocked priests were much in evidence in the streets as the mendicants solicited alms or the clergy went about their daily business.

Not all of the male clergy and perhaps not all nuns kept their vows of chastity. Just as in modern times there was a far higher proportion of homosexual men among the Catholic priesthood than in the Portuguese male population at large. The Church provided a niche for homosexual males – a place where they might acquire social respectability, even power, and be relieved of the pressures to marry. In a way the Church offered a means of dealing with troubling issues of sexuality. Priests who could not keep their vows of chastity often controlled spaces for the commission of sexuality with other males. In the denunciations and trials of sodomites in seventeenth-century Lisbon there is abundant evidence of clerical homosexual activity, just as the registers of solicitation show many thousands of women being used sexually by priests.

In the shifting conditions of life stages it might well be said of early modern Lisbon as it has of Renaissance Florence that for most males sodomy was a temporary and occasional transgression. If not sodomy at least mutual masturbation was common among youths. Participants in same-sex genital activities in the age cohort of adolescents and youths before marriage did not categorize themselves as a sexual orientation. However the son of the bailiff of the Inquisition in 1620 seemed to do just that when he spoke of 'many people of that type'[3] who went to the house of a great nobleman where they met in the room of his lackey. He entered into detail about sexual practices. Among the individuals was a priest, David Cardoso, accused of organizing a ring of youths for male prostitution. Another witness said that the priest Cardoso was very persistent both in sodomy and providing youths and a place to have sex, and that he procured them for money, and that many youths were urged to go to his house.[4] In Lisbon there was in 1620 a masculine society of lackeys and priests enticing younger males (*moços*) to be sexually available for money.

A leading figure in that society was a mulatto dancer, son of a black female slave and an unknown white father, who was called Domingos of the Dance.[5] The dances were known as being those of 'fairies' – *fanchonos* – and obviously attracted spectators. They were also called dances of the women, which stressed the gender switch of male participants. Domingos would be put to death and burned in 1621 aged 26. His trial took evidence from seven of his sexual partners: two priests, two married men and two lay bachelors plus a free mulatto. The sexual acts dated back as far as ten years previously, from the time Domingos was 15. In stating the sexual practices involved in his sexual curriculum a married man of 40 revealed that Domingos had started to sodomize him but that he could not stand it, and he the married man had not sodomized Domingos. The free mulatto said that when he was 62 he had once sodomized Domingos and Domingos had twice sodomized him. The other men all sodomized Domingos: one mentioned that he was then beardless (*desbarbeado*). This sexual activity took place in houses, significantly, save for the married man of 40 who said their sex acts took place outside a convent at Odivelas, some 10 kilometers inland, where he had gone to watch the Dance of the *Fanchonos*. The sixth man noted that he had first sodomized Domingos in 1614 in a house belonging to a priest. Two and a half years later he had sexual commerce with him in a house that Domingos had (*tinha*) on the rua dos Cavaleiros, an old street that still survives in Lisbon with this name, leading up towards the São Jorge castle and the Graça church where some neighbors testified that Domingos worshipped. This testimony also implied that Domingos was notoriously feminine in mannerism and mostly receptive in sodomy, but that he was also sometimes insertive with older men. Domingos never confessed during his trial. In his genealogy he explained that his name was really Domingos Rodrigues but that he was called Rocha which was the name of his owner, and that he earned his living as a dancer, that he was unmarried, had been baptized in São Julião church in Lisbon but did not know the Commandments of the Church.

Priests evidently controlled spaces to which young males could go. An Augustinian monk who lived in Lisbon at the College of Saint Anthony the Old confessed in 1644 to having, *c.* 1635, entertained a barber's boy in his cell, whose surname he remembered but not his given name, who was then a bachelor learning from his uncle and who was then 17, thin and light-skinned with green eyes, and that he then *did not have a beard* (my emphasis). He added that he now did. They had some sex but he could not remember details about ejaculations. The barber it transpired in other testimony from a second priest was married in 1644 with a place of business. The second priest said that ten months earlier the married man had been on the point of committing sodomy but there had not been penetration. The apprentice barber with the green eyes at 17 was having two-way sodomy with a 36-year-old priest; and as a married man of 25 was ready to sodomize a 41-year-old priest. Antonio Alvares Palhaço, 66 in 1644 who had been in trouble previously for sodomy in 1630, said that he did masturbation and was sodomized by the married barber Machado. He added that Machado had had a lot of sodomy with Antonio de Azevedo, who was responsible for the altar in the Cathedral (*altareiro da Sé*). This man actually confessed that Machado had been sodomizing him for eight years and as recently as eight months before his testimony in 1645, noting that it was once in the barber's house but also in the latrines (*necessárias*) of the Cathedral, and that he always gave the barber money.[6]

The barber's sexual services to priests extended to providing them with a member of his wife's family, a bachelor who was 20 years old when arrested. The younger man recalled that ten years earlier João Machado was engaged to his sister and the two boys regularly slept together in a bakery on rua da D. Mafaldo. Sixteen-year-old João touched his anus with his penis and asked him if he wanted to be sodomized: 10-year-old Luís declined and nothing else happened. An alternative version of the bed in the bakery was given by João who claimed that Luís had sodomized *him* but there was no spilling of seed because he was then only about 12 years of age. What seems indubitable is that long-term sleeping together of the two boys in the same bed had led to sexual intimacy and complicity which continued after the marriage of the older one to the sister of the younger. The barber when married seems to have pimped for the still bachelor Luís who had a job as a valet to the conde da Torre to customers like Padre Luís da Costa three years before. When Luís was 17 the priest asked the barber if he could 'fool around' with the youth, using a word that the notary explained as being a synonym for sodomy. The barber answered yes. The priest went off with his brother-in-law. The barber explicitly said he did not know what happened between them, but that it was for money.[7] When the barber was attending to the beard of Sanches de Almeida, a priest aged over 60, he told him that his brother in law was a *fanchono* and had done 'fairy stuff' (*fanchonices*) with him. The barber sent Luís to the house of Sanches who fellated him on from fifteen to twenty occasions while himself masturbating with the 'nature' of the youth in his mouth. It was because of this that the word for pimp *alcovitre* figured in the barber's sentence in the Auto-da-Fé, since having slept with Luís as a young boy he subsequently was setting up the teenager for paid sex with his clients.

The Early Modern paradigm of adult–youth sexual systems was, it has been argued, a small part of male–female relations where youths were an acceptable sexual choice for an older man in the absence of, or prior to, sustained sexual commerce with a wife. Youths might provide an ancillary sexual satisfaction. In that paradigm little or no emphasis was placed on the sexual pleasure or response of the younger partner. Neither participant thought of themselves as definitively homosexual or 'gay.' Youths as much as women and girls were subordinate objects to dominant males in the sexual arena, just as lord and vassal shared reciprocal obligations under feudalism.

We find in seventeenth-century Lisbon clear signs of the tension between the feudal model and that of a subculture identity. The count of Vila Franca engaged in a full repertoire of sexual acts with younger partners ranging from manual and inter-crural masturbation, fellatio, and sodomy in receptive and insertive roles. He was also married and had a son, the latter of whom appeared before the Inquisitors to say his father had masturbated and sodomized him. All of these partners said they had been forced to sin by the count. Even when admitting to repeated orgasms over long periods of time they denied any pleasure in these activities. The word *fanchono* is used nowhere in the trial.[8]

By contrast in other trials of a street society of hustlers, priests and laymen there was reference to a way of talking among homosexual men and to a social life. The *fanchonos* of Lisbon shared a complicity and an identity in homosexual practices at least from the sixteenth century. They called themselves and were called by others *fanchonos*. Many of them were married, or married when older. They were males who habitually and repeatedly engaged in sodomy with other males as well as other sexual practices. They seem to have recognized themselves as a group with shared sexual activities even if it was not a fixed social identity. It was a behavior which the Church taught was a sin, but some of the *fanchonos* remained exclusively oriented to other men. The exclusively male-oriented *fanchonos* who never married did not perhaps formulate any ideas of a right to do what they pleased, and perhaps they were burdened by a sense of guilt over repeated sin, but they defied social and religious constraints.

Seventy-eight years later, in 1698, another priest was picking up males younger than him but with no hint that he associated with other men who

shared his desires. He was a loner in his efforts to satisfy his personal sexual crav-
ings. In the trial of one of his catamites, a cavalryman of 16 whom he met by
calling to him from the window as the youth passed the house next to the Saint
Nicholas Church on horseback when returning to his barracks, we have the
succinct version recounted by the priest followed by the more detailed discussion
of what happened in the words of the young man. The priest said simply that
when alone together, and after some 'dishonest touchings,' he persuaded the
youth to take down his breeches and to lie face down on the bed and that he
mounted him twice and both times deposited seed in his 'rear vase.' The cavalryman was more expansive in giving the details of a homosexual encounter in
late seventeenth-century Lisbon:[9]

> He said that about a month ago more or less he the confessant was on
> horseback, passing in front of the house of a priest and he does not know
> his name nor where he was born, but he was young and a bit more than 25
> years old, tall body, not very fat, with a round pale face, and he goes about
> dressed in the Roman style in a cassock, and he lives next to the Church of
> Saint Nicholas...the priest called out to him from the window of his house
> to he the confessant as he passed by going on horseback to his
> barracks...going to the house of the priest at nightfall and going into his
> house without having any previous knowledge of him the priest asked him if
> he had gone back to the barracks already and he said yes. The said priest
> gave him sweets and wine of which he the confessant drank two big cups
> and became drunk, and in that sort the said priest took him to the bed
> which in this house was in an inner room and threw him down on it kissing
> him and taking hold of his virile member and ordered him to turn over with
> his breeches down, and putting himself on top of the confessant he put his
> virile member in the back vase of he the confessant, and penetrating him all
> the way in he scattered seed inside him and in the course of an hour more
> or less that he the confessant was with the said priest on the said bed they
> consummated three times one with another the sin of sodomy in the above-
> mentioned form, scattering always the said priest's seed in the rear vase of
> him the confessant and that in all of this the said [priest] was agent while he
> was receptive, and after this nothing more happened with the said priest.

Later in the trial he added that as well as the cakes and wine which brought him
to bed that after the sex was over he was *paid*, thus establishing a hustler–client
relationship between the priest whose clerical costume, house, interior bed all
marked his place in the world. He claimed the priest had paid more than
another priest with whom he had confined his activities to masturbation. His
sodomizer paid him a silver coin called a *pataca*, while the other client preferred
only a copper *tostão*, worth less than a seventh of the payment for anal sex.

The priest Sanches de Almeida in the 1630s provided both food and lodgings
for male sexual partners, and he also permitted the use of his premises for others
to have sex together. This point was specifically made by a 17-year-old, Francisco

Pacheco, who said that in the house of the royal chaplain Sanches de Almeida together with a 21-year-old valet (*moço da camara*) the priest gave them a light lunch and then whispered in the ear of the older youth who then took the younger boy to the bed of the priest. There they both had an orgasm from frottage. In his confession Francisco explicitly said the priest was not present, but that his partner had told him that the priest 'permitted youths who were his friends to use his house for such things.'[10] Other youths confirmed that they found refuge in the house where the priest helped them but also expected to fellate them. References to the priest's same-sex activities fell from *c*. 1624 to the 1640s. The house on the calçada de São Crispim near the Colegio of the Irish fathers – approximately where the present Escadinhas are – gave shelter to adolescents in the 15 to 20 years age range, including runaways like Manuel Gomes of 1640. Sanches de Almeida in 1630, when he was 50 years old, was often providing a bed for a 15-year-old as he did for another and repeatedly fellated them. They both gave the impression of a welcoming household for young boys, and that he knew perfectly well that they were masturbating each other, although they did not know if he knew of 'worse acts,' meaning sodomy. More information about the house was provided when a search party looked for a runaway slave cook with a 'bad' reputation as a 'fairy' (again using the word *fanchono*). They burst into the priest's house and found Almeida with one boy who seemed to be preparing supper, but inside another room with a locked door which they forced and went in with a candle they found a blonde white youth with some light beard getting out of the bed in his shirt and another boy also not fully dressed whose clothes were on a sideboard, and they deduced that it was clear that they all in the house slept in the single bed. Sanches de Almeida was chaplain of the royal chapel of Santa Barbara which was further up the hill inside the parameter of the Castelo of São Jorge (Castilho 1936: iv, 39). The chapel contained a remarkable statue of Our Lady of Poverty of which the French Theatine Bluteau said in 1707 that the rust on her crown symbolized perfectly her love of the needy. It seems that Almeida was protected in some way since his proclivities seem to have been well known to his neighbors.

What was the gay way of talking in Portugal that might 'sign' or mark space? Certainly from the sixteenth century to the first half of the nineteenth the word used in a 'third sex' sense of an effeminate man or 'fairy,' was *fanchono*. This meant someone whose preferred role was receptive in sodomy – *paciente* – or perhaps more accurately was an individual known to be available for receptive anal sex. That is, he was a man who wanted to take 'the woman's part' in a phallocratic culture. A notoriously effeminate (but fully bearded) Madeiran told the Inquisitors in 1570: 'The *fanchonos* are the patients, and never does a *fanchono* sin with a *fanchono* in committing this sin' (Dias 1989: 157). Literary scholars identified this usage of *fanchono* as an effeminate male in the sixteenth-century theater which suggests that it was not only a term used by effeminate homosexuals to describe others like themselves but also had this meaning to the larger heterosexual public (Teyssier 1982: 65–78).

Mott found the usage of *menino puto* for a younger boy who could be sodomized. The word for a female whore – *puta* – is easily masculinized by changing the last letter to *puto*, and thus makes a simple and obvious vehicle for describing a vulnerable or needy boy who agreed or was coerced as much as an adolescent who liked receptive anal sex. Street boys in general, ragamuffins on the look-out for a coin for an errand or other minor services, were also sometimes called *putos* with no obvious sexual meaning. In the 1891 novel discussed below when the baron finds that his catamite was sleeping with his wife as well as with him he calls the youth – *Puto indecente!* (Botelho 1979: 195). This wandering semantic field could thus mean either a catamite or a street urchin depending on context and speech situation. At another point in the story the youth Eugénio describes another noble who propositioned him in the street as a *gajo* which, as in the exchange from earlier in the book, is the street-boy's term for a client.[11]

In a testimony of 1643 by a 16-year-old boy we find a remarkable short description of suggestive talk among men who are on the look-out for homosexual acts:

> all of these men continued to meet in the house of João Mendonça, and when they are there they talk of these filthinesses, saying that such a queer (*bobija*) takes pleasure of this *bobija*, and that so-and-so was good in his time, and when a youth passed by in the street some of them say to the others that this is a good piece, the bugger, and that of these names and these words he the witness thought ill, and that they were directed always towards dishonest acts of the crime of sodomy....[12]

The notary made the odd observation that because of his youth the boy did not confess well but for the modern reader at least the adolescent was keenly aware of the difference between suggestive campy talk between *fanchonos* and accepted normal speech of 'macho' men outside of the sodomite's house.

The Auto da Fé was the locus classicus of the representative public sphere, to use the concept of Jurgen Habermas, of the absolutist monarchy consecrated by the Church. What would be called today the gay subculture of baroque Lisbon was surely rocked by the Auto of 25 June 1645. The event had all the elements of ceremony in the heart of the capital (Bethencourt 1994).

The sentences of eight sodomites and three judaizers who were to die were proclaimed in June on the square in front of the royal palace:

> in the presence of the King Our Lord, the Queen, crown prince and princes, the Most Reverend Senhor Bishop Inquisitor General, the members of the Council [of the Inquisition] Inquisitors, Deputies, Prosecutor, notaries, other ministers, familiars and officials of the Holy Office and a great many of the nobility of this kingdom and the people of this city of Lisbon.
>
> (Higgs 1993: 19)

Figure 5.1 Early eighteenth century print showing a Lisbon Auto da Fé procession of those condemned by the Inquisition, and clergy, and officials.

The fire that in the Old Testament punished those who sinned against nature in Sodom now consumed six laymen and two priests noted as incorrigible (*devasso*), that is to say, persistent homosexuals.

To my knowledge there is no eyewitness account of those proceedings. In a quaint instance of priestly hypocrisy the secular justices were always asked in the formulae of the sentences to treat the prisoner with care, and not to proceed to the death penalty or the spilling of blood. What this meant in fact was described by a British resident of Portugal recounting the punishment inflicted on two obdurate judaizers at the start of the eighteenth century. A letter of 15 January 1706 [*sic* but in fact 1707] written to Dr Gilbert Burnet by the minister to the English factory Wilcox, afterwards bishop of Rochester:

> My Lord, In obedience to your lordship's commands, of the 10th ult. I have here sent all that was printed concerning the last Auto da Fé [of 12 September 1706]. I saw the whole process, which was agreeable to what is published by Limborch [1633–1712] and others upon that subject. Of the five persons condemned there were but four burnt: Antonio Tavanes, [i.e. Tavares] by an unusual reprieve, being saved after the procession. Heytor Dias [da Paz] [Trial number 9776 of the Lisbon Inquisition], and Maria Pinteyra [i.e. Pinheira (Trial number 1537] were burnt alive, and the other two first strangled. The execution was very cruel. The woman was alive in the flames half an hour, and the man above an hour. The present king [João V, 1706–50] and his brothers were seated at a window so near, as to

be addressed to a considerable time, in very moving terms, by the man as he was burning. But though the favour he begged was only a few more faggots, yet he was not able to obtain it. Those which are burnt alive here, are seated on a bench twelve feet high, fastened to a pole, and above six feet higher than the faggots. The wind being a little fresh, the man's hinder parts were perfectly wasted; and as he turned himself, his ribs opened before he left speaking, the fire being recruited as it wasted to keep him just in the same degree of heat. But all his entreaties could not procure him a larger allowance of wood to shorten his misery and despatch him.

(Wright 1816: 247–8)

The significance of this description is that the Auto took place with the individuals named whose complete trials are available for inspection in Lisbon. In the bound collection of printed lists of participants in that particular Auto there is a manuscript annotation by the two names which reads '*queimado vivo*' – burnt alive. This would seem to suggest that this did not always take place. It also accords with the English spectator's description.

Sodomites were perhaps put to death in the same fashion without the prior strangulation, but I have not yet located a precise description of the burning of a sodomite. As the Englishman noted, the issue of prior strangulation, and the rapidity with which death was induced when the garotte was refused, were elements in the theatricality of the punishment. Given the popular hatred of sodomites they may well have been burned alive. The engraving by Bernard Picart (1673–1733) on the Terreiro do Paço depicts only male spectators although there is also a coach, and the windows of the royal palace are not depicted with spectators. Whether this was artistic economy by the engraver or an accurate analysis of a primarily male crowd is not easily decided. He also did not depict the 'bench' or 'elbow chair' mentioned by British observers. We do not now know if the burnings, floggings and other humiliation rituals of sodomites brought about a public catharsis in baroque Lisbon for those who thought male homosexuality an offense to God. The last sodomite to parade in a Lisbon Auto da Fé with the death sentence was in 1740: he was a straw-mat maker brought up as a foundling at the royal hospital in Lisbon who had been found guilty of sodomizing a 4-year-old infant boy. In fact his execution was commuted to a life sentence to the galleys. In 1745 two men in their fifties, a surgeon and a priest, appeared in the public Auto, and in 1748 a Brazilian mulatto and a black slave, both in their forties, processed in Lisbon. In an Auto in Lisbon of September 1754 a bachelor merchant who had emigrated from Minho to Mariana, M.G. in Brazil paraded before the scornful public.

Although the documentation on sodomy cases has existed for centuries, many earlier historians found them too distasteful to do more than mention them in passing. Mott used the material most intensively and militantly. For him the men arrested for sodomy in the past are the historical antecedents of the gay movement of the 1980s on. He brings to his views the special authority of someone who studied for eight years in a Dominican seminary, was married and fathered two daughters, founded the Atheist Group of Latin America, set up the Bahian Anti-AIDS Group, and enjoyed in 1994 a same-sex union with an Afro-Brazilian some twenty years his junior which had been recognized by his University as eligible for benefits coverage. Mott's work is sprinkled with mockery of Catholic clergy and rituals. He has perhaps not sufficiently stressed changes in the attitudes of the tribunal over time.

One of the most remarkable sodomy cases of late seventeenth century Lisbon has already been cited in the adventures of the cavalryman: the Azorean priest Father Machado and his thirteen catamites over a period of eight and a half years. The priest was insistent in his confession that once he had the boy in his house and bed he was always insertive. He dwelt next to the church where he officiated. He repeated in each description of his numerous sex acts that he was always 'the agent' while the boy was exclusively 'the patient.'

The circumstance of his confession on 13 February 1698 showed how carefully he planned to give the information without raising the alarm. He went out of his way to denounce them, even traveling from Lisbon to the city of Evora in the Alentejo to do so. The spatial significance of that is extraordinary: his church was located at no more than 10 minutes' walk from the main door of the Lisbon Estaus palace of the Holy Inquisition. His house was adjacent to his Lisbon church: that was the house from which he sent his manservant out on errands while he sodomized his catamites. Evora, by contrast, is 115 kilometers away from Lisbon. This was his small, special and penitent part of what Jean Delumeau has called the Western guilt culture (Delumeau, 1990). One can only speculate about his feelings, presumably of clerical compassion and unction, over the punishments, ruin and humiliations that would overtake his thirteen sexual partners. By traveling to Evora he was taking careful precautions that they should not be forewarned or able to flee from capture and punishment. On 9 November 1698 some ten months after their arrests ten youths and young men out of thirteen who had been sodomized in his Lisbon house by the Azorean priest were whipped through the streets of the Portuguese capital, sentenced to the galleys for various terms (and subsequently exiled for life). One of the thirteen, who came from a middle-class merchant background and had refused to confess even under torture, was sentenced in private (*na Mesa*) so that his family was not publicly disgraced. Two others, one a student of Latin and the other an apprentice silversmith, in the former case had been sodomized once long ago and the apprentice was no longer in the city. The boy the priest had sodomized most, he claimed a hundred times, had been seduced by him at age 14. At the time of his trial in 1698 this person was a married man with two daughters. After the Auto each of the convicted appealed for mercy in letters that often gave details of their family situation. They were exiled for life. The seducer and insertive sodomizer of the adolescents, being a priest was not whipped or tortured, was not in the public humiliation ritual at the Auto, but was subsequently secretly exiled from the kingdom.

The average age of the youths when they started being receptive in anal sex with this priest was a little over 16. (It is interesting to note that the median age of a sample of receptive partners in male sodomy in fifteenth-century Florence was also 16 (see Rocke 1996: 116). The youngest had been 14 when initiated, and the oldest 19. Clearly the priest was having sex with some of them concurrently on different days over the same time period. Of his occasional partners (with whom he had sex fewer than ten times), the professions were tailor, artillery soldier, cavalry soldier, post-office worker and three students. His repeat partners of between eleven to fifty acts each were a surgeon, a tailor, an apprentice silversmith and a grammar student. His most persistent partners, both with a score of between 51 to 100 receptive acts of sodomy, were a wax worker and an employee in a bookshop.

What is most striking is the relative inversion of the sentencing pattern from modern usage. A priest who sodomized thirteen teenagers while making use of his own premises, gradually extending the complicity with each from masturbations to sodomizing them, sometimes giving them money and bringing them back for more of the same, clearly in a calculating and predatory type of sexual activity might be expected to be punished more severely than his sexual prey. However that was not the assumption of the seventeenth-century Inquisitors. The priest was exiled to be sure, but without the public shaming that would cast light on his failings to his clerical vows of chastity. Another priest, Father Ascenção, was also not in the Auto although young men whom he had solicited to sodomize him were.

In fact the sentencing does not seem to fit with the number of sexual acts, or the age at initial seduction or the sexual role taken. Thus João Nunes Soares, who in his confession claimed to have been active with another partner, but *paciente* for Father Machado got a flogging and ten years in the galleys: he was 18 at the time of the Auto. The married man aged 23 with three daughters at the time of the Auto (the third of whom was born while he was in the Inquisition prison), had been seduced when 14. He had not had sex with Father Machado for years and said he had changed his sexual ways and was contrite. Nevertheless for this his property was confiscated, he was flogged through the streets, and was sentenced to eight years in the galleys. Doubtless he felt a little bemused at the workings of Father Machado's conscience, and that of the Inquisitors. We also cannot perhaps ever know if he felt any fellowship with the other convicted sodomites in the 1698 Auto as they processed before the church of Saint Dominic before a jeering mob, or whether he knew that they too had been used by the parish priest of Saint Nicholas.

Yet it is perhaps true that these grim ceremonials designed by priests to warn the spectators of the consequences of the unspeakable sin and the other offenses enumerated in the Edict of Faith had another result: they displayed in the heart of the city that there were individuals who could be their husbands, neighbors, fathers, brothers, their sons or their nephews who participated in this form of sexuality.

A century later in Lisbon there had been a big shift in praxis. In 1753 a priest who asked errand boys and casual laborers during confessions at the cathedral and elsewhere about their penis size, whether they masturbated and whether in the houses which they often shared in large numbers they played sexually when undressed for sleeping, was sentenced to eight years of exile. However various people petitioned the Inquisition on his behalf and he was excused much of his punishment.[13] The 1777–1807 Inquisition documentation includes a full case and sentence of a rural pedophile rapist accused of the *nefando*, an incomplete extra-judicial inquiry into a village butcher who as a widower propositioned the local bachelors, and a variety of denunciations and some voluntary confessions from Lisbon. This represents no more than 1 per cent of the business of the late Inquisition which manifestly was not greatly concerned with policing this particular activity in Lisbon or following up on denunciations.

Were those arrested for the *nefando* men who thought of themselves as homosexuals in the sense meant in the postmodern usage of gay men? We have a voluntary self-accusation in 1799 in Lisbon made by a Brazilian sailor over 40 for 'disorders' in religious matters, but he added his confession of 'innumerable complete sodomitic acts with persons of the same sex in the back passage' most recently with a boy in Oporto.

> neither could he specify, because of the multiplicity of places, times and the diversity of persons who were passive [*paciente*] with him in this fault, however the slackness of his conscience was such that he used all and every occasion convenient to this end…[14]

The sailor made no reference to sodomizing women.

Canon Antonio de Queirós Camacho Botelho, interrogated by the Inquisition as a freemason, confessed on 23 February 1792 to his 'enormous faults' in places and with men he could not name: 'knaves have no name….' He said that he was prey to the shameful and most degraded vice of sodomy where he was usually receptive for anonymous accomplices, but that he would provide those names and places he could remember.[15] As a priest his sexual encounters were generally nameless, furtive and brief and *outdoors* in Lisbon, and all those he admitted were recruited among his social inferiors. However it was not his homosexual activities but his Freemasonry that caused his arrest.

In the later eighteenth century in Portugal sodomy or homoerotic practices were prosecuted rarely by the Inquisition save in cases of child abuse, or sexual solicitation of male penitents by priests. Lay adults were left alone, or merely warned to mend their ways. Denunciations were not even investigated save for priests and in some matters of religious scandal. In short, during the post-Pombal period there was an end to the 'make an example' policy of earlier times. Inquisition records provide other examples of sodomites over the course of the eighteenth century. In 1790 a married surgeon from Lisbon aged 33 revealed 'that he had had sodomitic acts twice with some male nurses (*uns praticantes do Hospital*) some four to five years ago.'[16]

Self-denunciations might also provide information on the location of sex acts. It was in his own house and marital bed that the husband of a D. Margarida in the 1790s blamed too much wine with his dinner for his abominable advances to his wife. She wrote that he had been so insistent that he made me violate my own will in letting him serve himself of me by the back passage, and reminding him the next day of how much this had cost me he said that he only remembered in part and that he wished to see how it was, and once again he asked that I should consent to satisfy him in the same fashion, but now [July 1795] that I am informed that this offense belongs to the Holy Office I come to it to denounce myself so that by the love of God I shall be pardoned...[17]

The same husband wrote a revealing confession in the same month in which he added to the offense against his wife further details of a drunken nocturnal promenade when outdoors, in the Lisbon night, he met three soldiers, and propositioned them to agree to the same fault (*delicto*) as that which his wife denounced. He claimed that one soldier was agreeable to his request but that he could not 'achieve his desire.' With the other two he achieved what he wanted. His language contrasted desire and wish, with what he called fault and guilt (*culpa*) but not a sin, both in his own house and out of doors.

The most prominent name in the *cadernos do nefando*[18]of the late Inquisition was a leading member of the Academy of Sciences José Francisco Correa da Serra. He found himself sometimes present in elite space in company with a member of the royal family, the duque de Lafões. At other times he was in more plebeian circumstances when he had three or four times made a 'sin against nature' with Faustina, a woman from the Praça das Flores and had done the same with Ana Joaquina some years earlier. He said his most recent acts of sodomy in 1792–3 had been with 'unknown persons in the darkness of night' *outdoors*, and in particular five or six times with a youth (*moço*) whose name he gives and whom he had admitted *into his own house* [my emphasis].[19] The document was not annotated with any call for further inquiries.

It is possible that police records in Lisbon will yield information about homosexuality in the city after the abolition of the Inquisition in 1821. Something can also be gleaned from imaginative literature and also satire, prose, poetry and song on the feelings and activities of lesbians and gay men. Such writing was often oblique in its statement of meanings. Few things are more difficult for the historian to capture than irony on the part of the long dead.

The literary echoes of male homosexuality in Portugal in the seventeenth century were sparse and generally contemptuous in tone. They pointed often to the relations of adolescents and adults. The Jesuit António Vieira's comment on the presence of 'harpies' among the varieties of thieves is followed by observations about the rich house of a man whom he had first known 'yesterday' as the 'shameless page of a rich minister' – (*pagem safado de um ministro opulento*). The connection here of a loaded word, *safado*, in context of a page whose proximity to a rich minister leads on to an expensively furnished house points to the toy-boy/sugar Daddy duo which is one of the constants of the gay male European and American imagination of possible relationships. Vieira's description of the domestic interior in Lisbon of the ex-page provides a seventeenth-century version of the 'Queen's Nest':

I saw that he had wall-hangings and pictures, writing desks and chairs, monkeys at the windows and parrots in ivory cages, mirrors of *cristal* in the salon, clocks of mother-of-pearl and other furnishings such as are not owned by the king of China.

(Vieira 1937: 321–2)

There is a clear implication of the rewards amassed by a now superannuated catamite for sexual services.

Relations between male adolescents and older men reappeared in literature in the nineteenth century. Some theories of morbidity and degenerative sexuality found among doctors at the end of the nineteenth century inspired a novel published in 1891 at Oporto: *O Barão de Lavos* (the Baron from Lavos). Born in 1855, the author Abel Acácio de Almeida Botelho used his first and last names on his novels. He died in Argentina in 1917 where he was a Portuguese diplomat. He had a distinguished career as a military officer, journalist, politician, poet and novelist. *O Barão* is perhaps the first sustained book-length word portrait of a homosexual in Portuguese literature. In the case of the Portuguese and Brazilian world this was not a common subject at any time, despite the fairly high incidence of homosexual activity. Lisbon and Oporto in the nineteenth century certainly had hustlers (*putos*) available as a cheaper and ancillary form to heterosexual prostitution. Like many Portuguese men with strong homosexual inclinations in the past and present the baron married – a state he entered into after the death of his own parents.

O Barão raised a great hue and cry among the reading public. There were calls for its suppression on the grounds that a novel about a pederast was obscene. It was also a great commercial success and the first edition sold out in a fortnight. It was often reprinted in later editions as part of the set of social-realist novels which Botelho entitled 'Social Pathology.' *O Barão* was written between March 1888 and May 1889. To the best of my knowledge it was never translated.[20]

Botelho was, on the face of it, a heterosexual married man. His marriage was childless. There is little likelihood of knowing now whether Botelho had any participant observer knowledge of juvenile male homosexual prostitution in Lisbon. If he was himself bisexual he sought to conceal this from his public by his repeated expressions of disgust for the character he created. At the same time the reader received precise indications about where to look for hustlers in the Portuguese capital.

In the story the baron finds the major youth character, an orphan of 16 who is a street vendor called Eugénio, on the central avenue of Lisbon, that of Liberty. He meets the boy at night and persuades the boy to meet him at a rented apartment in another district, the Bairro Alto. There he makes him pose naked. The baron examines him, sketches him, and then takes him to bed and sodomizes him.

Lisbon's gay geography in the late nineteenth century is the backdrop to the unfolding of the story. The novel starts at rua do Salitre as people arrive for the circus with the night-time street pick-up of Eugénio. The novel ends with a scene near the rua dos Condes theater, a zone which was still listed in gay guides a century later as a cruising ground. These streets are on opposite sides of the wide Liberty Avenue which was laid out in its modern form at the end of the nineteenth century. There is an account of how the baron in 1867 (aged 32) scoured the streets for boys:

> It had to be a boy that he was looking for because the eyes of this tall dry man sought out the beardless faces, with a light fuzz, of adolescents. He stared at them for an instant with a greedy and dark fixation, and then quickly went elsewhere. It was possible to see after some minutes of observation that he did not look for anyone in particular. On the contrary, he seemed to compare, contrast, choose. If there were kids he rapidly walked past them after a furtive glance. There were others at whose discovery his face showed the most pungent sensuality. Then, with them, there was no means that he did not use to try to capture their attention. He lightly brushed them with his arm, he touched their thigh with his walking stick as if absent minded, he stood by their side giving them a dry, glassy and persistent look, and he blew a cloud of smoke at the nape of their necks as he passed by.

His attempt to pick up a 15-year-old who sold cakes is described; when the boy understood the baron's sexual intent he says rudely to the nobleman that he is mistaken.

Figure 5.2 A map of Lisbon, 1785, showing the central district with rectangular layout constructed after the earthquake.
Source: Murphy, *Travels in Portugal*

If the baron lived with his wife on the largo São Cristovão not far from the Saint George Castle with a view over the city, his apartment for assignations on the other side of the city was in the Bairro Alto on rua da Rosa, the name of an actual street. (This was a fairly obvious reference to the scandal of the Travessa da Espera in the same district which took place *c.* 1880 when a nobleman, the marquês de Vallada, was caught by the police having sex with a soldier.) Eugénio of the novel is lodged there. One night when the baron cannot find his kept catamite Eugénio he goes to the Arco da Bandeira and finds a scruffy boy for quick sex in the first squalid nook of a narrow alleyway he could discover. Eugénio is gradually introduced into the main household and in due course he cuckolds the baron. After the baron returns from foreign travel six months after the scandal when he had discovered his wife and Eugénio *in flagrante delicto*, he is to be seen every night in the theater staring through opera glasses at Eugénio, now on stage wearing tights. When the baron dropped still further in his world because of the scandal and his extravagant debauchery he sought out male pick-ups near the waterfront. His hunting ground was near the Tagus and the cheap wine bars. These *tascas* for drinking were on the Calçada do Garcia, beco do Forno and that of Ricarda. There the baron met sailors, soldiers and coachmen who were muscular and strong and to whom he wished to be receptive in anal sex.

Botelho 'explains' the baron's sexual drive as a result of a flawed genetic inheritance (from his decadent noble family) and his education in a Jesuit school where he masturbated a lot. If the alleys of Lisbon are the outdoor backdrop to the baron's pick-ups for sex there is the indoor symbolism of a Ganymede print which hangs on the baron's wall. The baron is particularly fond of this picture. It provides the opportunity for his discussion with some other male guests of how male bodies are much better looking than those of women. Later in the story, after the scandal, one of his guests inadvertently brings him the Rembrandt caricature of Ganymede (from Dresden) where the young boy being lifted up by the Eagle is urinating in fright. Later, even when in poverty and completely outcast from polite society, the baron still has the print on the wall in the room provided for him out of compassion by an old society associate. At the end of the novel he has finally sold it so that he can buy a hat to attend the wedding of a virginal daughter of his compassionate benefactor. In other words he kept his picture of the abduction of the beautiful youth after he had lost his wife, his palace, his social position and even his failed attempt to be a photographer. It was a remnant of a coded gay interior decoration of his living space as much as a metaphor for the passionate homoerotic ideal of his existence.

The *Barão de Lavos* thus reads as a classic account of the punishments visited upon the insertive pederast who gradually evolves into a receptive sodomite, and whose lineage ends with him. Like the *Présidente* of the *Liaisons Dangereuses* of Laclos he is disfigured by disease when he finally dies. On the other hand the book was relatively informative about how youths could be picked up by cruising on the main Liberty Avenue in Lisbon and on certain streets in the downtown core, that cheap hotels existed where no questions were asked, and that a discreet flat or room for special adventures could be rented in the Bairro Alto of Lisbon.

Figure 5.3 Early nineteenth-century neo-classical statue of the Love of
         Virtue from the Ajuda Palace, Lisbon.

The baron pursued obsessively another child labeled only as the 'boy in the vest,'
a particularly attractive youngster whom he finally succeeds in picking up at
night on the west side of rua Augusta, the main street of the business district.
They go to a hotel and the baron fellates the boy who tells him that a black priest
had done the same thing to him the day before. This surprises the baron but also
makes him think that this sort of thing is commonplace and should not be the
cause of a guilt complex.

   This long novel was very much of its period in that nobody is portrayed as
exclusively homosexual with long-term partners of the same sex or age group.
The baron's search for gay sex may be compulsive for him, and the 'feasting with

panthers' riveting, but it is not given a separate existence from that of heterosexuals. Like Oscar Wilde he had a wife and a place in heterosexual society. However, there are descriptions of the complicities and friendliness of feminine-acting men to be found in the streets of Lisbon:

> In the dark spot in the middle of the squares he began, lightly brushing against the effeminate beings that came to cross his path, with salient buttocks and a provocative look, an indecent nudging of the hips, hand in pocket, arching the back. Usually they were inferior types, kyphosis [?], irregular, with plastered locks of hair over the ears and a fur beret on the head, jacket, closely shaven, suspicious and skilled, swirling on the mosaic sidewalk, one eye on the loiterers and the other on the police.
>
> The baron spoke to them with some banal phrase to strike up a conversation: how the weather was, or a light for a cigarette, or were they taking a walk? – The crisis of abnormal excitement that racked the pederast at the first words of these unnameable beings was extraordinary. From thence it did not take long for them to understand each other, to become confident associates, friends. And the revels were launched. Afterwards, frolicking with one and the others as long as the cash held out, the night flew by in an instant. There were amatory preliminaries on public benches, they tippled in the wine shops, and they mounted arm in arm to the 'gods' of the theaters, going to hide the satisfaction of monstrous appetites in the shadows of debauched dens of vice.

The novelette of Mário de Sá-Carneiro, *The Confession of Lúcio*, written in 1916 shortly before the poet's suicide, contains at least a homosexual implication of the affection of the narrator for his friend, who is involved with a woman. It can be read as a discussion of same-sex affection but with the inevitable presence of women, that is, the angle of vision is never that of exclusively homosexual men. The novel is absorbed with the relationship between young men of bourgeois background and says almost nothing of setting. Family control meant that same-sex sustained affairs between school friends were problematic and at all times furtive and concealed. Death was the literary device for closing off the extension of an unimaginable love.

António Botto (1897–1959) was a dapper, clean-shaven poet whose unapologetic homosexuality was patent in his 1920 book of poetry entitled *Songs*. This led to a Church-encouraged student manifesto in 1923 calling for withdrawal of the book from sale as well as another volume which showed homosexual sympathies. Botto became an icon for the Lisbon anticlerical literati and often appeared in the cafés where they gathered. Jokes circulated about him like that told by the poet Fernando Pessoa in which a friend teased Botto for promenading arm-in-arm with a sailor on Good Friday. 'António, you are impossible. Eating meat on Good Friday!' to which Botto replied in his nelly voice 'But a Jack Tar [*Marujo*] is not meat. It's fish.'[21]

In the last third of the nineteenth century the French influence on Portuguese medical-social thinking was perhaps stronger than the German. Various investigations by Portuguese doctors and others echoed the kind of investigations which were beginning at that time in the French- and the German-speaking empires. Arlindo Camillo Monteiro referred to a study by Maximiliano de Lemos of the Medical Faculty in Oporto for an erudite monograph (Monteiro 1922: 154–5). Forty years later the Secretary General of the Lisbon Police, Alexandre Morgado, distinguished between kept 'fancy boys' and those who hustled because unemployed or homeless and on the streets. He noted that the latter were to be found late at night on public squares 'waiting for persons who come out of the urinals' (Monteiro 1922: 201). He said the majority of them were drawn from man servants, persons who had been in controlled institutions (*internatos*) meaning orphanages, colleges, prisons and barracks. What they might learn in such places was suggested by a news report of the 1870s about a reformatory for juvenile delinquents housed in the former convent of the Monicas in Lisbon. Seventy-one naked boys were locked up in the dormitory each night: their clothes were left outside so that they did not smell near the beds and because 'nobody flees in the nude.' [22] Poor boys and youths who hustled in the street were often drawn from trumpeters, soldiers and others in an age range of 15 to 30 years of age, and were mostly found in Lisbon and Oporto, according to Monteiro.

Much male prostitution was not the work of transvestites but of youths and young men who continued the *puto* tradition of the Portuguese capital which existed for centuries. Some were to be found near the River Tagus-side area of the executions of sodomites in the seventeenth century. It was an active cruising area as the *Barão de Lavos* novel said of the 1860s, and as did post 1960s gay guides to the city. Further along the river the area around the Casa Pia school for orphans and disadvantaged youths was known in the 1940s until the 1970s for two kinds of encounters: one with some of the adolescent male pupils (known as *casapianos*) but also with artillery men from a barracks situated up the hill. They loitered in the park in front of the Jeronimos monastery. A 1994 report on youths who worked as prostitutes in the Edward VII Park in central Lisbon described the way in which they were picked up by car drivers, the high incidence of drug use among them, the occasional scenes of violence and their ages, ranging from mid teens to early twenties. [23]

Some men on military service participated in prostitution on an occasional basis. Sailors loitered and displayed in the underground male urinals on Commerce Square hoping to meet a partner who would pay for sex. The river front along to the electric train station at Cais Sodré, and the urinals inside that station, were also a notorious venue for pick-ups, especially of conscripts, in the 1960s and 1970s. Teenaged marines, the Marinheiros-Fusileiros, would cross over from the south bank of the Tagus where their barracks were located to cruise in their white summer uniforms in the Baixa, on Rossio and as far as the Edward VII Park for same-sex encounters with paying civilians during the era of the colonial wars that ended in 1974. At the same time all these locations might have gays who sought egalitarian, non-venal sexual encounters. Indeed the last electric trains after midnight that ran along the bank of the Tagus to serve outlying dormitory towns were often heavily traveled in-bound to the capital by gay men on weekend nights as they arrived hoping for sexual adventure. The first train to make the outward bound trip in the morning, at around 5:30 a.m., carried its contingent of gay men, either sated or not, back to their homes outside the capital.

For those without a place to entertain sexual partners or city dwellers who were cautious about introducing strangers into their home the best-known cheap pensions for sex in Lisbon in 1994 were one on a square near the Cais do Sodré, another up the hill near the Chiado and a third on the Escadinhas do Duque stairways. All three were in the historic core of the city. (A room and bed fee of 1,000 escudos for half an hour was at that time effectively the same multiple Daniel Guérin once noted for street hustlers in Pigalle in Paris: twice the room rental as the price for a brief sexual encounter.)[24] In Lisbon better-dressed, better-educated male sex escorts who worked for guests from the five star hotels would expect much more money than the minimum for the park *putos* who accepted lifts and who lived in shacks or abandoned cars. Not only was the geography of pick-ups variegated but so too was the behavior and bargaining of the sexual actors in the arena at any given moment.

In modern Lisbon public urinals served as meeting places for non-commercial sexual relations between men. In the nineteenth century there were some cast-iron *vespasiennes* in central Lisbon in imitation of those found in Paris, like that on the Square outside the *Misericórdia*. Under the authoritarian government (1926–74) such male urinals both outdoors or indoors were relatively unsupervised. That was especially true for underground toilets near the river on the Praça do Comercio or those in the station at Cais do Sodré. Many public male urinals in Lisbon were demolished or closed after the 1974 Revolution of the Carnations. One of the first to be closed to the public was the large underground urinal with some thirty stands in a semicircular arrangement located on the main square of Lisbon, Rossio. Under fascism prior to 1974 this remained open long after midnight and was always very busy with an elderly attendant who saw nothing as long as behavior had a faint semblance of propriety. It served as a display cabinet both for sailors and street-boys looking for paying contacts with whom they went to cheap, nearby pensions as well as some egalitarian cruising. The masonry structures on the Campo Grande in Lisbon served a less urban public in a suburban park near the university, but those urinals were walled in with the advent of democracy to prevent their unsupervised nocturnal frequentation. As a result they became arid and impregnable stone boxes, menhirs of past masturbations and other forms of sexual expression, with no utility for contemporary promenaders by day or night. Subway urinals were closed at some stations. The washrooms in shopping malls were increasingly under surveillance by security staff.

As the toilet culture declined – was asphyxiated – as the principal site of furtive, silent and anonymous encounters for male same-sex activities in Lisbon there was a corresponding development of commercial and overt meeting places. Modern Lisbon inaugurated since the 1970s a series of gay bars and clubs in the Bairro Alto district in particular. This was strongly influenced by the tourist trade. Police patrols were discreetly posted near some of the bars most popular with tourists in order to ensure that they were not at risk in the streets. These bars operated late at night and sometimes included sections for dancing. The Brica Bar situated on a street in that district was for long a secretive and expensive bar with a middle-aged woman door-keeper who was an implacable barrier to low class or unsuitable individuals. However in Lisbon as in Paris during the 1980s bars became more open and accessible and the price of drinks fell. This was perceived by some Portuguese as the Americanization of the homosexual subculture in Lisbon. Many other bars were opened from 1974 on, for longer or shorter periods of time. One bar particularly patronized by foreigners looking for hustlers was owned by an Englishman. Various steam-baths with a gay clientele existed. Certain cafés flourished which, while not explicitly 'gay' establishments, were known to enjoy the patronage of men looking for sexual partners. The tendency after 1974 was for a diminution of the number of such large 'mixed' cafés as the Palladium on Restauradores Square which was remodeled into boutiques, or the Monumental near Saldanha Square which was demolished.

By the 1990s there were also increasing numbers of same sex co-resident adult couples in the city without large age discrepancies, some previously married. Typically both men work. Middle-class couples in Portugal often remain integrated in their family networks. Others, especially those partners of working-class origin from small towns, are sometimes rejected by their kin. Such couples confronted Iberian familialism and refused to defer to the lingering *macho* disapproval of a modern gay identity. In Portugal 50 per cent of the respondents to a survey taken in 1990 objected to homosexuals living next door to them. That contrasted with the average for fourteen European countries in which 28 per cent opposed homosexuals.[25] Notwithstanding the concentration of gay bars in the Bairro Alto there is nowhere in Lisbon as sharp a division between gay and straight districts as that found in some North American 'ghettos.' In November 1994 a bourgeois newspaper like *Público* could carry advertisements in its classified section aimed at men who hoped to make sexual contacts with other men by telephone rather than in bars, baths or the streets. One company subdivided an advertisement for contact telephone numbers in Lisbon and five other regions of Portugal with the headings (in English) of 'Big Bananas' followed by 'Man to Man' followed by 'Gay Dating.' The choice of different categories in the advertisements as much as the use of the International gay lingua franca showed that the envisaged public did not have identical tastes.

In 1997 the Portuguese gay movement showed its presence in daylight in the heart of Lisbon with an AIDS awareness march down Liberty Avenue in May and a Pride festival in June on a square in the Bairro Alto. A Portuguese language gay magazine (*Korpus*) was on sale in a few kiosks. In October a Gay and Lesbian Community Center opened in the presence of the Mayor in space provided by the City Council in the historic heart of Lisbon.

Conclusion

The Inquisition records showed that priests' houses or the cells of regulars were privileged sites for homosexual encounters in the seventeenth and eighteenth centuries. The alternatives were outdoor ill-lit locations, like the shrubs at the foot of the battlements of the Castle of São Jorge, or fields beyond the built-up limits of the city. During the nineteenth century the French style urinal in front of the Misericórdia in the Bairro Alto was notorious as were some others in the lower part of the city and on Restauradores Square. As a result the Bairro Alto had a reputation, echoed in the novel *Barão de Lavos*, as a district where homosexual encounters could be made in the interstices of urban heterosexual prostitution. In the first half of the twentieth century there was a café culture, primarily male in the case of its clients, in which literary bohemia rubbed shoulders with some bourgeois homosexuals. There was a lower-class matrix of wine-shops and outdoor cruising by the Tagus and in the urinals of the center of the city. In the post-1974 era, following the restoration of democratic government in Portugal, it was the Bairro Alto which emerged as the center for a nocturnal but overt culture of bars, cafés and restaurants for gays and lesbians in Lisbon.

Notes

1 Greenberg is misleading in his statement 'Napoleon struck a blow against religious repression by destroying the records of the Inquisition, thereby depriving us of records documenting the persecution of sodomites in early modern Europe' (Greenberg 1988:19). Much Inquisition documentation has been lost in different countries, especially in Italy where it was looted at the time of the French invasions. In 1998 the Vatican Archives opened more inquisitorial documents to scholars although it is not yet known if any of these concern sexual offenses.
2 National Archives of Portugal, Lisbon. Lisbon Inquisition, trial no. (henceforth IL) 6919.
3 IL 9467.
4 IL 9467.
5 IL 9469.
6 IL 8843.
7 '…perguntando-lhe se podia bobijar com ele que era o mesmo que cometer com ele o pecado nefando,' IL 3925.
8 IL 3529. Thanks to Prof. Alberto Vieiva for a photocopy of his transcription of the trial.
9 IL 939.
10 IL 17024.
11 This word is common Portuguese slang in the 1990s for a man, like 'guy' in American English, without any sexual connotations.
12 IL 6554.
13 IL 209.
14 IL 13638.
15 IL 13388 cited in Loja (1986: 343–4).
16 IL Livro 146.
17 IL Livro 145, fol. 364.

18 There is a gap in the documentation from 1778 to 1793 which may reflect the loss or even discarding of documentation. Possibly it may reflect consideration for the sensibilities of the royal council when Queen Maria ruled prior to her mental incapacity in 1792. See IL Caderno do Nefando 145.

19 IL Cadernos do Nefando 145.

20 See the introduction by Justino Mendes de Almeida to Botelho (1979). That edition has modernized spelling and a study of linguistic neologisms in volume one, pp. I–lix. References to the *Barão de Lavos* are translated by David Higgs from that edition.

21 *Jornal de Letras*, vol. XVII, no. 699, 30 July–12 August 1997 had a dossier on Botto.

22 *Jornal da Noite*, 11 May 1874, quoted in Leal (1875, vol. 5: 406).

23 Tereza Coelho, 'A prostituição masculina no Parque Eduardo VII,' *Público* 15 March 1994, 18–19.

24 Daniel Guérin, 'Chez Mado,' *Gai Pied Hebdo* (5–11 July 1986) 227: 39–40

25 *Globe and Mail* (Toronto) 11 July 1992, p. A11.

6   Rio de Janeiro

David Higgs

The earliest evidence of same-sex genital activity in sixteenth-century Brazil is scarce as a result of the disapproval of those who could record it. When Pero Vaz Caminha in 1500 wrote the famous letter which described the first contacts between the natives of Brazil and the bearded Portuguese sailors who made landfall on the coast of Bahia he was very attentive to the bodies of the Amerindian men and boys as well as the women who came out of the forest. He noticed that neither sex made any effort to cover their 'shames' and that the penises were not circumcised. He commented on the good bodies and smooth skins and affectionate disposition of the native peoples. While King Manuel was informed of the celebration of the First Mass in the new land his correspondent said nothing about when the first sexual interaction took place between sailors and Amerindians (Caminha 1985).

On 1 January 1502 a Portuguese fleet entered the bay of Guanabara, and, as it had the appearance of an estuary and a certain flow of tide, the commanding admiral misnamed the harbor River of January – Rio de Janeiro. The historic core of the present city was a mangrove swamp. The Europeans who came ashore soon had extensive contact with the Amerindians. Jean de Léry, a Huguenot who spent most of 1557 on the site of what is now Rio, recorded an insulting word in Tupi, *tyvire*, which he said meant bugger, from which he said one could conjecture that the 'abominable sin' was committed among the native people (Léry 1992: 153). Léry was a devout Calvinist who showed a limited but explicit ethnographical curiosity about sexuality. In 1565 the city of Saint Sebastian was formally established as a Portuguese municipality. In 1587 Soares de Souza said of the Amerindians who lived in the same general area that they were 'addicted to sodomy and do not consider it a shame…. In the bush some offer themselves to all who want them' (Murray 1995: 268). In parts of Brazil the custom of the pubescent Amerindian youths living and sleeping together in an all-male house meant that forms of adolescent sexuality between males before marriage existed. As late as the 1930s among the remnants of a nomadic tribe in Mato Grosso studied by a French anthropologist some unmarried young bachelors openly caressed each other by the camp fire. This behavior was restricted to adolescents who were brothers of girls who would later marry the youth from the other lineage. Lévi-Strauss claimed that even when adults it was not unusual to see two or three married men with children walking around in the evening tenderly entwined (Lévi-Strauss 1974: 313–14). If Christian shame and secrecy about physical pleasures did not inhibit the Nambikwara youths under the bespectacled gaze of a foreign anthropologist and their fellow band-members, we can reasonably conclude there were similar practices in the sixteenth century.

Some males functionally lived as Amerindian women. In general variations in gender behavior among Amerindians might also impinge on religious powers (Trexler 1995: 102–17). As so often in studies of the Amerindian past the history of their sexuality can only be known in the records of those who brought to them disease, exile and an alien religion.

Early European settlers imported many African slaves to work on sugar plantations in the area of Rio as well as at other suitable locations. Many of these slaves both female and male were used sexually by their masters. Inter-racial sodomy was encountered in Brazil by 1600 in the slave-owning colonial economy and this was primarily male same-sex. Given the great sexual imbalance among African slaves there may also have been sexual activities between males in the slave quarters.

By 1600 Rio had a population of some 2,000 with almost no European women, by 1700 it was no more than 10,000 and by 1800 the population had risen to 44,000. The nickname for a person born in Rio came to be *carioca*: a word derived from the Tupi expression for House of the Whites. The city housed religious institutions but also those of the government when the colonial capital moved south from Salvador in 1763. There was a constant movement from the port of Rio to the hinterland with the arrival of Portuguese immigrants and also of African slaves. The city had a large, indeed predominantly, slave population of African descent but also free blacks as well as people of Amerindian, European and mixed descents.

The main sources of written information on homosexuality in Brazil and in Rio during the colonial period are the papers of the Inquisition. These were always housed in Portugal since the monarchy never set up a sitting tribunal in 'Portuguese America.' They permit some 'micro-biography' of the lives of individuals of no social or political prominence. The Portuguese Inquisition exiled some convicted sodomites to Brazil: the first known was a surgeon from Evora in Alentejo in 1553.[1] The misfortunes of one of these men, Antonio Soares, was referred to in the chapter about Lisbon. Sentenced to exile to Brazil when under 20 for repeated acts of the abominable crime with a variety of partners he later lived at the Carmelite monastery in Rio from the 1630s for eighteen years. That building is today the university Faculdade Cândido Mendes and was close to the main square (now Praça XV de Novembro) and the principal thoroughfare of colonial Rio, the rua Direita. There he reverted to his homosexual activities:

> The truth is that he is known to carry on filthinesses with youths, and in respect to the same type of sin for which he came in exile [to Brazil] there are violent presuppositions against him with three accomplices with whom he shuts himself away for a long time, sometimes outside the Convent and

sometimes in the Convent, and being reproved never wished to correct himself, and those who complain of being propositioned by him are a further three or four…[2]

We know that the Catholic clergy provided a cover in the past just as in the present for more male homosexuals than in the male population at large, and therefore space controlled by priests is often sexualized: Antonio Soares in the Rio Carmelite Convent near the docks in the 1630s and 1640s was said to be corrupting '*moços*' a choice of word that suggested that as he aged the man convicted in Portugal as an adolescent for both insertive and receptive sodomy with other novices both in the Lisbon convent and at his father's house continued to seek out young partners under 20. Soares' repeated partnerships perhaps fell into the paradigm of the older man and younger ephebe which has so long exercised those who seek to establish the chronology of the idea of the homosexual as an orientation distinct from that of heterosexual males. Brother Antonio Soares' trial documentation contains pathetic reports of his condition after long imprisonment once he had reached Brazil, exiled for sodomy, covered with sores and bleeding ulcers. However, bound into the same documentation is a report by the Carmelite later sent to reform the monasteries of the Order in Brazil, which gave a radically different picture of what had happened to the monk after his exile. Soares had become very influential in the Rio convent because of his skill at business (and we can notice that the Carmo was literally steps from the docks where ships arrived and departed for other markets), and that he seems to have received protection from other members of the order against the rigors of the Inquisition, going as far as to solicit pardons and reinstatements directly from Rome.

Inquisition documents permit us to trace in detail the life of another seventeenth-century Portuguese sodomite, a violin player who later became a tobacco merchant, who lived in Rio during the second half of the seventeenth century. The city was then already more than a hundred years old.

The initial brush with the Inquisition of this violin player, Luiz Delgado, occurred in Evora, Portugal, when he was 21 years of age. He was denounced by another prisoner for his sexual relations when in prison with a putative future brother-in-law, aged 12, who squeezed through the bars to visit him. Delgado was found guilty of sodomizing the child and was exiled to Brazil. Delgado and a brother had been put in the secular prison in the first place because of involvement in thefts.

Upon arrival in Portuguese America Delgado first lived in Bahia, and was married there. However he was also involved with several white adolescent boys with whom he was passionately in love. The scandal about his behavior in Salvador da Bahia was such that he left for Rio in the company of a Portuguese-born Latin student named José Gonçalves who was not yet 18 when he first met the violin player who now traded in tobacco. Delgado left a previous flame with his wife to share the house he owned in Salvador, abandoning then both his domestic and sometimes gay space, and the public one of the streets of the colonial city where he was notorious.

He arrived in Rio, part of the movement of not only Portuguese migrants but also of sexual refugees. He set up a tobacco shop behind the Carmo Convent. A 26-year-old priest watched Delgado and his boyfriend from a first-floor window in the convent and testified that Delgado treated the student with great affection. He combed the youth's hair and tied ribbons on the sleeves of his shirt and on his small fans (*abanicos*), fans considered a part of a woman's dress, before the youth left the house. The prying eyes of the priest saw that Delgado had in effect at last created a gay domestic space where he could act as he wished with his beloved, including an encouragement of womanish behavior. A goldsmith aged 38 described the domestic living arrangements of Delgado with an emphasis on his bed:

> many times Luiz Delgado made accusations against Joseph Gonçalves who was a youth whom he called his nephew and treated with a great deal of friendship *in his own house on the second floor where he lived* [my emphasis] and not in the shop [where apprentices or assistants would normally sleep] and on the second floor he never saw more than one bed, but that it was certain that the youth Joseph Gonçalves did not sleep in the shop but rather on the second floor and he knew this because he often had dinner with the said Luiz Delgado and went to his house late at night, and left the said youth with him on the second floor....

This youth obviously provoked the more conventional males in the city by his costume. An official in Rio noted that he walked around with 'dishonest' colored silk britches, presumably meaning ones that were tightly revealing of his buttocks and penis, decorated with red and yellow ribbons, which he showed off when he pulled up his cassock. The bailiff noted that this costume scandalized the inhabitants. It was a disgraceful example to other students who behaved themselves, and in 1686 the judge ordered the beribboned tail of his costume to be cut since it caused 'scandal and was noted.' The flamboyant feminine-acting student was arrested and only released with the intervention of Benedictine fathers, doubtless his teachers.

Some months later however young Gonçalves decided to return to Portugal and went to the judge claiming that Delgado had hidden his clothes and books in order to prevent his departure. Delgado retorted that when he had first met Gonçalves the youth was dressed in rags and was hungry – in essence then claiming to own the property of the student – but the judge upheld the right of the young man to leave with his own things and some money. According to the Peeping Tom priest, Delgado wept copiously as he sought to persuade Gonçalves not to leave him, and even went so far as to try to enter the skiff which carried passengers out to ocean-going ships in a last frantic effort to persuade the youth to change his mind. Again Delgado was indifferent to public scandal and paid for it, since he was imprisoned for a time as a warning to change his behavior. Delgado was so affected by the departure of Gonçalves that he did not change the linens on the bed where they had slept together in their love nest. Delgado said he would not have them washed until the youth again returned to him. At this stage in his life he was 42, and notoriously a sodomite who liked somewhat feminine white youths.

He quickly found consolation in a public space, the theater, when on a summer night in 1686 he saw a 16-year-old boy playing the part of a woman. Delgado was passionate in his declarations to the boy and persuaded the young actor to leave the house of his father and to live in his shop with him. The father of this cross-dressing youth was a Portuguese immigrant grocer whose wife, Rio born, was already dead. Whether the conditions at home in the paternal house were uncomfortable for a theatrical son is unclear, but either because of paternal rejection or in response to a passionate admirer he moved in with Delgado and remained hidden for three months. In due course he moved freely around the house. A servant testified that he found the pair in the shop section of the house seated on a bench kissing and embracing. A law officer said that he had seen the boy walking around the house wearing merely a light undergarment and a shirt: that is, he noted the body language of a semi-dressed feminine-acting boy in an all-male domestic space. The father of the runaway lad turned to the law officer to investigate and the two accused, Delgado and his catamite, went to the Carmo convent to seek refuge. In due course they fled north to the town of Vitoria in Espirito Santo accompanied by a servant and a fugitive soldier. An order for their arrest followed them. The servant would later testify that the adult and the youth always slept together in Rio, and also during the journey to Vitoria either on land or in the boat, they were together in a bunk, or a hammock or sometimes entwined under a coverlet on the ground. The soldier mentioned he had seen them caressing each other and suspected that this was 'some filthinesses of "fairies" [*fanchonos*] and sodomites.' Later the couple traveled on to Salvador da Bahia and caused much scandal by their behavior leading to their arrest there on 5 February 1689. They were then shipped to Lisbon to stand trial before the Inquisition on the accusation of sodomy: Delgado was then 45 while his beloved Doroteu was 18 years of age.

They were described as 'sodomites who lived indoors like a husband and wife with general and public scandal' [sendo *vox et fama* que ambos eram sodomitas, vivendo de portas a dentro como marido e mulher, com geral e público escândalo].

The Inquisitors were well aware of the importance of a private and secure space to an expression of homosexuality. Indeed, Inquisition regulations made it an offense to provide space for the commission of the act of sodomy, so that a complaisant innkeeper or householder could not escape censure for what went on in a building for which he or she was responsible.

The testimony of Doroteu insisted that there was no ejaculation of semen inside his anus when Delgado, 'tempted by the Demon' penetrated him. This bizarre technical precision was a recognition that without ejaculation the Inquisition considered that the sinful wastage of semen had not taken place. He could not thus be found guilty of the sin which was punishable with the penalty of burning. In 1690 Doroteu was sentenced to the fairly mild punishment of three years exile to the Algarve in southern Portugal where he disappeared from the historical record.

Delgado was jailed in Lisbon in the Inquisition prison for three years. His trial was drawn out. He denied wrongdoing and alleged the malice of various individuals who lied about him, including Doroteu and the boy's father. This was a standard evasive procedure since the accused was, of course, never informed about the content of depositions against him. He was sentenced to ten years of exile in Angola.

Professor Luiz Mott's research allows us to deduce that Delgado, despite various punishments, continued to be involved in pederasty from his early twenties to the time when he vanished from the historical record in his early fifties. Throughout his life he looked for white partners who were more than a decade younger than him, who were only receptive in sodomy with him and who had somewhat feminine mannerisms. In Rio he finally achieved his aim of a gay domestic space, living with white boyfriends and a servant, whereas in Salvador he endured the presence of his wife. In his extravagant affections and in the ostentation of his catamites when in the public spaces of the colonial city, Delgado lived in a way that adumbrated a sustained male–male autonomy from heterosexist values. While Mott was not particularly concerned with the spatial elements in his account he mentioned that other students visited the house in Rio, and to that extent Delgado was an example of what was possible in a domestic sexual relationship with the same sex (Mott 1988: 75–129).[3]

Eighteenth-century Rio did not offer a great many diversions. As in Portugal respectable women were largely confined to their houses and much street sociability was exclusively masculine. The principal excursions for white women were trips to church. Many white men were unmarried, or found sexual release with slave women with whom they did not associate in any public space. In the interstices of this largely masculine public world individuals might find homosexual satisfactions.

Scraps of information are found dispersed in denunciations, but some offer more detailed accounts of individual whites accused of sodomy. A phonetic denunciation (*c.* 1781) from a detainee in prison in Rio professed horror at a homosexual love affair between two other prisoners, 'sharing friendship as if they were women and committing acts with each other by the back way.'[4] Denunciations provide clues about the sense of sinful sexuality in relation to sodomy in late colonial Brazil.

In 1790 one of the resident monks of the Carmelite convent in Rio was investigated for sodomizing young slaves. Although he crossed the racial line he retained the classic adult–ephebe balance, searching out adolescents for his sexual purposes. He was Father Tomé de Madre de Deus, a Brazilian born in Minas Gerais. There is a strong likelihood that the case was actually the result of a clerical squabble (the legendary *briga de frades*), since the accused was a brutal and peremptory member of the congregation and also the provincial president. However the inquiries appeared well founded. The witnesses were young: first was a slave born near Rio then aged 18. He described how two years earlier

Father Tomé had called him to his cell, locked the door, laid down on his bed without his habit while instructing the boy to rub his legs and then made him also lie on the bed on his side whereupon the priest sodomized him: 'and spilled inside the semen, consummating in this manner the horrendous and abominable sin of sodomy....' He noted that he had been used in the same fashion on three other occasions but then he was sent back to a country estate that belonged to the convent. The next witness was also a black slave boy, learning to be a carpenter, and he did not know how old he was although the scribe thought him about 15 to 16 years of age. This boy tried to deny that he had any complete experience of what the other boys of the same convent were saying that the priest did to another slave boy called Raimundo. He said he had often been to the house of the priest's mother with messages. He admitted that in his cell Father Tomé locked the door and made him take down his breeches but he added that he never consented to anything. Even so, he lamented, the other boys spread it about that the priest used him 'for bad ends.' As a result his own father had beaten him. Like the first witness the erstwhile carpenter was sent back to the country estate. Raimundo was the third and last witness and he said that two years earlier, when he was about 17, he too had been called to the cell of the priest, the door was locked once he was inside, and there was the same outcome. He admitted to having been sodomized seven times on different occasions by Father Tomé. He too was sent back to the country estate which, of course, was a demotion from urban domestic slave to rural laboring slave. The use of his cell for sexual relations with slave boys who belonged to the convent can be contrasted with the sending of them back to the country with its much quieter life. When the *comissario* made his wrap-up statement on the accusation he not only noted the professional failings of Tomé who avoided saying masses but added he was 'an enemy of the cloisters' who constantly went about outside the convent. He had lived for two months with a Protestant naval captain called Thomas Stephens in a *chácara* (country house often with an orchard).[5] As so often in Inquisition cases we have only the information in the inquiry and nothing with which to compare it. Certainly monks were accused of sexual abuse of black youths, as Pires de Almeida did in his book published a century later (Pires de Almeida 1906: 62–3). No further action was ordered against the priest, probably in order to prevent aggravating the scandal which, as Raimundo said: 'is notorious in the convent because he the witness made it known to some boys of the same Convent....'

As well as the trials and denunciations of sodomites as such, there is also scattered information where same-sex activities in Rio figured in documentation about individuals investigated for other reasons. Sometimes these fragments of historical information lend themselves to *bricolage* and link to each other. An example would be the young apothecary José Luís Mendes who was investigated for permitting gatherings of men in the shop where he worked as the cashier. This was a place known for irreligious conversations. This shop was on the rua Direita, steps away from the Carmo Convent from whose windows a priestly voyeur had spied on Delgado a century earlier as he showed his affection to his boyfriend. An apothecary's shop was not open to the public like a stall in the hot and dusty street with its noisy house slave customers. Neither was it private like an individual house. Individuals often foregathered when awaiting the grinding of drugs for a prescription or simply used the premises as a meeting place. Mendes was investigated for his sacrilegious talk but it also transpired, as one accuser put it, 'he does not have dealings with women but with men.' Two of these were mentioned, one a Brazilian-born black, and the other a *pardo* (mulatto) so his sexual dealings were inter-racial.[6] A married apothecary who lived nearby on the same street, the rua Direita, said that Mendes was guilty of *molicies* – which could mean fellatio and masturbation but not sodomy. He paid for his partner to go to the opera. Another individual said the sexual tastes of Mendes were notorious in the city. His own uncle said that Mendes talked a lot about Voltaire and his works, and had retorted that he heard from the Carmelite monks that Father Tomé owned the works of the sage of Ferney. Tomé was said to attend services in the choir where instead of reading his breviary he read Voltaire. There is here at least some circumstantial congruence between two individuals who were noted for same-sex genital activities with young non-whites, and both interested in prohibited foreign literary works, and who both lived within close walking distance. The Inquisition ordered no further inquiries into his sexual activities although Mendes was required to swear that he would cease to permit or to frequent the scandalous conversations in the apothecary's shop.[7] Almost a decade later Mendes briefly reappeared in the Rio historical records when he asked for exemption from the confiscation of the apartment in the house where he lived with his aged father and his 'numerous family'.

Towards the end of the eighteenth century Rio de Janeiro had a public garden laid out exclusively for strolling, that pleasure derived from the southern European custom of the family promenade, the *passegiata* or the *paseo*, which permitted inspection of other families. In a sense it was an institutionalized heterosexual cruising that might lead on to marriage, but it could also provide a cover for gay glances. The Viceroy Vasconcellos had ordered the draining of a fetid lagoon that was unsightly and suspected of causing illness. An architect who had studied in Europe designed a formal garden with French-style walkways and symmetrical plantings to put on the site. The French-inspired design would last until the middle of the nineteenth century (1862) when it was replaced by the more undisciplined layout of the English garden, characterized by curving pathways and uneven clusterings of vegetation (Delson 1979: 155). Whether French formal or English curvaceous the Passeio Público became a place of promenading which extended by analogy to street cruising by men looking for homosexual adventures. Within the space marked on one side by the eighteenth-century aqueduct which later became a track for *travesti* prostitution, the Passeio beyond which one reached the sea shore, and in another direction over to the Convent of the Carmelites near the main docks, this was a city zone of sexualized spaces.

As French troops under Marshal Junot marched into the outer suburbs of the Portuguese capital in November 1807 a great fleet set sail for Brazil carrying as many as 15,000 souls including the lunatic queen Maria I, her son the Prince Regent, courtiers, priests, diplomats and servants. After a stormy passage across the Atlantic and an unplanned stay in Salvador da Bahia the royal family and their entourage reached Rio de Janeiro in March 1808. This exodus was of great consequence to the city and to its homosexual spaces. Rio in 1800 numbered some 44,000 but when the Regent, now King John VI, returned to Portugal in 1821 the city had 100,000 residents. The French constituted the largest foreign component of Rio population and included shopkeepers, tailors, hairdressers and other completely urban occupations. There were also German and Irish mercenaries, Swiss colonists in transit, sailors and merchants from North America and elsewhere. With Brazilian independence in 1822 proclaimed by Prince Pedro, the rapid increase in city size continued. There were perhaps 150,000 *cariocas* in 1830. Already the city had a reputation for amusements, luxury and pleasure.

The Portuguese Inquisition was suppressed in 1821 and its documentation ceased. Written evidence about nineteenth-century homosexuality in Rio became very scattered and concealed by shame and furtiveness. Some literary evidence subsists, and perhaps more can be unearthed in newspapers of the time, but documenting where male homosexuals sought each other is necessarily characterized by much bricolage among mere fragments of information.

The colonial city in 1800 was primarily composed of a slave population of blacks and mulattos but during the nineteenth century as a result of European immigration and the marriage strategies in mulatto families the Rio population became steadily 'whiter' just as people of mixed racial origins were ever more numerous. By 1850 the old colonial city, the *várzea* flat area between Castelo, São Bento, Santo António, Conceição, was gradually superseded by more desirable living in the suburbs. In the colonial city social segregation had been more vertical than horizontal, with white families living on the upper floors, and servants, slaves and shops at street level. Increasingly, however, the better-off and established families made use of the street car, a system that first emerged in France at Nantes in 1826. By 1837 Rio had horse-drawn public carriages which passed at regular intervals, and while these were expensive they adumbrated a system of public transport which made the city grow. The slave sedan chair porters became a rarity. In 1849 80,000 blacks lived in Rio out of a total population of perhaps 200,000. There was a higher percentage of slaves in the urban population of Rio than any other city of the Americas *c.* 1850.

Homosexual activities across the divide of race and slavery and with a strong inequity between partners had been perhaps the most typical paradigm of colonial Rio. Under the Brazilian Empire (1822–89) homosexuality as the simple matter of sexual practices between consenting adults of the same sex in private was not a crime. If there was any scandal, however, individuals could be arrested. This happened in 1855 when the *crioulo* (Brazilian-born black) José Athanasso, was detained because he caused 'intrigues' in two convents where he was known as 'the servant (*criado*) of pederasts.' José had a host of protectors whose representations caused the Minister of Justice to order his release 'in order to be free of impertinencies and disagreeableness.' They made a huge fuss to prevent his recruitment for military service.[8]

The inter-racial paradigm of same-sex practices was not destined to remain the predominant one in a modernizing city. Foreign immigrants appeared in increasing numbers. Portuguese immigrants were the largest single category and many of them were young men and boys without families who lived in the crowded conditions of the *várzea* and who tried to save as much money as possible. More than half of the total of Portuguese immigrants to Rio in the years from 1820 to 1842 were from 10 to 20 years of age, and 87 per cent of them declared themselves to be unmarried. This age profile differed significantly in the case of other nationalities. Quite a few Portuguese youths, in the words of the consul in 1849, 'possessed no capacity nor aptness to employ themselves in any kind of application.' A sample of 170 wills made by Portuguese immigrants during the 1830s and 1840s showed that more than half were unmarried, although of those bachelors more than half left bequests to women and children (Nunes 1998).

The literates who arrived in greater numbers before 1850 often found work as cashiers or shop assistants, while the large-scale arrivals later in the century were landless illiterate peasants who found employment in the initial manufactories of the city which at that time were home to one-third of Brazilian industrial production. Others slept in the shops where they worked. Since many of these bachelors planned to return to Portugal with their earnings they lived in cheap and crowded boarding houses called *cortiços*, a kind of housing which gave the title to the famous novel by Aluísio Azevedo (1890). In that book there is a reference to an old man (Botelho) who sexually touches a male student, a feminine youth who likes being with washerwomen (Albino) and a lesbian prostitute who is after the girls (Léonie). There were real-life equivalents of these characters in São José parish where many Portuguese lived. The number of residents there in each household rose from 9.7 in 1890 to 19.2 in 1906. In those streets there was a *de facto* street familiarity between slaves, freedmen and the new arrivals. Among this floating population of men there were those who knew about the *puto* traditions of Oporto and Lisbon where adolescent boys sometimes hustled for instant sex with men. If the suburbs were becoming more desirable with the new sewage works and gas lines the central city was crowded, promiscuous and other. In Rio the square known as Rossio (Tiradentes) was a notorious place for cruising and pick-ups. Benches offered a place to sit and smoke, the statue in the middle of the square was a rendezvous point, and there was a public lavatory for men which, in the 1930s at least, required a modest payment for usage. The district of Botafogo had already gained the cachet of being the most aristocratic suburb of Rio by the 1890s. Sometimes a better-off male residents of Botafogo might go to the center to find a male immigrant for sex. Conversely immigrants might travel from northern working-class suburbs to find sexual contacts. An 18-year-old literate *galego* who dwelt in a house with a garden and who worked as a pharmacy cashier was expelled as an undesirable alien condemned for being a thief and a 'passive pederast.' He left on the steamship *Clyde* destined for Vigo in 1907. In 1912 two

Uruguayan bachelors who lived together on rua da Constituição in the center city, one of whom said he was a shop assistant while the other, aged 31, said he was a tailor, were expelled from Rio accused of being vagabonds and guilty of 'passive pederasty.'[9] In the same year a pornographic publication called *Naked Rio* contained a story about a youth who was picked up on a bench in Tiradentes square and taken to a room in Lapa where he was sodomized.[10]

By 1900 class and ethnic barriers in Rio society were evident. New forms of transportation and entertainment existed, and perhaps attitudes towards sexuality evolved. Slavery was abolished in Brazil when the princess regent Isabel signed the Golden Law on 13 May 1888 and the remaining population of 700,000 Brazilian slaves of full African descent were declared free. At the same time the upper classes in Rio had a long tradition of house servants who resided either under the same roof or in close proximity to their residences. The frequent use of black women as wet-nurses, the *ama de leite*, and as nursemaids, led to the kind of inter-racial heterosexual experimentation by employers and their sons which has been exalted by Gilberto Freyre and many other authors who stress the inter-racial eroticism of Brazil. Rapid increase in the Rio population continued during the second half of the nineteenth century: in 1870 Rio had 235,000 inhabitants and by 1890 this had more than doubled to 522,000.

In 1895, the year of Oscar Wilde's trial and conviction, the novel of Adolfo Caminha, *Bom-Crioulo*, was published in Rio de Janeiro by an impecunious young writer who died before he was 30 (Caminha n.d.).[11] Contemporary critics accused him of imitating the Portuguese naturalist novel of Botelho discussed in the Lisbon chapter above. Caminha certainly was well informed about the milieu he described. A doctor writing in 1872 commented on the high incidence of sodomy among the Brazilian military. Superiors demanded ('does not solicit but orders') this sexual service of those under their authority. Another doctor in the 1890s reported on the high incidence of anal venereal sores among military apprentices, most of whom were orphans subjected to 'humiliating sexual violation' (Beattie 1996: 442–3). Caminha had attended the naval school in Rio and served as a midshipman and officer in the Brazilian navy before being forced out of the service as a result of heterosexual scandal. Trevisan, a gay Brazilian critic, wrote that in his courageous treatment of homosexuality as a specific and irrefutable fact, Caminha was much ahead of his time and his work was banned for many years (Trevisan 1986 104–5).

Adolfo Caminha's novel about the strong black ex-slave Bom-Crioulo who fell passionately in love with the blonde cabin boy was set in Rio and its port. It presents the adult–adolescent paradigm of same-sex relationships, but here it is a 30-year-old ex-slave who is insertive and a white, European-looking 15-year-old adolescent boy who is receptive. Bom-Crioulo (Caminha n.d) possesses Aleixo for the first time on the navy ship – that is, in a place where there is only occasional privacy for sexual acts and where discovery can lead to a flogging – but subsequently establishes on land in Rio a love nest in a house belonging to a Portuguese woman who had seen better days when she was younger and slimmer and had many admirers.

Dona Carolina was Portuguese and rented out rooms on Misericórdia Street only to persons of a certain 'type,' people who weren't haughty or pretentious but all the same lads that could be trusted, good tenants, compatriots, old friends.... She wasn't concerned about color or class or profession of the individual. Sailor, soldier, ferryman, cashier from a corner store were all the same to her: she treated them all alike and affably.

This house where Dona Caroline rents rooms, by the month or by the hour was of the type known in Rio as *casas de cómodos* rather than the better accommodations offered in *estalagens*.

The Portuguese woman is beholden to Bom-Crioulo who had helped her when a robbery was attempted and was friendly but without any sexual overtones: 'she knew that the black man was not a man for women'. He asks her for a room:

'Just a little room without any frills for when we come ashore.'

'One bed or two?' asked the fortyish Carolina with a smile.... They laughed, in mutual understanding, while Aleixo, leaning over the windowsill, spat down into the small back yard of the Africans.

Caminha evokes the pleasure of Bom-Crioulo in his 'beloved refuge' in the room and he spends money on it:

All the money he could get was to buy furniture and little rococo objects of fantasy, figurines, decorations, things of no value, often brought from on board ship. Little by little the small room started to look like a Jewish bazaar as it filled up with bric-à-brac, and accumulated empty boxes, vulgar seashells and other ornamental accessories. The bed was an already much used camp bed over which Bom-Crioulo was careful to spread when he got up every morning, a thick red blanket 'to hide the stains.

Caminha describes the two sailors in their room in their underwear on the canvas bed which was cool in the hot weather with a bottle of white rum, feeling completely free and independent and with the door double locked as a precaution against being disturbed.

Only one thing vexed the cabin-boy – the black man's libertine caprices. Because Bom-Crioulo was not satisfied merely with possessing him sexually at any hour of the day or night. He wanted much more; he obliged the boy to go to extremes. He made him a slave, a whore, suggesting to him whatever extravagance came to his imagination. Right from the first night he insisted that the cabin boy strip, completely naked: he wanted to examine his body. Aleixo became sullen: this was not something that you asked a man to do!

But he submits and strips completely 'Sodom was now resurgent in a sad and desolate rooming house on Misericórdia Street where at this time of night all was in the soft quietness of a distant desert'.

They are very domesticated for a year and Dona Carolina would tease them saying that they would end up having children. but then Bom-Crioulo is reassigned and cannot come ashore with Aleixo: he is worried that the boy will become infatuated with some handsome young officer while Aleixo thinks of perhaps meeting some wealthy man with a position:

> He was already accustomed to doing 'that stuff.' Bom-Crioulo himself said that nobody paid attention to those things in Rio de Janeiro. And what could he ever hope for from Bom-Crioulo? Nothing, and meanwhile he was sacrificing his health, his body, his youth to him....Certainly it wasn't worth it!

The Portuguese woman Carolina finds the adolescent very attractive, makes up to him and seduces him, and he in turn comes to dislike Bom-Crioulo. This involves a statement about the room where they had been a sexual couple:

> The attic, the mysterious little attic, was abandoned now. Aleixo didn't want to know about it. He hated it, because it was there that he had become a slave to Bom-Crioulo; it was there that he had 'lost all shame.' The poor room was like a cursed place, always locked with a key, lugubrious and dusty. Dona Carolina scarcely opened it – only when she had to stow away some old utensil or some formless item of furniture. The emperor's portrait, the canvas folding bed, the old household goods of Bom-Crioulo and the cabin-boy, everything that before was the delight of the two friends, had long since disappeared. Nothing remained now of the life they lived in common.

Bom-Crioulo is hospitalized after a flogging, and he tries to contact Aleixo but his letter is destroyed by Dona Carolina. He then learns that Aleixo has become the lover of the Portuguese woman. He confronts the youth who is very handsome in his tight fitting white and blue sailor's uniform and grips him by the arm. When Aleixo asks him to let him go or he will cry out Bom-Crioulo tells him to call for the 'cow Carolina.' In the *dénouement*, Bom-Crioulo stabs and kills Aleixo: the description of the dead body even suggests perhaps sexual mutilation: 'His dark blue shirt and his white trousers bore great red stains...everyone wanted to *see* the corpse, to analyse the scar, to stick his nose in the wound'.

The story is thus an account of an inter-racial gay love affair in Rio that turns to tragedy, of an encounter between a strong black man and a white ephebe who as he matures is attracted to heterosexuality. It provides an imaginative rendition of the type of living arrangements and port zone tolerance that existed in the working-class areas of the city of Rio before its modernization.

The great dividing point between the old colonial city and the new urbanization inspired by the remodeling of Paris by Baron Haussmann came in 1902–6 with the plans prepared by Pereira Passos. In 1904 Olavo Bilac rejoiced at the noise of the falling masonry when old housing was cleared to make way for the new Avenida Central in Rio de Janeiro:

> It was the sad and lamenting groan of the Past, of Backwardness, of Shame. The colonial city, filthy, backward, obstinate in its old traditions, was weeping with the sobs of those rotten materials falling apart.
>
> (Needell 1987: 48)

In 1903 a Toronto-based company, the Rio de Janeiro Tramway Light and Power Company Limited, proposed to unify existing streetcar networks that served the *várzea* but also the northern suburbs. That proposal was made effective by 1907. The average vehicle carried 30 passengers and covered 8 to 10 kilometers an hour with a mule for traction, while electric trams ran at 15 to 20 kilometers per hour. By 1895 they already provided 82 million rides per year and no decline took place until the trams were gradually replaced by buses.

At the start of the twentieth century Rio had a new tramway system and a new democratic form of entertainment, the cinema. The streetcar to Copacabana was part of the rapid build-up of the beach suburb. The growth of Rio de Janeiro into a major tourist center brought many visitors to the city who in turn stimulated prostitution of both sexes. The separation of two major gay cruising tracks and hustling locales into Cinelândia in the center, near the Opera House and the National Library on the one hand, and on the other in parts of Copacabana near the beach was already incipient before World War II. Cinelândia had the reputation in a 1994 guide as being one of the oldest pick-up (*pegação*) areas in Rio where large numbers of male prostitutes went looking for clients on the streets. The toilet of the Bar Amarelinho was famous in legend although the same guide noted that it was not really very active. Instead it suggested the toilets in a nearby department store (Mesbla), the toilets at the station for the Santa Teresa streetcars and those in McDonalds. The square called largo do Machado in a mixed residential-commercial area in Flamengo became cruisy on Sunday afternoons when in-migrants from the Northeast were found 'paying attention.'

Rio acquired a world-famous sexual aura from its carnival (Parker 1991: 136–64). It gradually developed from an earlier celebration in which men and women threw water bombs at each other. The procession (*Desfile*) was the annual culmination of the festivities. The sweaty bodies of the dancers of both sexes and the *travestis* among the costumed *sambistas* proclaim eroticism. The carnival makes a street theater of the inversion of the roles of authority beginning on the Friday night when the keys of the city are given to King Momo. After 1888 and the end of slavery, and with increasing elaboration, the carnival celebrated reversals of the everyday black–white, male–female, rich–poor dyads of Brazil. The first Rio samba school was founded in 1928 with the name 'Let them Talk' (*Deixa Falar*) in the Estácio district.

This coincided with the development of radio stations in Brazil which broadcast music written and performed by Brazilians as well as foreigners. One composer assumed by at least part of his audience in the 1930s to be gay was the Rio-based Assis Valente. His song 'Striped Shirt' (*Camisa Listrada*) could be taken as addressed to a male companion/lover, and at least by some listeners was understood to be so. Other singers, like Cauby Peixoto in due course, would be identified as being gay even if, in the interests of larger sales, their publicity agents never propagated such identifications. By the 1980s the singer Cazuza, however, would not only flaunt his sexuality but he mediatized his own resistance to his oncoming death from AIDS. The radio and the gramophone made it possible to play music in a variety of urban spaces, both indoors and outdoors, and when the music was congenial to male homosexuals it might eroticize either discreetly or blatantly the location in which it was played.

Particularly from the 1930s the carnival fed on the imagery of Brazilian films which were giddy comedies of manners with a lot of popular songs. These films were known as *chanchadas* and the Rio Atlantida studios made about forty by 1943. No actress icon more encapsulated this genre than Carmen Miranda, with her headdress of tropical fruit. Made for domestic consumption these films contained a Brazilian mimicry-caricature of the Hollywood productions which circulated at that time. These giggly, kitsch productions often indirectly satirized Brazil but in a way that was inherently *carioca* and which entered the popular culture of the times. The *chanchadas* stopped production around 1960, at roughly the time when the television had made deep inroads into the leisure space of even the lower classes in Brazil.

The overacted heroines of the *chanchadas* provided a series of models for the symbolic vamping of the drag queens (*travestis*) of the carnival. The films and the *escolas de samba* won an impregnable public space for the transvestite man in a land famous for its machismo and its hyper-masculine men. Men who behaved in a feminine way were called *bicha* ('faggot'). The stand-out figure (*destaque*) who parades between sections (*alas*) of the procession is frequently a *travesti* with silicone implants to produce a caricature of breast development. The macho is known in Brazilian homosexual slang as *bofe*, (cf. 'butch' in North American English of the 1990s). Much of the oral culture of Brazilian men drawn to same-sex encounters revolved around the role playing of *bicha–bofe* discourses. Significantly, the emergent egalitarian couples to be found in Rio and some of the larger cities of Brazil attempted, from the 1960s on, to emulate the clones of North America, where both partners for instance would sport facial hair. In the popular imagination, however, it was the image of the *bicha* which predominated in ideas about gay identity.

A marked increase in the explicit gayness of carnival performers was a development of the 1980s. Since the 1960s a dance *baile dos enxutos* had been held in a cinema on Praça Tiradentes in the business district despite a *pro-forma* threat by the police to close it for indecency. By the late 1970s it was a major event which drew a large crowd to watch arrivals in drag, lesbians and others. By the 1980s it was held in a much larger space near the Rio Sul shopping center, closer to the Copacabana district. The publicity was blatant and obvious. This was a process whereby what had formerly been presented as playful gender-bending by straight men who hilariously vamped and camped as women, was now turned into part of an affirmative gay identity.

Rio became the world capital of male transvestites from the 1960s on. Of course men have dressed as women and women have dressed as men in many places and for many reasons, as the chevalier d'Eon and Saint Joan of Arc among others remind us. However, Rio has developed a culture of exuberant transvestites which commands even a modicum of social respect in certain spheres. Men go to Rio from all over Brazil in order that they may begin cross-dressing. Thanks to the television and to various references in tabloids the bohemian area called Lapa near the majestic aqueduct built in 1723 to bring water to the central city from the Carioca River is known as their particular domain. Lapa was from the late nineteenth century the district associated with 'rascals' – a particular Rio type, called in Portuguese *malandro* – who was a petty criminal, pimp, gambler and player of the street game *porrinha*. The *malandro* was to Rio what the *apache* was to the 1920s in Paris: imagined at least as young, sensual and even creative in his disobedience to the rules of the conventional citizen. The *malandro* also rejected the desire of the nineteenth-century Rio bourgeoisie to appear as 'European' as possible. He wore garishly colored clothes. An ethnographer who interviewed many *travestis* put forward the hypothesis that the slightly menacing unconventionality of a district favored by *malandros* also stimulated the transgressions of gender rules that lie at the core of the transvestite enterprise (Silva 1993). Between the 1940s and the 1960s the *travesti* themes of the carnival became a feature of some specialized shows in bars with musical accompaniment. A few *travestis* could work in the shadows of more conventional heterosexual prostitution; sometimes they loitered in the lamp-light, risking arrest for the crime of 'offending public decency.' Sometimes they twirled and danced in the lower-class *gafieiras* – dance-halls – without exciting the hostility of the (heterosexual) working-class couples around them.

During the 1960s there had been a *de facto* clean out of female prostitutes from Lapa by violence and threats. This was a conquest of a *travesti* space. The women had moved away: the relatively cheap, 'industrialized' heterosexual prostitutes worked at the Vila Mimosa close to the avenida Vargas which was the oldest red light district in the city. In the first days of January 1996 bulldozers knocked down the Vila Mimosa installations which had been used by prostitutes for more than a century. The 1,800 women who worked those beds were to be re-housed in Duque de Caxias district, although the municipality there was opposed to the move. Instead some of them managed to find a new site some 500 meters from the old where they could install themselves.[12] Lower-priced heterosexual prostitutes were found on certain streets and also at the main railway station, Central. Sex workers who wanted higher returns advertised in the newspapers or were organized by pimps to service hotels, or to attend particular nightclubs in the search for business. There was always something of a working acceptance between *travestis*, male hustlers and heterosexual prostitution. Two men might rent a room to have sex with each other in a primarily heterosexual 'hot pillow' hotel without difficulty. However the ethnographer particularly stressed the nervousness and shame of the clients of *travestis* compared with men using conventional women prostitutes.

Lapa was a section of Rio that became notorious throughout Brazil as the 'low end' of the *travesti* life, just as the visibility of *travestis* on Brazilian television and in certain clubs was the 'high end.' There were other 'strolls' for *travestis* from the 1970s on, like Quinta de Boa Vista, Madureira, Realengo, Avenida Atlântica and even places in Nova Iguaçu but Lapa was the most obvious. Many new *travestis* were young in-migrants from the Northeast, men with a low life expectancy as a result of drug-taking, violence, adverse reactions to silicon implants, unhygienic depilations, sexual mutilations and poor diet and living conditions. There were *travestis* of all races. For the youth who began cross-dressing the streets of Lapa and the denizens of that district were immediately accessible. From the arches of the eighteenth-century aqueduct of Lapa might come the contacts which lead to the fantastic world of elaborate clothes, luxurious living, international travel and money. Artistes like the witty Argentinian transvestite Patrício Bisso performed in shows at Copacabana and elsewhere in the 1980s, and appeared in the pages of news magazines. This publicity accorded to some *travestis* also bestowed a legitimation of sorts upon a career. Between the street and the tv screen was the world of the bars and pick-ups. Many *travestis* avoided places where there were many egalitarian male homosexuals who dressed like men: individuals they disdainfully called *bicha-homem*, i.e. 'fairy man' or *bicha de bigode* – 'fairy with a moustache,' or *maricão* -'big faggot.'

Lapa and the *travesti* beat was not far from the region known as Via Appia where young, athletic and masculine men displayed themselves along the pavement. They wore sports clothes and at night often showed their erect penis as they stood at the roadside hoping to attract the motorized potential clients who drove around the circuit. There is a sequence filmed in this zone in the German film (1992) *Via Appia*. The Via Appia men were more *bofe* (butch) than the younger adolescents who worked around Cinelândia, and also at Posto Seis in Copacabana. The adolescents, in particular, hoped to meet foreign tourists who paid a higher rate than Brazilians. Indeed the Brazilian clients of *travestis*, *bofes* and adolescents ('menores de rua' who provoked international concern over the widespread juvenile prostitution of both sexes in the 1990s) would often bargain hard. Much of this bargaining would be about sexual acts, especially for adolescent boys to be receptive in sodomy, or for *travestis* to sodomize apparently masculine clients. (One *travesti* gave up her 'husband' when the man asked to be sodomized (Silva 1993). There was a 'circuit' of relationships between minors, thieves, policemen, *travestis*, drug dealers, informal peddlers of various items from clothes to cigarette lighters along the streets and store fronts of Lapa.

Non-monetized sexual acts between males of similar ages especially among whites are the most hidden by discretion and reticence. Such activities could go on in known cinemas, either with sex acts on the premises or immediately after leaving. Indeed a psychology dissertation in 1989 carried the intriguing title: 'In the cinema twilight…orgiastic society on *carioca* afternoons.'[13]

During the nineteenth century and much of the twentieth Brazilian bourgeois males wore formal 'European' clothes as a sign of status. Under slavery blacks did not wear shoes but freemen and whites did. Costume carried a message about social authority. That was true for young and old. The Rio bourgeoisie was small – never more than 5 per cent of the population before 1940 – and so for much of the nineteenth and twentieth centuries the social labeling of an individual was obvious from his costume. It was a kind of social revolution when the middle-class young and aspirants to enter that class began to wear casual clothes, particularly blue jeans, and sports shirts. This was really an innovation of the 1960s.

The center of the city developed locales for gay meetings at night when the population of business people left the area. A classic illustration of this would be the vegetarian restaurant called Boêmio which at lunch-time served meals to office workers and at night became a place for flamboyant transvestites. One of the most striking was a university teacher of geography who changed his appearance totally in the evening and vamped at the restaurant. A video was made of his transformation in the 1980s. Tigresa on rua Riachuelo had transvestite clients.

The sexual culture of Brazil was always flamboyantly heterosexual as in the poetry of Carlos Drummond de Andrade. It was also perverse in its cult of the buttocks, as in that heterosexual author's poem playing with the slang word for buttocks, 'bum' – bunda:

> Bumhoney, bumlily, bumcolor, bumlove
> Bumlaw, bumlore, bumaniseed, bumbread
> Bum of a thousand versions, pluribum, unibum
> Bum in flower, bum somewhere else.

> (Andrade 1992: 50)

The stress on physical appearance was part of the modern Brazilian identity. This could easily link to a fluidity between genders and appearances. The development in the twentieth century of the fondness for beaches provided opportunities for display.

There was a widespread knowledge among *carioca* men and youths of a sexual economy for genital activity between males that was particularly complex in racial, age and class terms. What seems to have been rare prior to the post-World War II era was an on-going, egalitarian, sexual liaison between cohabiting adults of the same social background. The strong familialism of Brazilian life meant that late-night escapades could not easily be turned into the public and stable forms of a cohabiting gay couple in the modern sense. The announcement of a gay 'marriage' between a 29-year-old man and another of 23, one from São Paulo and the other from Bahia, who shared an apartment in Copacabana was sufficiently newsworthy to merit a picture of the couple in a news magazine in 1994.[14] The ceremony was to be 'officialized' with the participation of an ex-seminarist.

Brazilian modernization accelerated during the 1930s and especially after World War II. With the development of Rio's financial and commercial importance there were increasing numbers of office workers in the city core. A 'modern' model of cruising differed from the older forms of street loitering. The downtown time for cruising was from 5 p.m. to 8 p.m. when employees left work, as one Portuguese visitor noted in the 1970s contrasting it with Lisbon where serious homosexual cruising started at 11 p.m. He explained it by saying men who lived in the distant suburbs sought release before going back to their wives and dwellings (Gomes n.d.: 172).

By the 1960s there was a whole series of bars in Copacabana that were social centers as well as being pick-up places for sexual encounters. There were thus semi-private but obviously gay locations other than the outdoor cruising grounds of the city.

Another commercial institution which flourished in the 1960s and particularly the 1970s was the steam-bath which was obviously intended for a gay clientele. Since it was necessary to pay to go in, this immediately separated out much of the danger and uncertainty of pick-ups on the streets or in the parks of the city. The proximity of employees and other clients meant that the risk of theft or violence was reduced. Middle-class gay men were particularly drawn to these aspects of discretion, cleanliness and security. A number of steam-baths were in operation. One in the suburb of Gávea, for example, was in a residential street. Some 'registered' hustlers among the bathers wore a distinctive towel to indicate who was a sex worker if their services were required. Other clients might prefer to eye their fellows disposed to intimacy without additional expenditure. While the notion of such a steam-bath was a copy of a North American institution, its functioning in Rio had a Brazilian touch in background music and body types.

The growth of the gay movement in Brazil in the 1970s was affected by greater openness of intellectuals. Gasparino Damata (1917–) published in 1967 a collection of short extracts from other writers called 'stories of the accursed love.' Damata followed this with other works with homosexual themes.[15] The well-known painter Darcy Penteado made a positive proclamation of his homosexuality in an illustrated magazine, *Fatos e Fotos* and also in a 1976 book entitled *The Goal*. He followed this up with several other books on explicitly homosexual themes, with publicity photographs on the cover showing himself as a healthy, bare-chested bearded man over 50 noted as fond of surfing. His later death from AIDS was widely reported.

Lampião, named for a legendary 'Robin Hood' Brazilian bandit, was an explicitly self-identifying gay monthly newspaper which had a difficult birth. It was published in Rio for the first time in April of 1978 in a tabloid format.[16] The 25 May 1978 issue of *Lampião* carried a picture of a hustler who had killed a client on the front page under the headline 'Cinelândia, Alaska, São João [references to the two most notorious cruising grounds in Rio, and the last to an avenue in São Paulo]: dangerous relationships'. It also announced that it would deal with the church and homosexuals, poems and a play, and a revelation about the carnival in Rio. The bottom of the page carried the legend: 'How to operate in the *carioca* night.' This was exactly the unself-conscious type of wide-ranging public discussions that the military government of the day disliked. The mainline newsmagazine *IstoÉ* had already been prosecuted under the Press Law for a 1977 report on homosexuality in Brazil.[17] *Lampião* was also to be accused of 'offense to morals and good behavior.' This produced a widespread commentary in other newspapers. Even more to the point, the distribution map of the journal showed how a gay voice was read in Brazil. After three years it was, reported an editor, distributed from Oiapoque to Chui: that is, from the Uruguayan border to the Amazon, and there was a map of the nation in the editorial rooms. What was particularly striking was that the distribution was carried out through an informal network since the commercial distributors of newspapers refused to accept it. Thus the kiosk that sold the paper was itself defined as distributing louche materials, sometimes in conjunction with magazines of male nudes as well as similar heterosexual publications. The editor proclaimed himself sympathetic to feminism and the black movement and sought to draw together a national coalition of the excluded, and not just male homosexuals. He also made the traditional *carioca* claim to be light-hearted and not the producer of a rigid and crotchety official bulletin of homosexual activism. *Lampião* ceased publication after four years, partly because of political disputes among the editorial staff and partly for financial reasons due to the chronic inflation of the time (Trevisan 1986: 131–54). Throughout the 1980s and 1990s picture books of nude models destined for a homosexual male public were produced in Brazil and sold in Rio just as in other large cities. In 1995 *Sui Generis* a glossy magazine in color based in Rio, with many pictures of young male models, lesbians, figures from popular culture and transvestites, began publication. Nelson Feitosa, the editor, wrote of the production team that they were chic, showing their faces, and that their main aim was to amuse and inform the readers with a lot of good humor.[18]

A newspaper reader in Rio in June 1993 perusing the story of a municipal politician in Coqueiro Seco, a small town in the northern state of Alagoas, who was shot dead after he publicly admitted his homosexuality and his body dismembered and strewn about the place as a warning to others, would have a reinforced sense of sexual geography. Gay activists were reminded of the fact that figures in public office in much of rural Brazil still dare not 'come out' openly for fear of negative consequences at the ballot boxes and even physical attack. A broadly based opinion survey in Brazil of 1993 found that 56 per cent of the respondents did not agree that a homosexual could be voted president of the Republic, 47 per cent would change their vote if it came out that their candidate in an election was homosexual, and 45 per cent would change doctor if they found out that he was gay.[19]

The 1980s brought the onset of the AIDS crisis in Brazil which stimulated a more systematic study of male prostitution and of sexual practices with a view to warning sex workers and clients about dangerous behavior. A 1990 newspaper reported that 68.9 per cent of the male prostitutes in Rio were infected with AIDS. It added that Rio had ten areas of male prostitution where 500 youths mostly between 15 to 23 years of age each serviced on average 25 clients per month.[20]

A 1994 article on Brazilian juvenile prostitution noted that Rio had probably the largest population of male prostitutes (*michês*) in the country serving an extensive 'pornoturismo.' The number ranged from 1,000 in the low season to 4,000 in the high. The vast majority were adolescents under 20 who did not at all dress in a feminine way. Many took the receptive role in sodomy for a paying client, despite affecting an exaggeratedly macho discourse among their fellows. They often came from poor and disadvantaged backgrounds. They accepted the traditional role of a younger male before marriage without the strongly masculine body characteristics of heavy beards who served as an acceptable sexual object for an older male. They did not identify themselves as having a homosexual identity even if they engaged in prostitution with other men.

The article described a 17-year-old boy from the interior state of Minas Gerais who worked as the ticket seller on a bus until he was laid off because he had reached the age of his military service. He was the son of a carpenter and a house maid. He had initial sexual encounters with other males without asking for money. He then went to Rio at the invitation of a friend and for some months at Cinelândia was a prostitute for older Brazilian men ($US 8.00 for each encounter or if for a foreign client met on the street in Copacabana, $US 20.00). At the time of the article he had been working for two months and was concerned that his mother should not know that he was sodomized by his clients. He had been identified as at risk by an association which specialized in surveillance of male hustlers at the Central do Brasil railway station in and near the main urinal. That was a site of proletarian prostitution and very poor payment, sometimes nothing more than some bread and a boiled egg for sexual acts.[21] Generally in Brazil in many towns there were no public lavatories. Rio had none until the start of the twentieth century and of six public toilets opened during the remodeling constructions only one, by then with a user fee, survived in 1997. Men seeking anonymous sex made less use of such sites than in North America and Western Europe. However the washroom at Central was an exception for decades in Rio. A Portuguese tourist described it in the 1970s as two large rooms which held troughs against the walls without divisions. It was often busy from 6 a.m. in the morning. No feminine-acting men went there and there were often ten or twenty men looking at those who displayed an erect penis. There was an attendant; the police occasionally asked youths for their identity papers (Gomes n.d. 172–3).

A guide for 1994 noted that Central was the place to find very young poor boys on the hustle among large numbers of female prostitutes and street kids. Just as at the Gare du Nord urinal in Paris, a user fee was introduced at Central in the 1990s to discourage homosexual activity.

A retired official of the fire brigade from Brasília and previously married gave his negative views of Cinelândia, the Via Appia and Galeria Alaska, the three most notorious outdoor Rio cruising grounds. (He said nothing about the cruising area of Ipanema which was more bourgeois and egalitarian.) He thought that the Central railway station was much better for sexual encounters. Aged 65 he used a feminine nickname – Tonia Carrero Gay – and told the jour-

nalist that he could 'fuck all night' in the receptive role of anal sex. His preference ran to youths between 15 to 22 years of age, and he added that he
especially liked workers who are occasional hustlers and not 'professionals.' After
the separation from his wife, his son lived with him when twenty years earlier, at
age 45, he accepted his receptive sexual role with younger men. Before marriage
he had experimented with another male taking the insertive part, but then he
stopped and was married for ten years. He gave this interview about the stages of
his sexual development to a newspaper particularly active in the anti-AIDS
campaign.[22]

The intersection of developing forms of capitalism also affected Rio gay
space. Modern notorious cruising grounds like Cinelândia in the old center of
the city, the Galeria Alaska at Posto Seis in Copacabana, Farme beach near
Posto Nove in Ipanema and the Central Railway Station off Presidente Vargas
Avenue, did not exist before 1900. Cinelândia took its name from the cinemas
which only opened in the first decade of the twentieth century, Posto Seis was no
more than some beach houses, and what had formerly been the Pedro II railway
station was completely rebuilt in 1934. In 1995 a commercial guide described
the Galeria Alaska as the 'oldest area of [male] prostitution in Rio de Janeiro.'[23]
In 1970 a Portuguese-speaking visitor calculated that there were some twenty
homosexual nightclubs in Rio, none of which were lesbian, twenty seedy
cinemas where sexual acts took place on the balconies and thirty famous outdoor
cruising places. This shows a rather suspect fondness for round numbers but was
made by contrast with a larger city, São Paulo, said to have only six gay nightclubs and four cinemas known for sex. The Brazilian newspaper of record, the
Jornal do Brasil, regularly published during the 1980s advertisements for male
escorts who would visit prospective clients for gay sex in their homes or hotel
rooms.

In Rio the more theatrical side of homosexual males could be commercialized for an ostensibly heterosexual audience. One instance in January 1981 was
the show *Gay Fantasy* in the large theater in the Galeria Alaska in Copacabana
with numerous transvestite and 'beefcake' performances. Located in the theater
near the beach and presented as a form of ribald camp excess, male homosexuality became comic and diverting. Writing at the start of the 1980s Guy
Hocquenhem said of the dancing bar Sotão in the Alaska arcade that it was the
headquarters of Rio homosexual youth: 'It was situated in the Alaska arcade, a
promenade for picturesque old fairies, hustlers and transvestites who performed
in the theater under the arches' (Hocquenghem 1980: 158).

Little had changed by the time of the show called *The Leopards* in the same
theater at the end of the decade, which involved hilarious and risqué stand-up
transvestite comics and culminated with a procession across the stage of stark
naked, muscular young men sporting full erections. The audience included
heterosexual couples and the atmosphere was one of much camp hilarity and
knowing toleration rather than sexual titillation. However, by the late 1990s
aggressive real-estate purchases by a fundamentalist Protestant church had
stopped most of the gay cruising in the environs of the Galeria Alaska.

The beach and sea were already homoerotic in nineteenth-century Rio. From the quay-side around 1880 small dinghies left to row out to the Floating Palace, a large flatboat anchored in the middle of the Bay with tanks for sea baths and a bar service. This was something like a precursor of a modern swimming pool. On hot summer nights hundreds of bathers would congregate, mostly single men. Families at that time preferred to bathe on the beach of Santa Luzia or at Flamengo (Gerson n.d.: 35). The later beach display in Copacabana in front of the Palace Hotel was a known concentration of [possibly] available young men, some for money and others for looks or lust depending on social class, circumstance and behavior. Because of the variability of supply and demand it was known in gay slang as the Stock Exchange (*Bolsa de valores*).[24] The swimming and beaches of Rio always provided opportunities to watch attractive young men and to meet them. From the late 1970s another beach area in the Ipanema suburb became increasingly a magnet for gay sunbathers. The well-known Brazilian theater director Luiz Antônio Martinez Correa (1950–87) brought a 26-year-old man with curly blonde hair and a variety of tattoos on his muscular body from a beach to his small apartment in Ipanema in December 1987. This transfer from public eroticized shoreline to a private theater of desire proved fatal. There, when he was naked on his bed, his guest, perhaps with the help of an accomplice, murdered him for his video-cassette, a telephone answering machine and some cash.[25] The accused man and a fellow surfer had previously attacked a 38-year-old French male tourist with a knife but the latter escaped. The assailants were arrested and interrogated, and this facilitated the identification of the young man who was last seen with the director. The murdered theater director was popular and his brother was also well known in theatrical circles. A small but vociferous demonstration of men and women, primarily from the Rio arts community, demonstrated outside the Ipanema police station against what they saw as deliberate foot-dragging by the police in following up cases of the murders of homosexual men. In Rio as in São Paulo and Bahia it was believed by many gay men that the police, particularly since the start of the AIDS epidemic, were not assiduous in tracking down the killers of those gays they believed to be passive sodomites who were said to be vectors of the spread of the disease (Venciguerra 1988).

Of the photographs showing homosexual men in Brazil illustrating a big article in a magazine on 'What it is to be gay in Brazil' there was a clean-shaven Englishman aged 35 and his bearded white Brazilian companion aged 28,[26] a 39-year-old mulatto clean shaven, a cohabiting couple respectively 36 and 34 both bearded, and a 37-year-old white with a Groucho-style mustache. A collective photo of beach boys of Ipanema, which includes one girl in a skimpy bathing costume, shows one muscular figure with 'designer' facial stubble but the other men, apparently in their twenties, are muscular and clean shaven. One São Paulo clean-shaven white designer of 29 is shown with his mother. The widespread cultivation of facial hair by Brazilian homosexual men over 30 is part of a strategy of 'passing' as they age. That is, as men leave the 15 to 30 stage where their unmarried status does not perhaps demand explanation they add facial hair to keep a 'butch' *bofe* image so that they will not appear 'fairy' (*bicha*). One obvious exception is transvestites who seek facial and bodily depilation.

The fear of appearing effeminate can be noted among gay men who accept a domestic arrangement of living together. Various commentators on homosexuality in South America have stressed the inhibiting effect of familialism on relationships. To live together in broad daylight as a family unit with domestic routines in a way that became fairly banal in North American big-city gay districts and even the suburbs from the 1960s on is still unusual and reproved in much of Brazil in the 1990s. The article stressed that in 1993 there was a great deal of discrimination and social pressure against homosexual men and lesbians in Brazil. Rio de Janeiro is the most tolerant urban site in the nation in the opinion of Brazilian homosexuals.[27] For them Rio is more than the 'Marvellous City' of its official slogan, it is 'Our City' in the same way that gay Americans recognize the special quality of San Francisco. Much Brazilian gay slang – 'Portugayese' as Wayne R. Dynes called it in a compilation – derived from *carioca* wits (Murray 1995: 256–63). Like many North American cities, Rio de Janeiro has been reworked over time. Public spaces changed with the rebuilding of the old colonial city. Warehouse and market districts relocated, and inter-urban and intra-urban transportation nodes were built and rebuilt, from tramways to the bus station for long-distance travelers. Indeed, even the landscape was reworked with the flattening of some of the *morros* or small hills on the city site: that of the Castle was demolished between 1920 and 1922. Formerly it had been home to many poor residents and latterly its site served as an airport. By 1920 Rio de Janeiro exceeded 1 million in population, of whom almost a fifth were foreign-born.

Rio attracted gay pornographers like the Englishman who used the professional name Kristen Bjorn. His *Carnaval in Rio* (1989) showed men being cruised from an open sports car, views of Copacabana Beach, male dancers in the carnival who subsequently make love on camera, pick-ups at a street market and sex sequences in luxurious houses. The film-maker described the sexual attitudes of the local Brazilian models who were not gay but who participated in a full range of sexual acts with other male models in his film because of high pay (Jamoo 1997: 19–20). The film *Via Appia* (1992) with Peter Senner and Guilherme de Padua directed by Andreas Schreitmütter and Jochen Hick was in the form of docudrama about an infected German looking for the Mário in Rio whom he believes gave him AIDS on a previous visit. It showed many gay meeting places of Rio de Janeiro at that time.

As for the domestic space of gays and lesbians, there is by the 1990s nothing like the gay ghettos which enable some North American and European gays to feel safe from societal disapproval and even violence. Some Rio districts have prosperous gay couples who live in apartment blocks in Leme, Santa Teresa or in Copacabana but this is scarcely in a visible concentration of gay residents and services. They are less likely to employ servants than heterosexuals although well able to afford to pay them. Rio in many ways is still in the 1950s holding pattern where discreet, mostly white, prosperous gays could survive on the margins of bourgeois propriety by avoiding any challenge to the heterosexist ascendancy. Co-resident gay couples are virtually unknown in the *favelas* (semi-slum housing of the poor). Only the *travesti* can openly defy the traditional family model – and it is a defiance which is either a joke or an imitation which by definition can never reach its goal.

North Atlantic sexual groupings who eroticize painful sexuality with a panoply of whips, chains, studded collars and instruments of torture, the sado-masochists, have little resonance in Rio gay society where suffering and cruelty scream out from every crime tabloid. Yet there is a paradox here which is the core of the Rio gay experience. Rio offers a circuit of spaces for exuberant sensual sexual release which finds its greatest public unity with the cityscape in the annual carnival. Rio is also, in the 1990s, one of the most violent large cities in the world with around 7,000 homicides annually for a population of some 5.6 million, most of the deaths occurring among young black males in the 15 to 20 age bracket. There are many more lesser attacks, stray bullets, and hold-ups on the streets and by-ways.[28] The Marvellous City – *A Cidade Maravilhosa* – of sexuality and sun is also, and simultaneously, the city of fear and shadow.

Figure 6.1 Carnival on Rio, 1978. Photo by Pedro Lobo.

Notes

1 Pieroni (1996: 288) says 65 per cent of the known exiles to Brazil for sodomy were under 25 years of age.
2 IL (Lisbon Inquisition trial no.) 6919.
3 Luiz Mott drew his information from three trials: IL 4769 and 4230; Inquisition of Evora Trial no. 4995.
4 IL Liv. 146, undated, unnumbered, denunciation Antonio Coelho de Carvalho 'in the same prison.'
5 IL 16888.
6 IL 16177.
7 IL 411.
8 Chief of Police to Minister of Justice 2 April 1855, Novas Latas of the IHGB Arquivo de Nabuco. I am indebted to Roderick Barman for this reference.
9 Ex inf. Prof. Lená Medeiros de Menezes.
10 Ex inf. James N. Green, see *Beyond Carnival* forthcoming University of Chicago Press.
11 The following translations are by David Higgs from the Portuguese edition. An American translation was produced in California in 1981.
12 *Le Monde*, 8 January 1996, 1.
13 Veriano de Souza Terto Júnior, 'No escurinho do cinema...sociedade orgiástica nas tardes cariocas,' Psychology Dissertation, Rio de Janeiro, PUCRJ, 1989.
14 *Veja*, 6 April 1994, p. 91.
15 Gasparino Damata, *Histórias do amor maldito* (Rio de Janeiro, Record 1967); with Walmir Ayala, *Poemas do amor maldito* (1969). See also *As sobras do mar*, 1958, on homoerotic life in the navy, and *Os solteirões* (Rio de Janeiro, Pallas, 1976) about sexual encounters between men with youths set in Rio during the 1950s and 1960s. He also produced an *Antologia da Lapa Vida boêmia no Rio de Janeiro* (Rio de Janeiro, Leitura, 1965) which discussed the marginal world of prostitutes, pimps, thieves and homosexuals.
16 Number O of the newspaper appeared in April 1978.
17 *IstoÉ,* No. 53, 28 Dec. 1977.
18 *Sui Generis*, No. 8, December 1995, 3.
19 *Veja*, 12 May 1993, 53.
20 *Jornal do Brasil*, 2 February 1990.
21 *Veja* 16 March 1994, 70–2.
22 *Beijo da Rua* Year 1, No. 2 (July–August 1989), p. 7.
23 *Guia Gay: Rio*, 1994–5, p. 61.
24 *Guia Gay: Rio*, 1994–5, noted that it was called the Stock Exchange because of the large quantity of 'boys on the game' ('rapazes de programa') who frequented it.
25 *Jornal do Brasil*, 26 December 1987, B1.
26 *The Washington Blade*, 17 May 1996, p. 12 carried a news report that Maria Conceição Muller dos Reis, the mother of the Brazilian man, had agreed to marry the Englishman so that he might legally reside with her son in Brazil.
27 *Veja*, 12 May 1993, 52–9.
28 *Le Monde*, 30 November 1995, p. 2.

7   San Francisco

Les Wright

San Francisco is a peninsula. It's surrounded on three sides by water and on one side by reality.

Joseph Torchia, *As If After Sex*

The San Francisco of legend, myth and nostalgic remembrance has been far better documented than the day-to-day realities of most of its historical development. The only antidote to these romanticized visions of San Francisco is to live there. San Franciscans have been embellishing, exaggerating and eschewing the circumstances of their city since the Gold Rush days of 1848–9 to such a degree that the city's uncanny ability to reinvent itself is perhaps its most remarkable feature. Gay men not least have been happening upon this happy accident of San Francisco, inscribing their own queer visions on the palimpsest of this very young city for the past century and a half.

San Francisco's appeal has always been as a rough-and-tumble, morally wide-open frontier town. The first Anglo-American migrants, predominantly from Puritan New England, engaged in homosexual activity and created homosocial spaces within the liminal moral and social spaces created by San Francisco's vast geographic remove from the structured moral spaces of the urban and even rural communities of mid-nineteenth-century America.

True to the gold diggers, utopians, philosophers of Manifest Destiny, opportunists of every stripe and many a young man escaping dubious or intolerable personal situations, each arrived in San Francisco with distinctly preconceived notions of the place which rarely had the slightest correspondence with reality. The earliest Anglo-American migrants were, for all practical purposes, oblivious to the presence of the *californios*, the Spanish gentleman ranchers who settled Mexican Alta California following the Spanish missionaries' conversion of the native peoples. There had been Russian fur trappers just to the north and only a handful of Anglo-American settlers in the region when Mexico ceded California and Texas to the United States in 1848. Chinese miners, who also came in search of gold, found themselves relegated to second-class status, barred from most social spaces and sequestered in Chinatown, which sprang up next to the original Portsmouth Square.

No records of homoerotic dynamics from this founding era have come to light. Mid-century Americans were reticent to express any matters of a sexual nature. As George Chauncey (1994) documented through the case of New York City, a very different notion of sexual matters existed at this time. The phallocentric sexual economy of Gold Rush era San Francisco suggests that we distinguish between penetrative-masculine and receptive-feminine roles in male–male sexual encounters, and that sexual adventurism carried very different meanings to practitioners of the time than they do in American society today.

John D'Emilio (1983) employed a materialist model to articulate the shift to modern social classes and concomitant social and economic freedom. Men and women could live and work in the new industrial-era cities outside the social and economic unit of the extended family. When gold fever swept the nation, men were able to mobilize easily to head West to prospect. When gold was discovered at Sutter's Mill setting off the stampede of would-be prospectors in 1848–9, California's promise seemed fulfilled and San Francisco became a boom town. Bachelors and family men alike left by land and by sea for California, most intending to return home once they had made their fortunes. Some fled ruinous domestic or financial situations, some went for the adventure of it, some to cater to the needs of – or make their fortunes from – the '49ers. The earliest gold-miners, of the 1848 season, encountered a unique egalitarian camaraderie among their fellows in the gold fields. In the second season, of 1849, the gold fields grew crowded, competitive, dangerous, and vigilante rule took over in the mining camps and in San Francisco.

The city quickly transformed from a sleepy backwater to international port and cultural capital of the American West. For a while it was lawless. Gold Rush era San Francisco was an estimated 92 per cent (or higher) male, and the men mostly in their twenties. The men came from not only all over America, but many other parts of the world as well, especially Europe and China. The familiar comforts of home, hearth and womenfolk were virtually nonexistent, familiar social mores temporarily suspended. Dwellings were in short supply, and most men rented housing in leaky tents, wooden or muslin shanties, even table tops or planks laid across two chairs. In boarding houses and even in some of the hotels men slept in barracks-like conditions, a row of bunks along a wall or a row of cots on the floor. Boarding houses, public baths, sailors' and workingmen's clubs lent themselves to male–male socio-sexual meeting places.

The most popular pastimes were gambling, drinking and prostitution. During the Gold Rush days men would go to dances on Friday night. 'Sometimes some of the men would wear dresses, and sometimes a bandanna would be worn on the arm to indicate a man who would dance the woman's part' (Pennington n.d.). Up to a thousand gambling places, including the legendary El Dorado, operated in the early years, centered on and around Portsmouth Square – San Francisco's notorious Barbary Coast district, at that time adjacent to the waterfront. (Years later land and rubble from the 1906 earthquake were used as landfill, displacing the waterfront several blocks to the north.) Gambling, drinking, and sex could be and were pursued twenty-four hours a day, seven days a week. (Enforceable anti-gambling laws did not succeed until 1873.) Herbert

Ashbury reports the legendary San Francisco gambler as 'one of the queerest mixture in human nature' (Ashbury 1933: 23), stereotypically mercurial but with self-control, impulsive yet coolly cunning, ever ready with the pistol, able to go days without sleep and studiously neat, with a tendency toward the foppish.

Most inhabitants of the time, however, were lower- and working-class men: miners, ex-miners, odd-job workers, sailors. Desertion of sailors from ships began as soon as Americans took over San Francisco in 1846. The Gold Rush only made the problem worse. Sailors became unwilling chattels – the practice of shanghaiing sailors is virtually synonymous with San Francisco. As there was much easy money to be made in the practice, crimps (the procurers) and 'respectable' citizens (businessmen and politicians) made it into a common and unregulated practice which flourished there between 1850 and 1910.

A crimp was often a boardinghouse proprietor or the agent of a local business-man. Politicians were, in turn, bought off. Crimps would often lure their victim with promises, get him drunk, drug him or send out their 'runners' to meet and illegally board arriving ships, lure or threaten or render the sailor unconscious and drag him off ship. It is remarkable the numbers of sailors who knowingly put themselves in dangerous situations, where they could be victimized.

Keeping in mind Chauncey's concept of a phallocentric economy, several preliminary deductions may be drawn: male–male sexual activities, male–male affectional bondings (with and without a sexual component) undoubtedly occurred with some frequency. Waterfronts were well known as cruising areas to meet sailors and female prostitutes. A few records exist of the arrests of men dressed in female attire selling sexual services along the waterfront. One man fellating or manually masturbating another man, whether for money or love or lack of female 'companionship,' would not have been perceived as a 'perversion.' Chauncey describes an array of relationships in late nineteenth-century New York City among 'wolves' (working-class men who identified themselves as conventionally masculine) and 'fairies' (effeminate men who wore women's clothing) and 'punks' (younger male in a subordinate role to another man). Similar dynamics no doubt existed in San Francisco.

Walt Whitman, 'poet of the common man,' articulated his vision of an American democracy at mid nineteenth century, based, in part, on the 'comradely love' of men for each other. For Whitman, who drew so copiously upon his own sexual experiences among predominantly working-class men he met, 'homogenic' [male–male] love was explicitly sexual in nature, the expres-sion of a working-class ethos, and the cement that would glue together a truly democratic union among the citizens of the United States and among the states of the newly restored Union.

Most of the men arriving at San Francisco would not have read Whitman nor have been aware of the homoerotic content of his poetry. Among them, however, would have been men drawn to the exclusive company of other men (such as sailors), men encountering male–male sexual activities (away from home and family) while working in Eastern cities, men given to romantic attachment (anecdotal reports of later decades suggest the likelihood of coupled, if unacknowledged, male pairings), most of whom would not have found their activities worthy of or appropriate to social acknowledgment. Given the density of the city and the boom town population's overwhelming proportion of men in their teens and twenties, it is very likely that men with such desires – wolves, fairies, punks, sailors, prospectors, adventurers – could and did easily and frequently encounter each other in San Francisco, and in greater numbers than anywhere else – along the waterfront, in the saloons and gambling houses, on the thronging streets, in the overcrowded boarding houses. The prevalence of alcohol and drugs, the free-wheeling lifestyle of a frontier town would be conducive to such encounters and even to attracting those who might desire them. The frequency with which sailors and other rooming house boarders put themselves in situations to be shanghaied suggests that, at least in some cases, homoerotic allure may have been the precipitating factor.

Significantly, cross-gender expression was not a homosexually 'marked' activity. Indeed, it was a frequent, if relatively unremarkable feature 'in many parades, costume balls, vaudeville routines...and part of Sunday afternoon socializing with friends and family' (Stryker and Buskirk 1996: 17) in nineteenth-century America. San Francisco saloons often featured men in women's clothing as a staged entertainment. Vaudevillian Paul Vernon, for example, who often performed in female attire, was a celebrity in 1870s San Francisco.

During San Francisco's Gilded Age (1880–1906), reliable records of homo-sexual activity and homosocial arrangement emerge through bourgeois prisms. George Mosse (1985) pointed to the rise of the European 'cult of middle-class respectability,' buttressed by the development of public hygiene, medical doctrines of psychopathology, class- and race-based biologism, and the oft-cited Foucauldian observation of the medicalization of homosexuality and the creation of a distinct homosexual social type, among other tenets. San Francisco flowered as the United States' port to the Orient and cultural and financial capital on the Pacific. The city established a literary and journalistic bohemian culture, including the likes of Samuel Clemens. Along the Barbary Coast literary bohemia rubbed shoulders with the stage performers, prostitutes and saloon patrons of high and low station. It must be kept in mind that, although situated along the margin of middle-class respectability, when a literary bohemian milieu takes root in an established and prospering middle class – cultural bohemia is by definition an insider's revolt against prevalent middle-class mores or values.

While lower- and working-class San Francisco men were not minded to record their homoerotic experiences, the bohemian outsiders to proper society reveal their insider knowledge in circumspect manner. Oscar Wilde who uttered his memorable if cryptic pronouncement, that 'everyone who disappears is said to be seen at San Francisco. It must be a delightful city and possess all the attrac-tions of the next world,' visited the city in 1882. In 1896, a local San Franciscan wrote to Edward Carpenter, the English utopian socialist who championed Whitmanesque democracy and 'homogenic love,' to tell him 'really you have quite a following in San Francisco alone' (Katz 1983: 254; Stryker and Buskirk 1996: 19). The new science of sexology was coming into being toward the century's end. Charles Warren Stoddard's late autobiographical San Francisco novel *For the Pleasure of His Company: An Affair of the Misty City* (1903) offered the first glimpse of a respectably middle-class gay life among the new genteel society in Gilded Age San Francisco. Stoddard's protagonist, Paul Clitheroe, is a young writer, the homoerotic nature of the friendship with his two closest male friends is alluded to by Stoddard, 'girl-boys' are discussed with a female friend, and the novel ends with Paul jumping ship in pursuit of three naked Pacific Island chiefs. Stoddard's South Sea Islanders were related to Melville's *Typee* (1846), a romanticizing literary trope for projecting his own sexual difference onto exotic queer 'others.' (It would take the middle class to commit such fantasy and desire to paper and discreetly displace it on to absent 'inferior' races.)

In San Francisco the repercussions of the new sexological views led to profound changes in social perceptions and the organization of gay male social spaces, as occurred elsewhere in the United States and Western Europe. Even as 'respectable' people withdrew into social closets, politically radical individuals and small groups rose up to counter every move to isolate and stigmatize individuals now labeled 'sexually deviant.' The promulgation of 'third sex' theory, positing male homosexuals as psychological hermaphrodites, stigmatized effeminate males and cast a new homosexual pallor on cross-dressing. Among the middle class, distinction between the roles of the masculine-penetrator and feminine-receptor or young/mature male–male sexual couplings would be replaced with a more rigidly drawn distinction between homosexual persons and adventuring heterosexuals. Among San Francisco's middle classes, 'passing' (as heterosexual) became a necessary camouflage. Identifiably effeminate men could take refuge among the bohemian class as cross-dressers and dandies. Another consequence of the nascent gender identity formation of the time may be noted in the hypermasculinity cultivated by San Francisco-based writer Frank Norris and Oakland-native Jack London, who portrayed his days of youthful drinking and carousing among the sailors and fisherman along the Oakland waterfront in vociferously heterosexual terms.

Experimentation in utopian communities was at its height, and free love was often one of its components. Numerous intentional communities were founded in California at this time. The colonizing Spaniards' vision of California as El Dorado gave way to utopian Yankee visions of Arcadia. Free thinkers, often with nonconformist sexual philosophies, migrated to northern California and established numerous intentional communities during this period, among them Fountaingrove (founded 1875) in Santa Rosa (Sonoma County), Icaria Speranza (founded 1881) in Cloverdale (Sonoma County), or the Kaweah Co-operative Commonwealth (founded 1885) in what is now Sequoia National Park in the high Sierras. With the social gaze upon knowable homosexuals, an elaborate, complex homosexual subculture emerged. Men continued to meet in the Barbary Coast saloons; the Dash, a dance hall and saloon which featured female impersonation, became San Francisco's first identifiably 'gay' bar, opening and closing its doors in 1908. The Dash probably took its name as an open joke making fun of the Dashaways, the most prominent of San Francisco's temperance organizations in pre-Prohibition times. But an increasingly powerful, conservative middle class desired to rid their fair city of the low-class and debauched Barbary Coast. Trauma and confusion among San Franciscans following the 1906 earthquake was exacerbated by political scandal, a Red Light Abatement Act was passed in 1914 and was upheld by the California Supreme Court in 1917, dealing the Barbary Coast its final death blow. The passage of Prohibition in 1919 shut down completely legal drinking establishments. 'Vice,' – alcohol, gambling, prostitution – came under the control of the newly organized criminal class, old social habits became 'dirty,' 'immoral,' 'outrageous' – and illegal, and a new criminal class was born, the 'sexual deviant.' (No wonder much of America's and San Francisco's bohemian literati moved to Paris in the 1920s, including Bay Area notables Gertrude Stein and Alice Toklas, to ride out this wave of Puritanism.)

Designers intended Market Street to be the Champs Élysées of San Francisco. It was lavishly developed following the earthquake of 1906 as the main artery for commerce, business and government. Market Street originally was anchored by Rincon Hill, the original exclusive enclave of the city, adjacent to the waterfront ferry terminals at the Embarcadero. Market Street ran, and still runs, in a northeast–southwesterly direction from there past the Pacific Stock Exchange and financial center, the elegant Union Square at the bottom of Nob Hill and connectors to North Beach and Chinatown, the theater district, the bars, pool halls and transient hotels of the Tenderloin, the monumental, post-quake beaux-arts Civic Center, one of the few City Beautiful projects of the early century completed in the US. Past Van Ness Street trolley lines continued on to the summer residences of upper Haight Street and Golden Gate Park, Eureka Valley and other points West.

From the Gilded Age through post-quake San Francisco, men would find each other for sexual encounters along the new public transit routes. The transportation hub along the Embarcadero at the bottom of Market Street became a major complex sociosexual space of men to meet each other at this time. Most of the original waterfront was filled in between the 1860s and 1900s, and especially following the Earthquake of 1906, with the first Embarcadero Ferry Terminal completed in 1896. (Until the construction of the Golden Gate and Oakland–San Francisco Bay Bridges in 1933, ferries were the only way to reach Oakland and other points in the east and north Bay.) Lower Market Street was very popular for street cruising. The newly constructed Embarcadero YMCA served as a convenient meeting place and transient residence. Waterfront bars catering to a rough clientele of sailors, longshoremen and others were also nearby.

Trolleys departing the Ferry Building connected every major site along and on either side of Market Street. Sites for male–male encounters along this route included the open space of Union Square, public bath-houses and public toilets (an innovation of the hygienically minded middle class) in various spots, and – at the end of the Geary Street trolley line – the seaside attractions clustered at the far end of Golden Gate Park along Ocean Beach: the Sutro Baths, the Cliff House, Land's End and at the amusement park Playland-by-the-Sea. Lower- and working-class men, and their families, continued to live in the Tenderloin, South of Market and other locations within walking distance of Market Street. The higher classes lived in districts which overlapped, such as Nob Hill, or which were adjacent, such as Van Ness and South Van Ness Streets and the Western Addition, or connected by trolley. Rincon Hill was leveled and most of the Nob Hill mansions burned down as a firewall following the earthquake of 1906, and many of San Francisco's poshest residents relocated to Pacific Heights. The upper Fillmore, the commercial strip atop Pacific Heights, eventually became home to upscale gay bars, the still extant Lion's Pub being the one with greatest longevity.

As San Francisco grew into a modern American metropolis it did so organically, such that hetero and homo spaces, public and private spaces, upper- and lower-class spaces intermingled, invisible to the tourist's eye but assuredly known by the habitués.

A popular meeting place for male–male sexual activity was the bath-houses. During the Gilded Age, San Francisco's bath-houses began their transformation into distinctly gay male sociosexual sites. In the 1890s the Sutro Baths (near the Cliff House) was such a meeting place (Pennington). They offered a safer and more private alternative to the public venues, as the moral crackdown exposed men to arrest, blackmail, beatings, robbery and murder. Bérubé recounts the 1918 raid on the Baker Street Club, which was in fact a pair of flats rented by two men who had met at the Embarcadero Y and who held parties and rented out rooms for men to have sex in private. (The raid ultimately failed when the names of 'prominent citizens' appeared among the arrested and charges were dismissed when the word 'fellatio' could not be found in an English dictionary.) Informal arrangements for such 'favorite spots' evolved into 'early gay bath-houses' in the 1920s and 1930s in San Francisco when sex between men became permitted 'in closed and locked cubicles.' The baths remained subject to police raids (Bérubé 1984: 16–17).

With the birth of mass culture at century's start came predicable forms of erotic and semiologically coded communication among this new and newly invisible class of homosexual men. Homosexual pornography of this era has been recovered. A number of literary works written, published and circulated among gay men have been rediscovered. Both high- and low-brow gay male readers and writers, as Joseph Cady argued, 'had to be self-relying and self-inventing in finding and learning from this literature' (Summers 1995: 31).

San Francisco's first movie house, the Cinograph, opened its doors in 1905 on Market Street, between Third and Fourth Streets. Admission was 10 cents. The original novelty quickly wore off, but technology and artistic innovation developed at a rapid pace and, by the 1920s, the moving pictures were talking. Early serious film-making included German films dealing with the 'problem of homosexuality' (notably, arguing for social acceptance of homosexuals' 'difference') and in the United States serious attempts were made in film to deal with a range of social issues of the day, including vice, prostitution, venereal disease, unmarried mothers and the like. In San Francisco, movie palladiums lined Market

Street and almost immediately the back rows of the balconies were appropriated for homosexual meetings and activities.

The expansive optimism of the 1920s gave way to the somber and desperate 1930s and the cheek-by-jowl proximity of San Francisco's urban districts fostered the development of an unprecedentedly extensive 'gay world.' Social conservatives had their way – the Motion Picture Production Code (the infamous Hays Code established by Postmaster General Will H. Hays) of 1930 introduced far-reaching censorship of film content, building on the precedent established by the Comstock Law of 1873, which 'gave [the US] post office the power to decide what was obscene' (Brownlow 1990: 4) and which by the 1930s led to the destruction of 160 tons of information on sex and birth control throughout the US. Magnus Hirschfeld, the German leader of the Scientific Humanitarian Committee for the legal rights of German homosexuals, visited San Francisco in 1931, denouncing both Comstock and Prohibition. Attempts at tighter policing of sexual mores only increased gay cynicism toward government and 'found it increasingly easy to question the legitimacy of the established social order' (Stryker and Buskirk 1996: 26). Drinking was no longer illegal, but jobs were scarce, people fell back into poverty, the Dust Bowl forced many impoverished Midwesterners to migrate to California. In San Francisco organized labor and the principles of socialism, once bohemian drawing-room conversation, had become the last hope for the working man. The San Francisco General Strike of 1933 shocked the city and the nation when police opened fire and killed unarmed longshoremen. (Allen Bérubé's recent work on the Maritime Stewards Union attests to the social cohesion among its black, homosexual and left-radical rank-and-file.)

Gay life flourished in San Francisco. Homosexuals spoke, in a camp manner, of 'coming out into' 'the gay world.' The coded film language of movies, as a strategy adopted by film directors to circumvent the Hays Code censorship, uncannily parallels the discursive 'closet' – the coded language of camp and gay argot – homosexual men adopted to safeguard their 'gay world' from the prying eyes of Lilly Law. The first two explicitly gay male bath-houses opened in the 1930s – Jack's Turkish Baths and the Third Street Baths. Gay bars, catering to self-selected crowds, flourished in the City and some featured drag queens. As Esther Newton has suggested, the early gay drag queens, especially the professional ones, served as gay male cultural heroes, in part because they were 'overt' about their inclinations (Garber 1988: 4).

By the 1930s two major changes influenced the direction of gay life in San Francisco. Prohibition was repealed – people could drink and congregate in bars openly. San Francisco's legendary Finocchio's opened in 1929 on the Barbary Coast as a speakeasy that featured entertainment by female impersonators. Finnochio's was *the* symbol of late 1930s and 1940s San Francisco gay life. It catered to the tourist trade but when it became a legal establishment in 1933 it became one of the city's most popular sites for homosexual men and women to socialize and featured legendary female impersonators, such as Rae Bourbon, Walter Hart and Lucian Phelps. Only now the Barbary Coast had become the Italian North End, popular with the literary bohemian crowd.

From a bird's-eye point of view, we can sketch a *gay map of 1930s San Francisco* using a clock whose center is at the top of Nob Hill with Market Street a perpendicular line touching below Union Square at 6 o'clock. Let us begin at the old Barbary Coast/bohemian North Beach district at 2 o'clock, site of Finnochio's (first at 406 Stockton Street, moved to 506 Broadway in 1936), Mona's (the city's first lesbian bar) and the legendary Black Cat Café. At 4 o'clock we find the Embarcadero waterfront, the immensely popular Embarcadero YMCA and, in 1938, the Sailor Boy Tavern (others followed), which catered to a rough-trade crowd. The Third Street Baths were within walking distance. At 6 o'clock we are in the heart of the bar and street cruising area – Union Square and its elegant hotel bars, what would become a strip of gay bars (beginning with the Old Crow in 1935). Movie houses, and the most popular street cruising area in the 1930s, 1940s and 1950s along the Market Street (roughly, Powell Street to Civic Center). Gay men lived in the neighborhoods straddling this stretch of Market Street. South of Market lower- and working-class and transient single men lived in boarding houses. Residential hotels and apartment buildings mingled with gay bars in the Tenderloin immediately north of Market. As the slope of Nob Hill rose, so too did the social class of its gay residents. At about 9 o'clock we find Polk Gulch and the back side of Nob Hill, which became a bustling commercial district and gay residential enclave. Jack's Baths was located here on Post Street between Polk and Van Ness. At 10 o'clock we find the more genteel Nob Hill/Pacific Heights junction and the Fireside bar and restaurant (1319 California Street) which opened in 1937. By the end of the 1930s the simulacrum of the modern gay community had taken distinct shape in the urban cauldron of San Francisco.

The universal practice of al fresco cruising adapted itself to the shifting environs of San Francisco, from the waterfront to city sidewalks, public toilets, city parks and movie balconies. Of the numerous public baths (Turkish, Finnish, Russian and American-style), always sites of occasional male–male sexual encounters, some became known by the 1930s to cater to an exclusively homosexual male clientele. Similarly, the institution of the gay bar emerged from an unbroken tradition of saloons, dance halls, and speakeasies. The entertainment form of female impersonation and its blurring with effeminacy and dandyism solidified into one of a series of modern gay typologies. Gay enclaves, clusters of commercial establishments and residential neighborhoods emerged, again with differing typologies. A gay dialect, an argot impenetrable by the uninitiated had risen, in keeping with the increasing censorship of the times, to forge a prototypical bond of community. Public scandal and cynicism induced by government failure in the face of the Great Depression accelerated a sense of difference among homosexuals, a sense of outrage at being stereotyped and marginalized, and laid the groundwork for political response to increasing social repression. Previously visible, in the late 1930s gays began going underground in keeping with the times.

San Francisco's gay world changed abruptly after the declaration of war on Japan. The US mobilization for World War II uprooted the entire social order in

America. Millions of young men, in their late teens and twenties (and older) were suddenly thrown together. Women were left to take over 'men's work' in their absence. San Francisco was a major departure and returning point for the Pacific theater of war. Much like the Gold Rush days, men found themselves thrust into unfamiliar and confusing situations, in all-male company. For the first time, the US military sought out and dishonorably discharged service members solely on the basis of their sexuality. Wartime San Francisco became filled with servicemen, dishonorably discharged homosexuals, and bars and restaurants catering to the wartime population. At this time, elegant hotel bars, such as the Top of the Mark, became popular as a place to mingle discreetly and to avoid being caught in raids on known gay bars. Scholars D'Emilio (1983) and Bérubé (1984) posited that the mass mobilization of World War II led directly to a dawning realization by homosexuals of their numbers, which in turn led to the formation of the post-war self-conception of gays as a quasi-ethnic minority.

Many homosexual men and women discharged, honorably or dishonorably, chose to remain in San Francisco at war's end. They were taken by the city's charm, the relatively free gay life, and in many cases wanting to avoid returning to their hometown in disgrace. The freewheeling gay town of San Francisco's wartime years, however, did not last long. Both the large numbers of gay men (and lesbians) transplanted to San Francisco and the established enclaves of homosexual San Francisco quickly found themselves under renewed siege by the law. The hearings of the House Un-American Activities Committee, later known as the 'McCarthy witch hunts,' were televised live from Washington, DC, and quickly turned post-war USA into a paranoid state. Communists and homosexuals were denounced, careers, families and lives were destroyed, in a dynamic oddly not unlike the denunciatory practices of Nazi Germany or Stalinist Russia. The 1949 California State Penal Code proscribed sodomy 'in its narrow and historical sense' (that is, anal sex or male–male sex of any sort) (Stryker and Buskirk 1996: 33). Raids on bars and public meeting places intensified, and numerous litigation efforts were pursued in an attempt to shut down San Francisco's gay bars; in 1958 homosexuals won a victory in a ruling on the Black Cat that 'the commission of illegal or immoral acts was necessary to close a gay bar' (Pennington n.d.).

Homosexuals, like communists and communist 'sympathizers,' became 'fellow travelers,' who were forced into the proverbial 'closets' where they hid for dear life. The 1939 MGM film *The Wizard of Oz*, starring a young Judy Garland, reverberated for post-war gay insiders – 'Are you a friend of Dorothy's?' became a universally recognized code. Bruce Rodgers records usage of 'Dorothy and Toto' to refer to male couples in which the effeminate partner dominated (Rodgers 1972: 66). Garland became the most beloved camp idol to several post-war generations of homosexual men. San Francisco became the land of Oz, the Technicolor world over the rainbow where gays would finally find a home. Over the next several decades the Oz/San Francisco metaphor took deep root, and no doubt was in mind when the rainbow flag was designed in 1978 by San Francisco resident Gilbert Baker.

Socio-politically, two divergent philosophical stands and political strategies emerged in the 1950s, the accommodation politics of the homophile movement and the left-radical activism of Harry Hay and the early Mattachine Society. Both philosophies were bolstered by the 1948 publication of the Kinsey report, which purported to prove through science and statistics that homosexuality was a natural and universal expression of human sexuality. In 1951 Donald Webster Cory published *The Homosexual in America*, written from the subjective perspective of twenty-five years of one homosexual's life experience, describing 'the hostility gay men encountered, the persecution and discrimination they faced, the variety of homosexual lifestyles, and the institutions of the gay subculture...as a polemic...designed to win acceptance for a new view of the homosexual' (D'Emilio 1983: 33). Cory was lionized by the homophile movement for this. A decade later he fell into disrepute when he reversed his position, asserting that homosexuals were ill and in need of professional help.

A small circle of friends, including Harry Hay, formed the Mattachine Society in Los Angeles in 1950, and chapters quickly opened elsewhere including San Francisco. Hay was radicalized as a participant in the San Francisco General Strike of 1934 and became a communist shortly after that. From a historical materialist perspective, Hay extrapolated that 10 per cent of the population was gay and from that he argued that gays formed a cultural minority since there was a common language, 'a psychological make-up in common, and in the cruise-necessities of the *double entendres* of CAMP...a common culture.' Most lesbian and gay organizations and culture even now continue to work through these ideas' (Shiveley 1997: 222). The intensifying red-baiting caused Hay and other Marxist-oriented founders to resign, and the Society's national offices relocated to San Francisco by 1957. Mattachine itself grew steadily more conservative and asserted itself as a homophile organization. (In 1955 eight lesbians, including Phyllis Lyon and Del Martin, founded the Daughters of Bilitis in San Francisco, as a social and political organization for lesbians.) As in the 1930s, the radical impulse was driven into oblivion, but the homophile organizations worked quietly with allies within the medical, legal, religious, political and scientific fields to effect gradual change for the betterment of the homosexual in society.

In 1950s San Francisco, as elsewhere in America, the white middle class was migrating out of the urban center to tract housing subdivisions, reachable only by car. Much of San Francisco went into economic decline during this time. Immigrants began leaving their enclaves, including the Italians from North Beach, the Chinese (for the very first time) from Chinatown, the Irish from Eureka Valley. North Beach, with its bars, jazz clubs and comedy clubs, attracted a range of anti-establishment, nomadic individuals, including notables from the Beat generation. Several key Beat figures, such as Allen Ginsberg, William Burroughs, Jack Kerouac and Neal Cassidy, were homosexual or bisexual. Although they did not stay long in San Francisco, their anarchic and iconoclastic presence took root. Ginsberg read *Howl* for the first time in public in San Francisco in 1955. This became an immediate *cause célèbre*, led to a legal battle over obscenity (Ginsberg won), and re-established San Francisco's reputation as a bohemian haven. Lenny Bruce and other comedians practiced their politically radical craft in North Beach comedy clubs.

From 1957 to 1960:

> the media's spotlight glared upon North Beach. A diffuse and diverse literary movement, bound more by locale and by what it stood against than by anything else, suddenly became 'beat,' representative of a nationwide generation rebellion against the values of the middle class. Journalists collapsed the San Francisco renaissance and the beat generation into one and then outdid each other in casting furious, scornful invective at it.
>
> (D'Emilio 1983: 178–9)

> The unique visibility of the burgeoning beat subculture in North Beach had a more than incidental impact upon gay male consciousness in San Francisco. Homosexuality weaved [sic] its way through descriptions of the North Beach scene as a persistent, albeit minor, leitmotif.
>
> (D'Emilio 1983: 179–80)

The sobriquet 'homosexual' was used to denigrate any beat or San Francisco bohemian artist. Much like the European expressionists of the 1920s, many avant-garde homosexuals of the era reveled in their being labeled 'sick,' wearing it as a badge of honor. In the beat era to be 'sick' in the gay subculture was camp and meant 'Cool, clever, brash, insulting, and outrageous' (Fritscher 1989: 111). Herein lay the birth of the romanticizing self-image of the homosexual as sexual outlaw.

Unlike the East Coast, where political activism remained divorced from the bar culture, rather like the classic left schism between laborers and intellectuals, in San Francisco a very different socio-sexual-political arrangement took root. Entrapment by police became common practice, as well as raids on gay bars. Those arrested sometimes found their name, address and profession listed in the next day's newspaper. Nonetheless, numerous gay and lesbian couples lived quietly, gathering socially at bars, clubs, coffee houses and other commercial venues, and calling lower Nob Hill, Polk Gulch, the Tenderloin and Telegraph Hill (above North Beach) home.

Gay bars remained a fixture in North Beach. And the Black Cat Café was the most popular. '[A]ll the gay screaming queens,' mixed with, 'heterosexual gray flannel suit types, the longshoremen' (D'Emilio quoting Allen Ginsberg, in Duberman *et al.* 1989: 463). Coming from the bottom up, radical gay political organizing began at the Black Cat when Jose Sarria ran for the public office of city Supervisor in 1961. Sarria reigned over weekend festivities at the Black Cat, singing camp queered arias in full costume to adoring fans. Sarria was deemed Empress to legendary Emperor Norton of San Francisco, declaring herself the Widow Norton, first Empress of the gay imperial court system which spread to many parts of the United States in the post-war years.

Gay men organized in reaction to increased police harassment. The extent of official corruption first became known when, in the 1961 'gayola' scandal, it was revealed that police and ABC officers were taking bribes from gay bar owners in exchange for not being raided. In response to this, the Tavern Guild, an organization of predominantly gay owners of gay bars organized in 1961. The Tavern Guild, a businessman's association, became the first legal and social agency run by gays for the benefit of its gay community, following closely the model of earlier immigrant agencies for the political and economic refugees from abroad. In this case, the Tavern Guild spoke 'gay'. They fought the Alcoholic Beverage Commission, the legal arm that raided and shut down bars. They retained a lawyer, distributed legal information and assisted with posting bond when someone was arrested near a gay bar. They sponsored popular community events such as the Beaux Arts Ball and the Tavern Guild Picnic. They worked closely with the Imperial Court of San Francisco to develop 'reliable mechanisms for charitable fund-raising and political leveraging within the queer community' (Stryker and Buskirk 1996: 44). The Society for Individual Rights (SIR) led by William Beardemphl, formed in 1964 in response to a police raid on the Tay-Bush, an all-night gay coffee house in the Tenderloin. SIR opened a gay community center, the first in America, in 1966, located South of Market on Sixth Street. The Citizens' Alert, a 24-hour hot line 'responded to incidents of police brutality against gays and lesbians' (Stryker and Buskirk 1996), began operating in 1965.

Life magazine's identification of San Francisco as the 'Gay Capital' of the United States in its 26 June 1964 issue was both an observation of the facts of San Francisco as well as fuel to the flames of official resentment of the visible gay presence in the city. The California Hall incident can be understood as police retaliation for such publicity. The Council on Religion and the Homosexual formed in 1964. That New Year's Eve the CRH sponsored a dance for gays and lesbians at California Hall, located behind Civic Center near the Tenderloin and Polk Gulch. The police showed up in force and attempted to intimidate party-goers by photographing them as they entered California Hall. Later the police attempted entry, but were stopped by three lawyers, on grounds that the police did not have a search warrant. The police raided the dance anyway. The event received massive coverage in the local press. The fact that several heterosexuals had been among those intimidated in the crowd fueled the sense of outrage.

The 26 June issue of *Life* in 1964 was a watershed for the leather community of San Francisco. The lead photo, an interior shot of the Tool Box and the mural of Chuck Arnett, served as beacon to show the world that in San Francisco 'there was an alternative homomasculine style' (Thompson 1991: 107). Jack Fritscher observed that 'No longer did men have to use the cruising code one-liner "Are you a friend of Dorothy?" to figure out if a masculine man was queer' (Thompson 1991: 109). In the sadomasochist (SM) community 'work' in the 1940s and 1950s became play for the next generation. Thom Magister noted:

In the early 1950s the leather scene in California was a strictly serious business...everything was passed on by legend and word-of-mouth tradition –
just like any other nomad tribe. The world of S/M, leathermen and leather-
bikermen were intertwined. Gay bikers and straight bikers commingled with
little conflict. Their commonality was leather, Harley-Davidson bikes, and
painful memories of a war that had disfigured them physically, emotionally,
and spiritually. This was not a carefree youth on a spree.

(Thompson 1991: 96–7)

It was 1960s indigenous radical sexual politics in the making.

Sex parties existed before leather bars and were crucial to the development of
leather social life. The first leather bar was the Why Not? in the Tenderloin, and
opened in 1958, but closed soon after. The Tool Box, at 399 Fourth Street at
Townsend Street, was the first leather bar South of Market. Other leather bars
followed in the mid-1960s. Gayle Rubin reported 'Leather establishments flourished in an area that sprawled between Howard and Bryant streets, from Sixth to
Twelfth. At night, leathermen owned those streets, prowling easily among the
bars, sex clubs, bathhouses, and back alleys' (Thompson 1991: 120).

All of these elements taken together, 'bars, baths, adult bookstores and heavily
coded mail order services, most of which operated on the margins of legality'
(Gluckman and Reed 1997: 123), comprised what Jeffrey Escoffier has dubbed
the 'closet economy' of the post-war gay culture. Commercial enterprises began
to come together for mutual protection and to extend such legal protections to
their customers. A burgeoning political awareness among assimilationist
homophiles led to the development of elementary social, legal and other custo-
dial agencies, creating an economy parallel to the social mainstream, but still
invisible, or downright incomprehensible, to outsiders. The queer outsiders
turned inward collectively. They began to see themselves and each other as a
quasi-ethnic minority and to behave so, rather than as the isolated criminals and
mentally ill patients which society through its agencies had attempted to disarm
and destroy. The social rhetoric of 1950s American society described homosexuality as a scourge not unlike Hitler's caricatures of 'Jews.' On the other hand a
legacy of civil rights and *de facto* practices by business people to protect their
financial interests caused the post-war tactic of the demonization of homosexuals to backfire both in the short and the long run. Denigration led directly to
practices of resistance among lesbians and gay men which produced the
conscious idea of self-identifying as a member of a quasi-ethnic minority. Let us
be clear: this closet economy and its self-chosen, quasi-ethnic minority members
were almost exclusively white, but originally spanned the middle range social
classes, from service industry to office workers, to professionals and professional
celebrities.

The multiple terrains of San Francisco naturally create community (in a
valley, on a hilltop, along a level connecting corridor). Each of those pockets is
inhabited by a proliferation of ethnic enclaves of residence, commerce, political
and social agencies. In the mid-1960s distinct gay enclaves shifted again. Polk

Street became the commercial center, and included numerous bars, restaurants and businesses which catered to the white-collar and professional gays settled in the area. Polk Street runs in a valley between the west side of Nob Hill and the east side of Pacific Heights. The Tenderloin, geographically the bottom of Nob Hill, was a mixed neighborhood of bars, restaurants and residential hotels for the gay poor and the sexually marginal – transvestites and male hustlers. South of Market had some residential presence, but was mostly home to bath-houses, sex clubs and the burgeoning leather subculture.

In the mid-1960s bohemian San Francisco would reinvent itself, spawning the Love Generation of the Haight-Ashbury district. The once upscale district of the Haight-Ashbury with its summer homes had gone into decline during the 1930s. It was settled by black armaments factory workers during World War II, and ended up a black slum after the wartime employment opportunities disappeared. In this neighborhood in quintessentially 1960s urban decay two beat coffee houses opened in 1965. Seminal San Francisco rock bands emerged, Victorian-era clothing from local second-hand shops became trendy. In 1966 the 'world's first psychedelic shop' opened on Haight Street (R Rand, 232), new drugs (such as LSD) became prevalent and the hippies moved in. By the late 1960s queers were a presence among the new 'hippie' movement, the bohemian reinvention of the Beats combined with, at least on the surface, a rejection of the post-war values of materialism, rejection of official authorities, embracing of social differences of all kinds in a utopian vision of peace, love and harmony. Experimentation with sex and drugs, and communication through rock music were also key. In early 1967 tens of thousands attended the first human Be-in in Golden Gate Park (adjacent to the Haight), presided over by Allen Ginsberg and others. The naive phase of this movement peaked with the Summer of Love in 1967, in which Allen Ginsberg, openly homosexual and reborn as a hippie, participated. Androgyny became a fashionable look, although some men sported full, flowing beards as well. Rock music served as advertising and propaganda internationally. A new mythic San Francisco was invented, drawing another Gold Rush-like wave of immigrants to the city in search of sex, drugs, rock and roll, and the opportunity to reinvent themselves, for the first time including homosexuals and bisexuals under their rainbow banner. By August 1967 the 'Summer of Love had turned ugly' (Richards 1995: 232). In 1968 things got even worse, shop windows were smashed following the assassination of Martin Luther King, crime and violence arose due to the drug abuse, and some store owners installed metal gratings, while many other stores became vacant and were boarded up. At this time, the gay contingent looked elsewhere for safety and a more stable place to live. Queer hippies began trekking over the hill to Eureka Valley with its commercial strip along Castro Street where there was already a small gay presence. (The first gay bar in the Castro, the Missouri Mule, opened in 1963.) The latest hippie-faggot immigrants were about to meet the politicized and organized homophile old guard. It would come as news to this 'old guard' that they were as yet 'unliberated'.

All but forgotten now, Carl Wittman's 'Refugees from Amerika: A Gay

Manifesto' (published in *SF Free Press*, 22 Dec. 1969–7 Jan. 1970), called the 'bible of the Gay Liberation Movement' (McCaffrey 1972: 157), would be the first call initiating the most massive gay immigration San Francisco had ever seen. 'San Francisco is a refugee camp for homosexuals,' wrote the gay liberationist Wittman:

> We have fled here from every part of the nation, and like refugees elsewhere, we came not because it is so great here, but because it was so bad there….And we have formed a ghetto, out of self protection. It is a ghetto, rather than a free territory, because it is still theirs [heterosexuals']. Straight cops patrol us, straight legislators make our laws, straight employers keep us in line, straight money exploits us.
>
> (McCaffrey 1972: 157)

These ideas 'reflect the perspective of only one person, and are determined not only by my homosexuality, but my being white, male, and middle class' (McCaffrey 1972: 158).

'For all its radical rhetoric, gay liberation in the Bay Area relied primarily on picketing, publishing, and public assembly to advance its causes' (Stryker and Buskirk 1996: 54). It was predominantly middle class in its social values as well, although the hippie movement created space for inclusion of genderfuck drag as political statement, and out of this tradition came the likes of the Cockettes, the Angels of Light and the Sister of Perpetual Indulgence. The Imperial Court society combined drag and leather elements in continuing gay social support, political fundraising and other charitable work. The Society of Janus formed in SF in 1974 as a 'pansexual' organization for SM, the first on the West Coast and arguably the second SM organization in the world (Stryker and Buskirk 1996: 62). To a degree the now established homosexual community resented the maverick liberationists, and for their part, as younger gay men flooded into San Francisco, a migrants' camp of often unemployed or marginally employed 'full-time gay men' moved into the Castro district in particular. This was the time of gay San Francisco's liberation economy, of 'proliferating retail businesses – bars, bookstores, baths and consumer services that emerged from the confines of semi-legality. Political and other voluntary organizations also provided previously unavailable public services' (Gluckman and Reed 1997: 123).

The early 1970s witnessed an unparalleled transformation of urban gay life in America and, as a consequence of San Francisco's lavender gold rush, it would eventually surpass New York City and Amsterdam as an urban gay center. There was a distinguishable gay minority group with a geographically definable neighborhood and all the appurtenances of a community. The 'white flight' to suburbs further out in the 1950s led to a dramatic drop in real estate prices and numerous empty buildings in the Castro, making it increasingly attractive as a cheap area for homosexuals to live in. As Kath Weston has described this phenomenon:

countless individuals launched themselves into a quest for community in Benedict Anderson's sense of the term. As 'members' of an imagined community people feel an attachment to a necessarily fictional group...[and] interpret themselves *through* that attachment, so that their subjectivity becomes inseparable from constructions of 'we-ness.'

(Weston 1995: 257)

The Castro would emerge as a gay city-within-a-city, a phenomenon as strong as ever today, over twenty-five years later.

In 1970 Rev. Troy Perry founded the San Francisco chapter of Metropolitan Community Church, the first gay (ecumenical Protestant) church in the Castro; arsonists would burn it in 1972 and 1973. *Gay Sunshine* began publishing in 1970 as a hippie-gay liberationist newsletter, in honor of the first anniversary of Stonewall a gay parade along Polk Street and a 'gay-in' were held which would lead, after several permutations, to the annual San Francisco Lesbian, Bisexual, Gay and Transgender Pride Parade, since the late 1970s the single largest-drawing event of the city. Three gay bars opened in the Castro. Rev. Ray Broshears began gay radio with a gay news program on radio station KSAN.

The following year brought increasing political agitation. Gay men began to gain real political power working through mainstream and protest avenues. Diane Feinstein and Willie Brown, both future mayors of San Francisco, worked on behalf of gay interest. Feinstein in particular was later rewarded by being voted into the office of mayor, in part due to gay block voting patterns. The Alice B. Toklas Democratic Club, the first of three gay Democratic Party groups in San Francisco, was founded. Four more gay bars opened in the Castro, and the *Bay Area Reporter*, arguably the gay newspaper of record, began publication. The stations KPFA-FM began gay radio programming, rotating between the Society for Individual Responsibility (SIR), the Daughters of Bilitis (DOB), Gay Alliance and *Gay Sunshine*. The SIR Center (at 83 Sixth Street) was torched by an angry member. The gay community pursued talks with the San Francisco Police Department to deal with anti-gay violence in the Castro area. The San Francisco Public Health Department estimated in 1971 the gay population of the city at 90,000. (By 1977 it was 120,000 and by 1978 about 150,000 out of a total of 750,000. This constituted 20 per cent of the city.)

In 1973 Pride Foundation was incorporated as a gay service organization, the Community Softball League was formed and Toad Hall, perhaps the most popular gay bar on Castro Street, was set on fire by arsonists three times. Also in 1973 a serial murderer known as the Doodler began a three-year spree of murdering gay men in San Francisco. The American Psychology Association formally voted in the same year to remove homosexuality *per se* from its list of mental illnesses. Among the bars were the Twin Peaks, the first gay bar with all plate-glass windows along its two walls facing the street, and the Midnight Sun, the neighborhood's first video bar. There were numerous restaurants and two sex venues, the Castro Baths and the Jaguar Bookstore. The Castro Street Fair began in 1974, the first lesbian club, Full Moon Coffeehouse, operated between 1974 and 1978. A Mardi Gras-like atmosphere prevailed along Castro Street. The late 1970s fulfilled Escoffier's territorial economy phase, although it might appear to be the beginning of an ideological consumer-capitalist takeover which led the way to a full-fledged economic appropriation by national franchises of gay-owned small businesses.

Known worldwide as the premier 'gay hometown,' the Castro is a roughly 34-block neighborhood in the geographic center of San Francisco. Originally known as Eureka Valley and formally demarcated by the Most Holy Redeemer Church parish boundaries of Sixteenth, Dolores, Twenty-Second and Douglass Streets, the Castro took its name from the movie palace which anchored the commercial corridor of Castro and upper Market Streets. The later 1970s became the phase of territorial economy, 'marked by the spread of gentrification and neighborhood developments' (Gluckman and Reed 1997: 124). During the late 1970s the gay community assumed full-fledged institutional dimensions. The San Francisco *Sentinel* began in 1974, and *Coming Up!* (later *Bay Times*) in 1979. Gay small presses flourished, *Gay Sunshine* focused on in-depth literary interviews and cultural-political articles. Frameline's first annual SFINtlLandG Film Festival was held in 1977, and Theater Rhino staged its first public performances in 1977 as well. Gyms and coffee houses complemented the bars, bath-houses and discos, for the most part all located in the Castro, Polk Gulch and South of Market areas. Serializing daily life for local residents in his *Examiner* newspaper column 'Tales of the City,' Armistead Maupin precipitated another flood of gay immigrants through this open advertisement of an imaginary yet uncannily accurate portrayal of middle-class San Francisco. Ironically, the new immigrants in search of Maupin's gay San Francisco generally found themselves in the Castro camp. No statistical study has yet been undertaken to determine actual numbers of gay professionals (i.e. who found appropriate professional-level employment) and professional gays, the legendary PhD taxi-drivers' clan of over-educated and under-employed migrants who moved to San Francisco intentionally to 'be gay.' San Francisco continued to serve as a sort of gay finishing school to the world's queer population for much of the last quarter of the twentieth century.

In Jane Jacobs' highly regarded study of *The Death and Life of Great American Cities* (1961/1992), she spelled out necessary elements for workable cities and neighborhoods. Transposing these terms slightly to a gay context, we find them very much at play in the Castro. Here I invoke the ethnosemantic analysis of a folk category – San Francisco men, including myself, when referring to 'gay community.' 'Gay self-identification,' remarked Stephen Murray, 'has been and continues to be the most important criterion of membership in the native view' (Herdt 1982: 107). The first element Jacobs identified was the role of sidewalks in achieving safety. Gay settlers persisted and eventually succeeded in forcing the SFPD to respond to homophobic violence on the neighborhood's streets. The political and economic importance of the gay population was established. In day-to-day living, Castro Street made a safety asset out of the presence of strangers. There are eyes on the street everywhere, generally eyes which Jacob's dubs 'natural proprietors of the street' (Jacobs 1961/1992: 35) – dozens of small businesses, heavy foot traffic of both neighborhood residents and various kinds of visitors (gay residents from other parts of the city, elsewhere in the Bay Area, gay friends and friends of friends and friends of friends of friends) and tourists (gay, straight, sexual), almost around the clock. The neighborhood is beloved by many different people for many different reasons, even though the tie to a gay neighborhood is the original and abiding draw.

'The sight of people attracts other people' (Jacobs 1961/1992: 37) and this is highly significant in the Castro. The wide-open frontier spirit has by no means completely disappeared in San Francisco. San Franciscans tend to be warm and open, and to pride themselves on their hospitality. Casual verbal exchanges can easily become hours'-long conversation upon first encounter. Despite the proliferation of designated sexual and sexual contact spaces (bars, sex clubs, parks), meeting someone for on-the-spot sex or arranging to meet at a later time for sex is a frequent occurrence. Cruising the Castro for sex, or 'merely window-shopping' is one of its hallmark pastimes. Except for the excesses of the late 1970s, sexual intercourse on a public street in the Castro in broad daylight tends to be a rare occurrence. While the tourist or visitor may feel anonymous on Castro Street, local residents and visiting former residents tend to recognize each other on sight, and often know a surprising amount of personal information on many fellow residents whom they have never met. Despite a certain fishbowl feeling, this does have the effect of increasing the sense of safety. The Castro resident knows his neighbor is keeping an eye out for him.

The neighborhood is nestled in a small valley, surrounded on three sides by steep hills, dotted with parks and outcroppings of rocks. Remarks Jacobs:

> San Francisco gives an impression of much verdure and relief from city stoniness. Yet San Francisco is a crowded city and little ground is used to convey this impression. The effect arises mainly form small bits of intensive cultivation, and it is multiplied because so much of San Francisco's greenery is vertical-window boxes, trees, vines, thick ground cover on little patches of 'waste' slopes.
>
> (Jacobs 1961/1992: 107)

Castro Street is the site of several neighborhood institutions. 'Hibernia Beach' on the northeast corner of Castro and Eighteenth Streets is local Speaker's Corner, where organized and free-thinking political activism – the ironing boards, cookie sales and ticket sales are staged. The annual lighting of the community Christmas tree takes place on this site. It contains a bus shelter, rows of ATM machines, some fenced-in bushes which suggest the ambiance of a park. It's a spot to meet friends, run into friends, turn a trick, and is at the heart of the Castro, the annual Castro Street Fair and the annual Halloween street party. This is where revelers rush out into the street at the stroke of midnight on New Year's Eve, and Castro Street is where gay people have headed whenever something of import to the community has happened. To find out what is happening in the gay community, all anyone needs to do is to head to Castro and Eighteenth Street and to listen to the word on the street.

Privacy is precious for urban dwellers, Jacobs observes. Castro residents may be seemingly ubiquitous on the streets, but never divulge where they live. Most San Franciscans have unlisted phone numbers. Except at times of extreme housing shortage, gay San Franciscans have tended to move often. The Castro, at the geographic center of the city, has the unique advantage of being at the hub of public transit – all five MUNI Metro trolley lines serve the Castro, the nearest BART station is but a half dozen blocks away, and several cross-town bus lines intersect the subway system and each other.

The denizens of 1970s Castro became known as 'clones.' The term embraces gay-pride, self-parody and pejorative perspectives. On one level the Castro clone 'look' was an urban street fashion:

> of a body-hugging ensemble – plaid shirt or tight-fitting tee shirt, tight-fitting 501 (button-up fly) blue jeans, sneakers or construction boots, a hat or cap, an earring, and facial hair, usually a mustache. The uniformity of the look and the fact the look was worn as a uniform…as if every individual were an exact copy of some original 'liberated gay man, 5'9", 29-inch waist, 29 years old gay white male.
>
> (Wright, forthcoming)

From the point of view of the Castro insiders, this was a new sociosexual gay male archetype – all-American middle-class male in blue-collar guise, assertively proud and aggressively sexual. From many an outsider's point of view the look manifested a stultifying group-think culture, an irritating or antagonizing exclusiveness or the complete transformation of the homosexual male into consumer-capitalist sexual object, ironically the exact opposite of gay liberationist ideals. During the 1970s a handful of bars served as cultural spaces for non-white gay men, among them Esta Noche in the Inner Mission (for Hispanic Americans) and the Pendulum (for African Americans) in the Castro. Racial discrimination by white bar owners and patrons against non-white potential patrons remained a social reality throughout this time. Practices such as subjecting black patrons to the three-photo ID policy while ignoring it for white patrons or point blank refusing entrance to women and mixed groups of gay men and women (lesbian or straight), were prevalent. Individual instances sometimes provoked heated letters to the editor in the *Bay Area Reporter* denouncing these practices and the racism and sexism behind them, and calls to boycott such establishments. As the tide changed in the multicultural 1980s, such blatant practices were dropped and 'mixed' (catering to an ethnically diversified and co-gendered crowd) bars, notably the Café San Marcos, became trendy among the younger generation. Social organizations, such as Black and White Men Together (later Men of All Colors Together), Gay Asian and Pacific Islanders Alliance and Trikone (South Asians), served as alternate social spaces for non-white gay men and to educate and work for social equality for non-white gay men within the larger gay community.

There are several novels, slightly to heavily autobiographical, which offer readers varying perspectives on life in the Castro. Paul Reed's *Longing* (1988) attacked the clone mentality. Joseph Torchia's *As If After Sex* (1983) gave a complex and ambivalent, although generally sanguine account of a typical 'Castro Street romance.' Jack Fritscher's still under-rated epic novel *Some Dance to Remember* (1989) described in great detail many neighborhood personalities, characters and institutions, from the pioneering days to the advent of AIDS. It too is a 'Castro Street romance,' but one which captured the sexually obsessive environment. Finally, Mike Hippler's *...So Little Time* (1990) was a collection of personal-opinion columns written by a kind of Castro Street gay everyman observing the AIDS epidemic around him as he anticipates his own death.

The Castro itself forms the hub of a continuously spreading gay metropolis within the city of San Francisco. From the mid-1970s through the 1990s, these gay urban suburbs proliferated in a pattern similar to the 1950s, and include Buena Vista Heights, Corona Heights, Diamond Heights, Twin Peaks, the Duboce Triangle, as well as surrounding Eureka Valley, Valencia Street/Inner Mission, Hayes Valley, the upper Haight (Haight-Ashbury), the lower Haight (Haight-Fillmore) and Noe Valley, with further extensions into the Potrero Hill district and Bernal Heights. Most of these areas, although identified somewhat differently by Stephen Murrray (1996), had a minimum of 25 per cent gay-identified population in 1990.

Let us evoke the rise of Harvey Milk, 'the mayor of Castro Street' in the 1970s, who was instrumental in transforming the burgeoning gay enclave in San Francisco's Eureka Valley into the unique gay community of the Castro. In 1972, after drifting across America, Milk had moved to Castro Street and opened a camera shop. Milk was not much of a businessman, but his shop served him well as he pursued his own version of gay politics. Originally a well-to-do conservative East Coast Jew, upon arrival in San Francisco:

> Milk threw his lot with the radical new 'gay' populace migrating to Castro Street. Milk created the first alliance between gays and San Francisco's blue-collar unions, organizing a boycott of Coors Beer. While mingling with Marxist-oriented gay liberationists and using the fiscal conservatism of the Republican Party of his youth, he mobilized as a coalitionist Democrat.
>
> (Wright, forthcoming)

Milk was elected, on his third try, to the Board of Supervisors in 1977. It was the first time district elections were held in San Francisco, and Milk campaigned for his constituents, both the gay voters of the Castro as well as the (mostly Irish-Catholic) working men of the old Eureka Valley enclave.

The massive influx of gays was not welcomed in many quarters. By 1976 gay murders 'accounted for 10 percent of the city's homicide rate' (Stryker and Buskirk 1996: 77) and gay businesses were the target of arsonists. In 1977 and 1978 arson fires at Ritch Street Baths, Castro Rock Baths, Turkish Baths left one dead after each blaze. After less than a year in office Milk was felled by an assassin's bullet. Dan White, representing another working-class Irish-Catholic constituency, but acting on his own, would galvanize the next radical transformation of San Francisco's gay community. Under the now-infamous 'twinkie' defense (i.e. White's ability to control his emotions was compromised by a high blood-sugar level induced from binge eating junk food), White received a very mild prison sentence for having murdered Mayor George Moscone and Supervisor Harvey Milk. Following the announcement of the verdict, San Francisco's gay community gathered at City Hall in a protest which erupted into the full-fledged 'White Night Riots,' echoing the race riots of the 1960s. Once again, San Francisco's police retaliated with an impromptu raid on the Elephant Walk, a bar at the corner of Castro and Eighteenth Streets. This attack went far in generating a deeper sense of the Castro as a gay community and gay neighborhood, and a profound feeling of violation and lack of safety. Middle-class gay men had more to fear from their legal 'protectors,' together with poor African Americans and Latinos, than from their 'natural' homophobe enemies (male youths in general, although Latino males fought a turf war against gay men around Dolores Park, which during the 1970s was the boundary between the Castro and the Inner Mission).

Milk's murder became an icon of martyrdom which was as powerful in San Francisco as the accounts of the 1969 Stonewall Riots were in New York. An emergent post-GLF, assimilationist gay-rights iconography found expression in the gay rainbow flag, designed in 1978. Gilbert Baker, a local San Francisco artist was contacted by a friend and asked to create a 'community symbol' for gay San Francisco. Baker's original design included eight different colored stripes, was reduced to seven for commercial production ('hot pink' could not be reproduced), and by the time the Gay Pride Parade adopted it for use in 1979, they had reduced the number of stripes to six. Through a local gay connection, the first contract to mass produce the flag went to San Francisco's Paramount Flag Company, and the same contact parlayed this local invention into the officially recognized symbol of the gay movement by the International Congress of Flag Makers.

By the late 1970s gay pride began taking new shapes. One key development was the realization that heavy consumption of alcohol and recreational drugs was leading to serious addiction problems. Alcoholism had been a serious problem among gay men for many decades, but not until the full blossoming of the perpetual party that was Castro Street did it get addressed. Gay meetings of Alcoholics Anonymous began proliferating in the Castro and throughout San Francisco (which is often cited as the American city with the highest rates of suicide and alcoholism). The growth of the recovery movement among the gay community led to major transformations within AA itself. Separate gay meetings started originally because homosexuals were not welcomed, and gay-related social issues not gladly entertained at regular AA meetings. Also, gay men of this generation often sought recovery form a dual addiction to alcohol and drugs. Old-time AA felt drug-related issues had no place in AA. Over the next decade, gay AA would grow as part of a national trend. By the early 1980s sobriety through AA was not only 'politically correct,' it was a social movement everyone wanted to join.

The proliferation of gay AA, Al-Anon, NA and Nar-Anon, CoDA, and numerous other Twelve-Step programs created another layer of community network within gay San Francisco. At the end of the 1970s and in tandem with the advent of the AIDS epidemic, a significant social regrouping took place. Former bar habitués replaced the bars with AA meetings and other social gatherings. Many cut back or abstained from drinking or avoided bars and potential sexual contacts altogether to stave off infection from HIV. For a few years, bars were mostly empty, and only the most hardened drinkers and alcoholics patronized them on a regular basis.

In the spring of 1981 rumors about a mysterious 'gay cancer' began circulating on Castro Street and throughout the gay community. By the time 'GRID' came to public attention in 1982, gay San Francisco was in a state of shock. Numerous gay men had died of mysterious 'gay pneumonias' and 'gay cancers,' more men were falling sick and no treatments seemed to arrest whatever was killing these men. In the early years of the epidemic fear and panic came to the fore. Some suspected it was a conspiracy of biological warfare against homosexuals. Many thought it was a result of immune systems exhausted by all the sex and drugs and antibiotics. (San Francisco had been number one for venereal diseases in the 1970s, and the VD clinic, located South of Market, was a popular place to cruise for sex while waiting to see a doctor. Several bath-houses were just around the corner.)

San Francisco, along with New York and Los Angeles, became ground zero for the first wave of the AIDS epidemic. There was the belief that AIDS could eradicate the entire population of homosexual men and quite likely would destroy the gay community. By 1984 Castro Street was virtually a ghost town. Businesses boarded up, fear gripped the community as at first hundreds and then thousands of gay men died. Before efficacious treatments were developed, HIV antibody testing was held by many San Franciscans, gay and straight, to be counterproductive, very likely to drive HIV+ people underground.

Erupting in this unique community, AIDS was devastating beyond comprehension – for sheer numbers of men struck down, needs (medical, emotional, practical) rising exponentially, faster than could be met. The *Bay Area Reporter*, the local newspaper of gay record, began printing obituaries in the early 1980s. (In 1995, they still filled one to three pages.) The gay community did not disintegrate as some had feared, but awareness of the Castro as a traumatized community was inadequate. Being gay in 1980s San Francisco meant living, working and playing with AIDS.

Initially, numerous community-based organizations were created to deal with the crisis when no one else was willing to step in. Among them, the San Francisco AIDS Foundation (SFAF) is the largest such organization, providing many services. The Shanti Project offers practical and emotional support for terminally ill PWAs. Other groups include the AIDS Fund, the Food Bank, Stop AIDS Project and Mobilization Against AIDS. The NAMES Project's AIDS Quilt, perhaps the world's largest folk art, has given a community outlet to collective grief. The NAMES Quilt has emerged as an early expression of the postmodern era's local/global consciousness.

The AIDS Office of the San Francisco Department of Public Health, coordinating community-based and governmental agencies, spearheaded a prevention and risk-reduction program between 1982 and 1989 – known as the 'San Francisco model,' which effected fundamental changes in the sexual behavior of gay men, reducing the spread of HIV. Innovative in addressing discrete audiences through a variety of approaches, they delivered these messages in subcultural-appropriate language. Local government, and the medical and the gay communities' mutual cooperation contributed to the success. This strategy was subsequently threatened when state and federal government stepped in to censor content. By the mid 1990s the initial success of this approach was viewed as a long-term failure, as the third generation of young gay men reinvented for themselves a new hedonism reminiscent of the 1970s.

Outreach to ethnic communities and cultural diversification began in 1986. Community-based organizations addressed community-specific issues, while organizations such as SFAF expanded and restructured to become all-inclusive. ACT-UP activism and its spin-off Queer Nationalism revitalized, if only briefly, political activism, albeit in a decidedly middle-of-the-road, collaborationist manner. ACT-UP blamed the federal government and its bureaucracy for the consequences of the epidemic and demanded from the government either as privileged offspring of a paternalistic society or as highly dissatisfied consumers that money and legislation be mobilized to deal with AIDS.

San Francisco Queer Nationalism realigned sexual identity politics with a philosophy of multiculturalism and a version of queer theory, which foregrounded the role of sexual desire and the ability to reinvent oneself, to pursue a classically San Francisco style of rainbow coalition sexual politics. By 1991, when the Gay Pride Parade Committee proclaimed the 'Year of the Queer,' the make-up of the gay community has changed profoundly once again. The new queer coalition embraced 'All' sexual queers (except, as always, the pedophiles) and 'all' colors, creeds and races (though, by and large, middle-class).

In the 1980s the 'clone' look was rejected by the younger generation as it came to symbolize a tainted, self-absorbed urban gay white male subculture, which some blamed for the epidemic. The look would re-emerge in a modified 'ACT UP' version – shaved head, goatee, gym-toned body, baseball cap worn backwards, tattoos and/or body piercings. While a 'street-wise' gay San Francisco look tended toward a sexually scruffy and traditionally blue-collar masculine more than in other urban area of the United States, it also witnessed the sleek and angular 'Chelsea' (New York City spawned) look of the 1990s, without the accompanying rigid group-think clone mentality of, for example, 1990s Boston or Los Angeles.

The AIDS crisis led to three significant changes in the gay landscape. In 1984, the bath-house controversy deeply divided the gay community and the City. Eventually, the bath-houses closed for want of business and, by the early 1990s, the ban on gay bath-houses had been thoroughly circumvented with the establishment of a new system of private and 'private' sex clubs. Membership fees were nominal, the practice of phoning in reservations was adumbrated with lists of paid club members at the door or the mere formality of collecting a (forged) signature and entry fee, much as the old bath-houses had done in the time before AIDS. New bars opened and a new club scene started up, several dance clubs gathering at the same site but each having its own night of the week. By the late 1990s a sexual culture, with concomitant public debate over 'circuit parties' and 'barebacking' (anal intercourse without a condom), emerged, which bore striking similarities to its 1970s precursor.

Along with the collapse of the commercial sex spaces south-of-Market, the once burgeoning leather community collapsed. The leather community suffered proportionately the greatest numbers of AIDS deaths. Most leather bars and sex clubs South of Market, such as Febe's, the Anvil, the Catacombs, the Cauldron folded in the early 1980s. For a time, the district was the nightclub district for heterosexual suburbia. San Franciscan Geoff Mains argued in the early 1980s that the gay male SM or 'leathersex' scene was about transcendence:

> leatherspace is a movement that is both tribal and magical....Although [SM] experiences are usually sexual and intimate, they are far more than that. These activities share strong social, intellectual and emotional mean-ings, and common knowledge of both activities and meanings is freely shared within the tribe.
>
> (Mains 1984: 40)

Of the dozens of leather bars along or near the Folsom Street corridor, only a few among them, including the San Francisco Eagle, at the corner of Twelfth and Harrison Streets, survived. The leather community never died out completely. For a few years during the 1980s the Folsom Street Fair attempted to shift its focus from the leather community exclusively to be inclusive of all south-of-Market residents. In 1985 Up Your Alley established a leathersex street fair on Ringold Alley, and moved in 1987 to Dore Alley. The Folsom Fair returned to its leather roots. According to Gayle Rubin (Levine Nardi Gagnon 1997: 130–1), as the leather community grew smaller in number, it grew more cohesive and socially integrated, gay men and lesbians, bisexuals and heterosexuals and racial diversity became apparent as well. In the 1990s the Folsom Street Fair expanded into a full Leather Pride Week, drawing tens of thousands of leather friends from around the world to its events.

A new masculine culture of gay 'bears' emerged during the mid 1980s. Four elements came together to create this new social space in *San Francisco – Bear* magazine (as a local sex contact resource), Bear Hug play parties (as part of the emergent private sex party scene), the emergence of cyberspace (and the preva-lence of self-identifying bears who used electronic bulletin boards or worked in the Silicon Valley computer technology industry) and a new kind of bar South of Market. Billing itself as a 'bear bar,' the Lone Star Saloon opened its doors in 1989, only to be destroyed a few months later in the Prieta Loma Earthquake of 1989. The Lone Star re-opened in a new location on Twelfth Street, and went on to become the anchor bar of a nascent bear zone. During the 1990s, South-

of-Market was established as the core commercial space for bear-related sociability and the bear culture, of self-identifying individuals, commercial sites and
sexual activities, overlapped with a re-emergent leather and S/M community, as
well as with the girth-and-mirth community.

In the late 1980s, as if following an all-out nuclear attack, gay San Francisco
began coming out again, as the survivors of AIDS, perhaps the worst epidemic
of the twentieth century as it affected gay men. Along with the new radicals
came a new class of gay neo-conservatives. Left-oriented gays were momentarily
pressured into silence in the aftermath of the collapse of Soviet communism.
Personal and political fashion, in a form of niche marketing emerged, among
them the piercing and tattooing fashion of queer 'modern primitives,' lipstick
lesbians and daddy dykes, boy toys and bears. The hyper-commodification
economy of consumer capitalism boomed.

As the 1990s come to a close, San Francisco is the most expensive city in the
United States in which to live. It is experiencing the tightest housing market ever,
and real estate prices have not stopped spiraling since the 1973–4 boom. Gay
men are moving out to relatively more affordable housing in the Bay Area
suburbs, while other gays of all ages continue to immigrate, though in smaller
numbers. The young and unaffluent are making their home in the Valencia
Street/Inner Mission, Tenderloin, and other pockets. The Castro has become
one of the most affluent residential areas of the city, but the neighborhood is still
home to queers of every description. Sexual spaces of many sorts, from various
kinds of socialization, continue to flourish, from the cruising grounds in Golden
Gate Park and Land's End to the Eros Club and numerous other sex clubs in the
Castro. A reinaugurated 'F' trolley-car line now shuttles tourists to Fisherman's
Wharf and Pier 39 from Union Square and the Embarcadero right to Castro
Street, along a newly beautified Market Street resplendent with mature royal
palm trees. Polk Gulch is no longer gay, South of Market is not as great as it
once was but thriving after dark as always. In the Castro, even as the locally
owned gay small businesses are replaced by national franchises and gimmicky
tourist traps, a certain feeling of nostalgia for its gay heyday remains. As author
Frank Browning commented, 'We know as good postmodernists that we are all
performers and viewers, foreground and background, subjects and objects'
(Browning 1996: 22). Every day the San Francisco gay man lives is another day
he takes part in creating an urban gay history.

Notes

1 Clemens, incidentally, recorded sharing a room and bed in his early California days
   with a male companion. Whether this was of practical necessity or erotic desire is not
   now clear.

Some suggestions for further reading

The literature on lesbian and gay historical studies grew by leaps and bounds from the 1970s on. An interested reader should consult an up-to-date bibliography. For books in print as this volume goes to press the bibliographies in Rudi C. Bleys, *The Geography of Perversion: Male-to-Male Sexual Behaviour Outside the West and the Ethnographic Imagination, 1750–1918*, London, Cassell, 1996; Henning Bech, *When Men Meet: Homosexuality and Modernity*, Chicago, University of Chicago Press, 1997, can be recommended.

For insight into the uses made of gay space in a primarily contemporary discussion readers should consult David Bell and Gill Valentine, *Mapping Desire; Geographies of Sexualities*, London and New York, Routledge, 1995, and its remarkable bibliography. The articles edited by Gordon Ingram, Anne-Marie Bouthillette and Yolanda Retter, *Queers in Space: Communities, Public Places, Sites of Resistance*, Seattle, Bay Press, 1997, are disparate but stimulating and well illustrated. Aaron Betsky, *Queer Space: Architecture and Same-Sex Desire*, New York, William Morrow and Company, 1997, is an elegant and highly contemporary essay.

Perhaps the first overtly sympathetic 'gay' urban portrait was Magnus Hirschfeld's short account of Berlin, first published in German in 1904. This book was a plea for majority tolerance and repeal of the anti-homosexual article 175 of the German criminal code. The book described Berlin, at that time about 2.5 million in population, but it was cautiously vague in identifying exact locations. A pastry shop frequented by middle-class Jewish lesbians was noted only as being in north Berlin. The book pointed out that there were twenty 'uranian' taverns in the city, but did not give their addresses. Hirschfeld claimed there were 50,000 homosexuals in Berlin which made them approximately 2 per cent of the urban population there. Later writers also engaged the 'How many?' question which is an initial step to many forms of social history. Hirschfeld simply left out references to male public urinals in Berlin which at the time were, in fact, the 'busiest' of all male same-sex pick-up venues in the city. He did not want to disgust or displease the heterosexual men and women whose acceptance of gays he craved. A 1906 book on male prostitution in Berlin was distanced in its subtitle: *First Comprehensive Overview and Lively Description of the Pernicious Phenomenon* (Ostwald 1906). Later writers evoked the homosexual ambiance of Berlin and its hustlers and photographers between the wars and afterwards (Persky 1995).

The study of the gay urban past beyond living witness was relatively undeveloped in English language scholarship until the 1990s. Garry Wotherspoon's 1991 study of Sydney dealt mainly with the twentieth century and made use of oral histories. George Chauncey's 1994 book on Gay New York from 1890 to 1940 relied primarily on documentation prior to 1940 about dead individuals. Michael Rocke's study of Renaissance Florence (1996) made use of a remarkable body of documentation which survived for more than five centuries. The 'Officers of the Night' kept records of their efforts to combat sodomy in the city between 1432 and 1502. Rocke consulted additional sources which permitted him to provide detailed analysis of homosexual activities at a time in the European and Italian past for which such evidence is extremely rare, or non-existent.

For the contemporary era after World War II studies of homosexual behavior between North American males reflected changing attitudes. Laud Humphreys made a plea for tolerance of the frequently married men who during the 1960s sought out impersonal sex in park restrooms in St Louis, Missouri, although the first edition of the book did not permit identification of the site of his research (Humphreys 1975).

Such work suggests the question of the difference between attempting to write historical urban sociology about male homosexuals and the recounting the gay urban history of a particular place. A kind of abstract gay urban sociology of a generic North American city ('metropolis') was produced by John Allen Lee, *Getting Sex*, Toronto, Musson Book Company, 1978. Shortly before the onset of the AIDS epidemic Lee pointed out contemporary types of meeting places for sexual interactions: his subtitle was *A New Approach: More Fun Less Guilt*. Such a technique is at least suggestive of the locations to observe to amass information on a city in North America. It is of course quite deaf to the specific attributes of a city and a historical moment, geography, climate, cultural setting and place as evoked in these essays.

Readers who themselves wish to investigate aspects of gay urban history over past centuries to the present will need to consult ecclesiastical and legal records of persecution where those subsist. The essays in *The Pursuit of Sodomy: Male Homosexuality in Renaissance and Enlightenment Europe*, Kent Gerard and Gert Hekma (eds), New York, 1989 (originally published as *Journal of Homosexuality*, volume 16, numbers 1/2, 1988) contain a variety of insights into the problems of sources and their interpretation. Other written documents without narrative intent may provide information on the gay past: one thinks of the use Chauncey made of applications for permits for bars in New York.

The collective work on Cologne homosexuals under the Third Reich is a modern instance of what can be learned from extant documentation on a particular city: *Verführte Männer: das leben der Kölner Homosexuellen im Dritten Reich*, Cornelia Limpricht *et al.* (eds), Cologne, 1991.

Sometimes documents surviving from the urban past can be supplemented with literary descriptions of gay life in poetry, novels and the like. The explicit evocation of the gay 'world' in a particular city was initially more likely to be the work of novelists than historians of urbanism. There is also a genre of historical novels with a sense of gay space. Novels occasionally provide accounts of coming out in particular cities like that by Michel Tremblay (1995) set in Montreal, *La Nuit des princes charmants*.

Much investigation in sparse and unsystematic records is best described as *bricolage* since in the more remote past one is inevitably forced to speculate and underline the plausible in the absence of unambiguous statements. Much collective work needs to be done to identify and make available sources of lesbian and gay history.

There is also a literature dealing with the use that can be made of pictures of various kinds, ranging from Old Master renditions of homosexual themes to sketches and caricatures. Some of those pictures provide clues about Early Modern gay spaces. Something of the same can be said of statuary which in its rendition of neo-classical or homo-erotic themes provided a vehicle for displaying the kind of iconography attractive to gay men. Since the invention of photography many individuals have made collections of erotic photographs and some of these are preserved in gay archives. David Leddick, *The Male Nude*, Cologne, Taschen, 1998, published a collection of such photographs arranged by decades since the nineteenth century.

In the century since the invention of the movies in 1895 there have been explicit film depictions of homosexuals, starting with *Anders als die Andern* (1919) which has partially survived in a copy held in Eastern Europe. A range of films have been made, in Europe particularly, which provide a sympathetic rendition of homo-eroticism including the seven cities of this book. There is also a much larger field of implicit renditions of homosexual stereotypes purveyed by Hollywood. These were brought to the screen in *The Celluloid Closet* by R. Epstein and J. Friedman, based on the book by Vito Russo (1981).

The technology of the videotape made possible from the 1970s the mass consumption of pornography in a home setting as well as in cinemas which showed such films. The video-porn market grew at a very rapid rate. Some films were set in the cities discussed in this book.

Finally readers can consult a developing body of first-person lesbian and gay published ego-documents in which individuals discuss their tastes and experiences in same-sex sexuality and its significance to their lives, outlook and work. There is a first-hand documentary residue of gay life ranging from personal letters, diaries, to formal memoirs. Those accounts also convey something of the locations and settings of individual existences: the queer spaces in which lesbians and gay men recount themselves. These are few indeed before 1970. The *Memoirs* of John Addington Symonds (1840–93) published in 1984 provide an exceptional insight into initial self-hatred and guilt, followed by growing self-knowledge, of a married English bisexual, written between 1889 and his death. Perhaps more unpublished manuscripts await editing and to enter the public domain. One masterpiece of gay autobiography was by the English critic, J.R. Ackerley (1896–1967), *My Father and Myself*, with much information about London life. It was published posthumously in 1968. A collection of transcribed interviews with men in Great Britain of various social backgrounds shows what can be learned from oral history: *Between the Acts [of the British Parliament]: Lives of Homosexual Men 1885–1967*, Kevin Porter and Jeffrey Weeks (eds.), London, 1991.

An amazing specimen of a gay man's self-chronicle in a set of diaries closely associated with a place, Washington D.C., unfortunately marred by extremely intrusive editing and in-fill writing and simplification of a text which itself is not open to consultation in a public deposit, dealt with the life of a civil servant 'Jeb Alexander' and his friends. It appeared in 1993 under the title *Jeb and Dash*. If this document was in fact even partially what it is represented as being in its selective and mutilated publication by its editor and publisher it is perhaps the most remarkable sustained self-description by a twentieth-century North American gay man prior to 1960 that is now known to exist. It can also be read as a guide to the use made of queer sites in the US capital in the 1920s and 1930s by one rather timid and awkward gay man. By the 1990s there was a steady increase in semi-popular accounts of gay communities in cities in the US and elsewhere. Representative specimens are Michelangelo Signorile, (1960–) *Life Outside: The Signorile Report on Gay Men [in the USA]: Sex, Drugs, Muscles, and the Passages of Life*, New York, Harper Collins, 1997; Charles Kaiser, *The Gay Metropolis, 1940–1996*, Boston, Houghton Mifflin Company, 1997, put a particular stress on the gay intelligentsia of New York.

Bibliography

Ackerley, J.R. (1968) *My Father and Myself*, London: The Bodley Head.

Aldrich, R. (1993) *The Seduction of the Mediterranean: Writing, Art and Homosexual Fantasy*, London: Routledge.

Alexander, J. (1993) *Jeb and Dash: A Diary of Gay Life, 1918–1945*, (edited by Ina Russell), Boston, Faber and Faber.

Altman, D.(1982) *The Homosexualization of America, the Americanization of the Homosexual*, New York: St Martin's Press.

Anderson, S.W. (1993) 'The rainbow flag,' *Gaze* (Minneapolis) 191, 25.

Andrade, C. Drummond de (1992) *O Amor Natural*, Rio de Janeiro: Editora Record.

Andrews, M.W. (1995) 'Public toilets and Victorian mores in London' (Northwest Conference on British Studies, Spokane, Wash.)

Angeli, M. (1974) *Guide du Paris Secret*, Paris: Société Européenne de Distribution.

Ashbury, H. (1933) *The Barbary Coast*, Garden City, NY: Garden City Publishing.

Aston, T.H. (1965) *Crisis in Europe, 1560–1660: Eassays from Past and Present*, London: Routledge and Kegan Paul.

Azevedo, A. (1939) *O Cortiço*, 8th edn, Rio de Janeiro: Briguiet.

Baker, T. (1703) *Tunbridge-Walks; or the Yeoman of Kent: A Comedy*, London: Bernard Lintot.

Balser, K., Kramp, M., Müller, J. and Gotzmann, J. (eds) (1994) *'Himmel und Hölle.' Das Leben Kölner Homosexuellen 1945–1969*, Köln: Emons Verlag.

Barbedette, G. and Carassou, M. (1981) *Paris Gay 1925*, Paris: Presses de la Renaissance.

Barker, M. E. (compiler) (1994) *San Francisco Memoirs, 1835–1851*, San Francisco: Londonborn.

Barker, M.E. (compiler) (1996) *More San Francisco Memoirs, 1852–1899*, San Francisco: Londonborn.

Baron, S. (ed.)(1967) *The Travels of Olearius in Seventeenth-Century Russia*, Stanford, CA: Stanford University Press.

Bartlett, N. (1988) *Who was that Man? A Present for Mr. Oscar Wilde*, London: Serpent's Tail.

Bastiani, A. (1968) *Les Mauvais Lieux de Paris*, Paris: A. Balland.

Beard, R. and Berlowitz, L.C. (eds) (1993) *Greenwich Village: Culture and Counterculture*, New Brunswick, NJ: Rutgers University Press.

Beattie, P.M. (1996) 'The house, the street, and the barracks: reform and honorable masculine social space in Brazil, 1864–1945,' *Hispanic American Historical Review* 76, 3, 439–73.

Bech, H. (1997) *When Men Meet: Homosexuality and Modernity*, Chicago: University of Chicago Press.

Beebe, L. and Clegg, C. (1960) *San Francisco's Golden Era*, Berkeley, CA: Howell-North.

Bekhterev, V.M. (1898) 'Lechenie vnusheniem prevratnykh polovykh vlechenii i onanizma,' *Obozrenie Psikhiatrii* (8), 1–11.

Bell, D. and Valentine, G. (eds) (1995) *Mapping Desire: Geographies of Sexuality*, London: Routledge.

Bennassar, B. (1978) *L'Inquisition Espagnole XVE–XIXe Siècle*, Paris: Hachette.

Bérubé, A. (1984) 'The history of gay bathhouses,' *Coming Up!* December, 15–19.

Bethencourt, F. (1994) *História das Inquisições: Portugal, Espanha e Itália*, Lisbon: Círculo dos Leitores.

Betsky, A. (1997) *Queer Space: Architecture and Same-Sex Desire*, New York: William Morrow.

Binnie, J. (1995) 'Trading places: consumption, sexuality and the production of queer space,' in D. Bell and G. Valentine (eds) *Mapping Desire: Geographies of Sexuality*, London: Routledge.

Biriukov, A.A. (1991) *Eta volshebnitsa bania*, Moscow: Sovetskii sport.

Bleys, R.C. (1995) *The Geography of Perversion: Male-to-Male Behaviour Outside the West and the Ethnographic Imagination, 1750–1918*, New York: New York University Press.

Boomgaard, J.E.A. (1992) *Misdaad en Straf in Amsterdam. Een Onderzoek naar de Strafrechspleging van de Amsterdamse Schepenbank 1490–1552*, Zwolle: Waanders.

Boon, L.J. (1997) *'Dien godlosen hoop van menschen' Vervolging van homoseksuelen in de Republiek in de Jaren dertig van de Achttiende Eeuw*, Amsterdam: De Bataafsche Leeuw.

Boswell, J. (1980) *Christianity, Social Tolerance, and Homosexuality: Gay People in Western Europe from the Beginning of the Christian Era to the Fourteenth Century*, Chicago: University of Chicago Press.

Boswell, J. (1994) *Same-Sex Unions in Premodern Europe*, New York: Villard.

Botelho, A. (1979) *O Barão de Lavos*, in *Obras*, Oporto: Lello and Irmão.

Botto, A. (1980) *As Canções…com um estudo Crítico de Fernando Pessoa*, Lisbon: Presença.

Bourdieu, P. (1984) *Distinction: A Social Critique of the Judgement of Taste*, Cambridge, MA: Harvard University Press.

Boyd, N.A. (1997) "Homos invade S.F.!" San Francisco's history as a wide-open town,' in Brett Beemyn (ed.) *Creating a Place for Ourselves: Lesbian, Gay and Bisexual Community Histories*, New York: Routledge, 73–95.

Brassaï, G. (1976) *The Secret Paris of the '30s*, London: Thames and Hudson.

Bravmann, S. (1997) *Queer Fictions of the Past: History, Culture, and Difference*, Cambridge: Cambridge University Press.

Bray, A. (1995) *Homosexuality in Renaissance England*, 2nd edn with a new afterword and updated bibliography. New York: Columbia University Press.

Bronstein, P. (1980) 'Muggings: Gay-Latino confrontations or no?' *San Francisco Examiner* 11 November, B1.

Brotz, H. (1992) *African-American Social and Political Thought 1850–1920*, New Brunswick, NJ: Transaction Publishers.

Brown, F. (1968) *An Impersonation of Angels: A Biography of Jean Cocteau*, New York: Viking Press.

Browning, F. (1996) *A Queer Geography: Journeys Toward a Sexual Self*, New York: Crown.

Brownlow, K., (1990) *Behind the Mask of Innocence*, New York: Knopf.

Burg, B.R. (1995) *Sodomy and the Pirate Tradition: English Sea Rovers in the Seventeenth-Century Caribbean*, New York: New York University Press.

Burke, P. (1978) *Popular Culture in Early Modern Europe*, New York: Harper and Row.

Butler, K. and Evans, G. (1979) 'Gay migration into black neighborhoods,' *San Francisco Chronicle* (1 September) 1, 5.

Caminha, A. (n.d.) *Bom Crioulo*, Rio de Janeiro: Olivé.

Caminha, P.V. de (1985) *A Carta de Pero Vaz de Caminha: o Descobrimento do Brasil*, Porto Alegre: Land PM Editores.

Campbell, R. (1747/1969) *The London Tradesman*, New York: A.M. Kelley.

'Can you remember when?' (1996) (master list of all known gay bars in San Francisco, compiled by Jim 'Betty' Bonko), *San Francisco Frontiers* (26 June), 38–9.

Can't Stop the Music (1980) Nancy Walker (dir.) Videocassette.

Canler, L. (1968) *Mémoires de Canler ancien chef du Service de Sûreté*, Paris: Mercure de France.

Canosa, R. (1986) *Storia dell'Inquisizione in Italia dalla Metà del Cinquecento all fine del Settecento*, Rome: Sapere 2000.

Carbery, G. (1992) 'Some Melbourne beats: a "map" of a subculture from the 1930s to the 1950s,' in R. Aldrich and G. Wotherspoon (eds) *Gay Perspectives: Essays in Australian Gay Culture*, Sydney: Department of Economic History, University of Sydney.

Carbery, G. (1995) *A History of the Sydney Gay and Lesbian Mardi Gras*, Melbourne: Australian Lesbian and Gay Archives Inc.

Carco, Francis (1914) *Jésus-la-Caille*, Paris: Mercure de France.

Carlier, F. (1887) *Les Deux Prostitutions*, Paris: E. Dentu.

Castells, M. (1983) *The City and the Grassroots: A Cross-Cultural Theory of Urban Social Movements*, Berkeley: University of California Press.

Castells, M. and Murphy, K. (1982) 'Cultural identity and urban structure: the spatial organization of San Francisco's gay community,' *Urban Affairs Review* 22, 237–59.

Castilho, J. de (1936) *Lisboa Antiga: Segunda Parte. Bairros Orientais...*, 2nd edn, Lisbon: Industrias da C.M.L.

Cavailhes, J., Dutey, P. and Bach-Ignasse, G. (1984) *Rapport Gai: enquête sur les modes de vie homosexuels en France*, Paris: Persona.

Chaikovskii, P.I. (1923) *Dnevniki 1873–1891*, Moscow-Petrograd: Gos. iz-vo Muzykal'nyi sektor, reprint 1993.

Chauncey, G. (1994) *Gay New York: Gender, Urban Culture, and the Making of the Gay Male World, 1890–1940*, New York: Basic Books.

Chauncey, G. (1996) 'Privacy could only be had in public: gay uses of the streets,' in Joel Sanders (ed.) *Stud: Architectures of Masculinity*, Princeton, NJ: Princeton University Press.

Clark, A. (1987) 'Womanhood and manhood in the transition from plebian to working-class culture: London, 1780–1845,' Unpublished PhD thesis, Rutgers University.

Ciliga, A. (1979) *The Russian Enigma*, London: Ink Links.

Coblentz, S.A. (1961) *Villains and Vigilantes: The Story of James King of William and Pioneer Justice in California*, New York: A.S. Barnes.

Coffignon, A. (1890) *Paris vivant: la corruption à Paris*, 6th edn, Paris: Librairie Illustrée.

Coglay, M. du (1937) *Chez les mauvais garçons*, Paris: Raoul Gaillard.

Coming Out Under Fire (1994) Arthur Dong (dir.) videocassette.

Common Threads: Stories from the Quilt (1989) R. Epstein and J. Friedman (dir.) videocassette.

Cory, D. W. pseud. (1951) *The Homosexual in America: A Subjective Approach*, New York: Greenberg.

Costlow, J.T., Sandler, S. and Vowles, J. (eds) (1993) *Sexuality and the Body in Russian Culture*, Stanford, CA: Stanford University Press.

Courouve, C. *Vocabulaire de l'homosexualité masculine*, Paris: Payot.

Crew, L. (ed.) (1978) *The Gay Academic*, Palm Springs, CA: ETC Publications.

Crompton, L. (1983) '*Don Leon*, Byron and Homosexual Law Reform,' *Journal of Homosexuality* 8, 53–71.

Crompton, L. (1985) *Byron and Greek Love: Homophobia in Nineteenth-Century England*, Berkeley: University of California Press.

Csergo, J. (1988) *Liberté, égalité, propreté: la morale de l'hygiène au XIXe siècle*, Paris: A. Michel.

Damata, G. (1967) *Histórias do Amor Maldito*, Rio de Janeiro: Graf Record.

David, H. (1997) *On Queer Street: A Social History of British Homosexuality 1895–1995*, London: Harper Collins.

Delcourt, P. (1888) *Le Vice à Paris*, 2nd edn, Paris: A. Piaget.

Delpêche, R. (1955) *Les Dessous de Paris*, Paris: Editions du Scorpion.

Delson, R.M. (1979) *New Towns for Colonial Brazil: Spatial and Social Planning of the Eighteenth Century*, Ann Arbor, MI: University Microfilms.

Delumeau, J. (1990) *Sin and Fear: the Emergence of a Western Guilt Culture 13th–18th Centuries*, translated by Eric Nicholson, New York: St Martin's Press.

D'Emilio, J. (1983) *Sexual Politics, Sexual Communities: The Making of a Homosexual Minority in the United States, 1940–1970*, Chicago: University of Chicago Press.

D'Emilio, J. and Freedman, E.B. (1988) *Intimate Matters: A History of Sexuality in America*, New York: Harper and Row.

Devaux, P. ('Dr Luiz') (1888) *Les Fellators: moeurs de la décadence*, Paris: Union des Bibliophiles.

De Vries, J. (1984) *European Urbanization 1500–1800*, Cambridge, MA: Harvard University Press.

Diaman, N.A. (1988) *Castro Street Memories*, San Francisco: Persona Press.

Dias, J.J. Alves (1989) 'Para uma abordagem do sexo proibido em Portugal, no século xvi,' in M.H. Carvalho dos Santos (ed.) *Inquisição* 1, 151–9, Lisbon: Universitária Editora.

Dilallo, K. and Krumholtz, J. (1994) *The Unofficial Gay Manual*, New York: Doubleday.

Dispot, L. (1986) *Manifeste archaïque: pour une morale de la modernité*, Paris: Grasset.

Donoghue, E. (1993) *Passions between Women: British Lesbian Culture 1668–1801*, London:

Dowling, L. (1994) *Hellenism and Homosexuality in Victorian Oxford*, Ithaca, NY: Cornell University Press.

Duberman, M. (1991) *Cures: A Gay Man's Odyssey*, New York: Dutton.

Duberman, M., Vicinus, M. and Chauncey, G. (1989) *Hidden from History: Reclaiming the Gay and Lesbian Past*, New York: Meridian.

Dubois, C. (1997) *La Bastoche: bal-musette, plaisir et crime 1750–1939*, Paris: Editions du Félin.

Du Dognon, A. (1948) *Les Amours buissonières*, Paris: Editions du Scorpion.

Dufour, G. (1996) *Clero y Sexto Mandamiento: la Confesión en la España del Siglo XVIII*, Madrid:

Duplay, M. (1928) *Adonis-Bar*, Paris: Albin Michel.

Duve, P. de (1994) *L'Orage de vivre*, Paris: Lattès.

Duyves, M. (1989) 'Sodom in Maccom. Homoseksualiteit in de stadscultuur,' in G. Hekma, D. Kraakman, A. van Lieshout and J. Radersma (eds) *Goed verkeerd. Een geschiedenis van homoseksuele mannen en lesbische vrouwen in Nederland* Amsterdam: Meulenhoff, 235–48.

Duyves, M. (1993) 'The Minitel: the glittering future of a new invention,' in R. Mendès-Leite and P.O. de Busscher (eds) *Gay Studies from the French Cultures*, New York and London: Harrington Park Press, 193–203.

Duyves, M. (1992) 'In de ban van de bak. Openbaar ruimtegebruik naar homoseksuele voorkeur in Amsterdam', in Jack Burgers (ed) *De uitstad. Over stedelijk vermaak*, Utrecht: Van Arkel, 73–98.

Dynes, W.R. (ed.) (1990) *Encyclopedia of Homosexuality*, New York: Garland Publishing.

Engelstein, L. (1993) 'Combined underdevelopment: discipline and the law in Imperial and Soviet Russia,' *American Historial Review* 98, 2: 338–53.

Erikson, K. (1995) 'Notes on trauma and community,' in *Trauma: Explorations in Memory*, Baltimore, MD: Johns Hopkins University Press, 183–99.

Estrée, P. d' (1902/1994) *Les Infâmes sous l'ancien régime, Cahiers* No. 24, Lille: Gai-Kitsch-Camp.

Ethington, P.J. (1996) *The Public City: The Political Construction of Urban Life in San Francisco, 1850–1900*, New York: Cambridge University Press.

Etzioni, A. (1993) *The Spirit of Community: The Reinvention of American Society*, New York: Touchstone.

Evans, D.T. (1993) *Sexual Citizenship: The Material Construction of Sexualities*, London: Routledge.

Everard, M. (1994) *Ziel en zinnen. Over liefde en lust tussen vrouwen in de tweede helft van de achttiende eeuw*, Groningen: Historische Uitgeverij.

Farinha, M. do C.J. Dias (1990) *Os Arquivos da Inquisição*, Lisbon: Arquivo Nacional da Torre do Tombo.

Faure, A. (1978) *Paris carême-prenant: du carnaval à Paris au XIXe siècle*, Paris: Hachette.

Faust, L. and Schiphorst, F.X.M. (n.d.) *Parijs bij Nacht* Amsterdam: Schettens & Giltay.

Fernandes, J.M. (1989) *Lisboa Arquitectura e Património*, Lisbon: Livros Horizonte.

Fierro, M. (1996) *Histoire et dictionnaire de Paris*, Paris: Robert Laffont.

Fischer, C.S. (1982) *To Dwell Among Friends: Personal Networks in Town and City*, Chicago: University of Chicago Press.

Fischer, H. (1977) *Gay Semiotics: A Photographic Study of Visual Coding among Homosexual Men*, San Francisco: NFS Press.

Fischer, H. (1978) *18th near Castro St. x 24*, San Francisco: NFS Press.

Fitzgerald, F. (1986) *Cities on a Hill: A Journey through Contemporary American Cultures*, New York: Touchstone.

Flamm, J. (1978) *Good Life in Hard Times: San Francisco's '20s and '30s*, San Francisco: Chronicle Books.

Freire de Oliveira, E. (1882–1911) *Elementos para a História do Município de Lisboa* Lisbon: Typographia Universal.

Friedrichs, C.R. (1995) *The Early Modern City 1450–1750*, London: Longmans.

Fritscher, J. (1989) *Some Dance to Remember*, Stamford, CT: Knights Press.

Fry, H. (1910) *London in 1910*, London: Simpkin, Marshall, Hamilton, Kent and Co.

A Full and True Account of the Discovery and Apprehending a Notorious Gang of Sodomites in St. James's London, 1709.

'G' (1980) 'The secret life of Moscow,' *Christopher Street* June: 15–21.

Gai Pied Hebdo, Paris: 1979–91.

Garber, E. (1988) 'Finocchio's: a gay community landmark,' *SFBAGLHS Newsletter* 3, 4 (June), 1ff.

Gardiner, J. (1992) *A Class Apart: The Private Pictures of Montague Glover*, London: Serpent's Tail.

'Gay power, gay politics,' (1980) Television documentary, CBS News special report.

Gemert, F. van (1994) 'Chicken Kills Hawk: Gay Murders During the Eighties in Amsterdam,' *Journal of Homosexuality* 26, 4, 149–74.

Genet, J. (1963) *Our Lady of the Flowers*, trans. Bernard, New York: Grove Press.

Georges-Anquetil (1925) *Satan conduit le bal*, Paris: Editions Georges-Anquetil.

Gerard, K. and Hekma, G. (eds) (1989) *The pursuit of sodomy: male homosexuality in Renaissance and Enlightenment Europe*, Kent Gerard and Gert Hekma (eds), New York: Harrington (originally published as *Journal of Homosexuality*, volume 16, numbers 1/2, 1988).

Gerson, B. (1954) *História das Ruas do Rio de Janeiro*, 3rd edn, Rio de Janeiro: Souza.

Gessen, M. (1990) 'We have no sex: soviet gays and AIDS in the era of Glasnost,' *Outlook* 3, 1, 42–54.

Girard, D. (1986) *Cher David: les nuits de citizen gay*, Paris: Ramsey.

Gluckman, A. and Reed, B. (eds) (1997) *Homo Economicus: Capitalism, Community, and Lesbian and Gay Life*, New York: Routledge.

Godfrey, B.J. (1988) *Neighborhoods in Transition: The Making of San Francisco's Ethnic and Nonconformist Communities*, Berkeley: University of California Press.

Gomes, J. (n.d.) *A Homossexualidade no Mundo* vol. 1, Lisbon: Autor.

Gorman, M.R. (1998) *The Empress Is a Man: Stories from the Life of Jose Sarria*, New York: Haworth.

Greenberg, D.F. (1988) *The Construction of Homosexuality*, Chicago: University of Chicago Press.

Grève, C. de (ed.) (1990) *Le Voyage en Russie. Anthologie des voyageurs français aux XVIIIe et XIXe siècles*, Paris: Robert Laffont.

Gromyko, M.M. (1986) *Traditsionnye formy povedeniia i formy obshcheniia russkikh krest'ian XIX v.*, Moscow: Nauka.

Groth, P. (1994) *Living Downtown: The History of Residential Hotels in the United States*, Berkeley: University of California Press.

Guerrand, R.H. (1985) *Les Lieux: histoire des commodités*, Paris: Editions de la Découverte.

Guersant, Marcel (1953) *Jean-Paul*, Paris: Éditions de Minuit.

Guillebaud, J.C. (1989) *Atlas mondial des libertés*, Paris: Editions Arléa.

Guyon, L. (1826) *Biographie des commissaires de police et des officiers de paix de la ville de Paris*, Paris: Mme Groullet.

Habermas, J. (1988) *The Structured Transformation of the Public Sphere: An Enquiry into a Category of Bourgeois Society*, Cambridge, Mass.: MIT Press.

Haine, S.W. (1996) *The World of the Paris Café: Sociability among the French Working Class, 1789–1914*, Baltimore, MD: Johns Hopkins University Press.

Halidzer, S. (1990) *Inquisition and Society in the Kingdom of Valencia 1478–1834*, Berkeley: University of California Press.

Hallam, P. (1993) *The Book of Sodom*, London: Verso.

Hannerz, U. (1980) *Exploring the City: Inquiries Toward an Urban Anthropology*, New York: Columbia University Press.

Hansen, G. (1995) *San Francisco Almanac: Everything You Want to Know About Everybody's Favorite City*, San Francisco: Chronicle Books.

Harding, A., Dawson, J., Evans, R. and Parkinson, M. (eds) (1994) *European Cities towards 2000: Profiles, Policies and Prospects*, Manchester: Manchester University Press.

Harris, M. (1973) *The Dilly Boys: Male Prostitution in Piccadilly*, London: New Perspectives.

Harvey, A.D. (1978) 'Prosecutions for sodomy in England at the beginning of the nineteenth century,' *The Historical Journal* 21, 939–48.

Healey, D. (1993) 'The Russian Revolution and the decriminalisation of homosexuality,' *Revolutionary Russia* 6, 1, 26–54.

Healey, D. (1997) 'Evgeniia/Evgenii: queer case histories in the first years of Soviet power,' *Gender and History* (1): 83–106.

Hekma, G. (1987) *Homoseksualiteit, een medische reputatie. De uitdoktering van de homoseksueel in negentiende-eeuws Nederland*, Amsterdam: SUA.

Hekma, G. (1992) *De roze rand van donker Amsterdam. De opkomst van een homoseksuele kroegcultuur 1930–1980*, Amsterdam: Van Gennep.

Hekma, G., Kraakman, D., Lieshout, A. van and Radersma, J. (eds) (1989) *Goed verkeerd. Een geschiedenis van homoseksuele mannen en lesbische vrouwen in Nederland* Amsterdam: Meulenhoff.

Hekma, G., Stolk, B. van, Heerikhuizen, B. van and Kruithof, B. (eds) (1990a) *Het verlies van de onschuld. Seks in Nederland*, Groningen: Wolters Noordhoff.

Hekma, G., Kraakman, D. and Melching, W. (eds) (1990b) *Grensgeschillen in de seks*, Amsterdam: Rodopi.

Herdt, G. (ed.) (1992) *Gay Culture in America: Essays from the Field*, Boston, MA: Beacon Press.

Herodotus, (1972) *The Histories*, translated by Aubrey de Sélincourt, Harmondsworth: Penguin.

Hickson, A. (1995) *The Poisoned Bowl: Sex and the Public School*, London: Constable.

Higgins, P. (1993) *A Queer Reader*, London: Fourth Estate.

Higgins, P. (1996) *Heterosexual Dictatorship: Male Homosexuality in Post-War Britain*, London: Fourth Estate.

Higgs, D. (1993) 'Inquisition, gender and genealogy in seventeenth-century Portugal,' *Portuguese Studies Review* 2, 2, 12–29.

Hilliard, D. (1982) 'UnEnglish and unmanly: Anglo-Catholicism and homosexuality,' *Victorian Studies* 25, 181–210.

Hippler, M. (1990) *So Little Time: Essays on Gay Life*, Berkeley: Celestial Arts.

Hirschfeld, M. (1993) *Le Troisième Sexe: les homosexuels de Berlin 1908 deuxième édition revue et corrigée, présentation Patrick Cardon*, Cahiers No. 17, Lille: Gai-Kitsch-Camp.

Hitchcock, T. (1996) 'Redefining sex in eighteenth-century England,' *History Workshop Journal* 41, Spring.

Hocquenghem, G.H. (1980) *Le Gay Voyage: guide et regard homosexuels sur les grandes métropoles*, Paris: Albin Michel.

Hoffbauer, F. (1875–82) *Paris à travers les ages*, Paris.

Hoffmann, D.L. (1994) *Peasant Metropolis: Social Identities in Moscow, 1929–1941*, Ithaca, NY: Cornell University Press.

Hoffschildt, R. (1992) *Geheim Olivia. Die bisher geheime Geschichte des Tabus Homosexualität und der Verfolgung der Homosexuellen in Hannover*, Hanover: Selbstverlag.

Hohenberg, P.M. and Lees, L.H. (1995) *The Making of Urban Europe 1000–1994*, Cambridge, MA: Harvard University Press.

Hollinghurst, A. (1988) *The Swimming Pool Library*, London: Chatto and Windus.

Holloway, R. (1813) *The Phoenix of Sodom, or the Vere Street Coterie*, London: J. Cook.

Hooker, E. (1956) 'A preliminary analysis of group behavior of homosexuals,' *Journal of Psychology* 42, 217–25.

Hoover, M.B., H.E. Rensch and E.G. Rensch (1948) *Historic Spots in California*, Stanford, CA: Stanford University Press, 3 vols.

Howson, G. (1970) *Thief-Taker General: Jonathan Wild and the Emergence of Crime and Corruption as a Way of Life*, New Brunswick, NJ: Transaction Books.

Huddleston, S. (1928) *Paris Salons, Cafés, Studios, Being Social, Artistic and Literary Memories*, Philadelphia, PA: J.B. Lippincott Co.

Hufton, O. (1995) *The Prospect before Her: A History of Women in Western Europe, vol. 1, 1500–1800*, London: HarperCollins.

Humphreys, L. (1975) *Tearoom Trade: Impersonal Sex in Public Places*, New York: Aldine de Gruyter.

Hyde, H.M. (1962) *Famous Trials, vol. 7, Oscar Wilde*, Baltimore: Penguin Books.

Hyde, H. M. (1970) *The Love that Dared Not Speak its Name*, Boston: Little Brown.

Hyde, H.M. (1976) *The Cleveland Street Scandal*, London: W.H. Allen.

Ingram, G.B., Bouthillette, A.M. and Retter, Y. (eds) (1997) *Queers in Space: Communities, Public Places, Sites of Resistance*, Seattle, WA: Bay Press.

Isherwood, Christopher (1997) *Diaries, vol. 1: 1939–1960*, edited by K. Bucknell, London: HarperCollins.

Jacobs, J. (1961/1992) *The Death and Life of Great American Cities*, New York: Vintage.

Jamoo (1997) *The Films of Kristen Bjorn*, with a foreword by William Higgins, Laguna Hills, CA: Companion Press.

Jeb, A. (1993) *Jeb and Dash: A Diary of Gay Life, 1918–1945*, edited by Ina Russell, Boston, MA: Faber and Faber.

Jeffrey-Poulter, S. (1991) *Peers, Queers and Commons*, New York: Routledge.

Johnson, R. and Stam, R. (1995) *Brazilian Cinema*, New York: Columbia University Press.

Kagan, P. (1975) *New World Utopias: A Photographic History of the Search for Community*, New York: Penguin.

Kaiser, C. (1997) *The Gay Metropolis 1940–1996*, Boston, MA: Houghton Mifflin Company.

Karlinsky, S. (1976) 'Russia's gay literature and history,' *Gay Sunshine* 29/30.

Karlinsky, S. (1982) 'Gay life before the Soviets: revisionism revised,' *The Advocate* 339, 1 April, 31–4.

Karlinsky, S. (1989) 'Russia's gay literature and culture: the impact of the October Revolution,' in M. Duberman, M. Vicinus and G. Chauncey (eds) *Hidden From History: Reclaiming the Gay and Lesbian Past*, New York: Penguin.

Katz, J. (1976) *Gay American History: Lesbians and Gay Men in the USA*, New York: Avon.

Katz, J. (1983) *Gay/Lesbian Almanac: A New Documentary*, New York: Harper and Row.

Keller, S. (1968) *The Urban Neighborhood: A Sociological Perspective*, New York: Random House.

Kennedy, E.L. and Davis, M.D. (1993) *Boots of Leather, Slippers of Gold: The History of a Lesbian Community*, New York: Routledge.

Kennedy, H. (1989) 'German gay activist visits San Francisco – in 1931,' *SFBAGLHS Newsletter* 5, 2 (Winter), 1ff.

Kinsey, A.C. Pomeroy, W.B. and Martin, E.E. (1948) *Sexual Behavior in the Human Male*, Philadelphia, PA: W.B. Saunders.

Koenders, P. (1987) *Het homomonument/The Homomonument*, Amsterdam: Stichting Homomonument.

Koenders, P. (1996) *Tussen Christelijk Réveil en Seksuele Revolutie*, Amsterdam: IISG.

Koni, A.F. (1912) *Na zhiznennom puti* vol. I, St Petersburg: Trud.

Kooten Niekerk, A. van and Wijmer, S. (1985) *Verkeerde vriendschap. Lesbisch leven in de jaren 1920–1960*, Amsterdam: Sara.

Kotkin, S. (1995) *Magnetic Mountain: Stalinism as a Civilization*, Berkeley: University of California Press.

Kozlovskii, V. (1986) *Argo russkoi gomoseksual'noi subkul'tury: materialy k izucheniiu*, Benson, VT: Chalidze Publications.

Kramer, J.L. (1995) 'Bachelor farmers and spinsters: gay and lesbian identities and communities in rural North Dakota,' in D. Bell and G. Valentine (eds) *Mapping Desire: Geographies of Sexuality*, London: Routledge, 200–13.

LaGory, M. and Pipkin, J. (1981) *Urban Social Space*, Belmont, CA: Wadsworth.

Lamothe Langon, E.L. (1830) *Voyage à Paris*, Paris: Veuve Lepetit.

Landers J. (1993) *Death and the Metropolis: the Demographic History of London 1670–1830*, Cambridge: Cambridge University Press.

Lanegran, D.A. and Palm, R. (eds) (1977) *An Invitation to Geography*, New York: McGraw Hill.

Leach, E. (1969) *Genesis as Myth and Other Essays*, London: Cape.

Leal, A.S. d'Azevedo Barbosa de Pinho (1875) *Portugal Antigo e Moderno* Lisbon: Mattos Moreira.

Leap, W.L. (1996) *Word's Out: Gay Men's English*, Minneapolis: University of Minnesota Press.

Leddick, D. (1998) *The Male Nude*, Cologne: Taschen.

Lee, J.A. (1978) *Getting Sex, a New Approach: More Fun, Less Guilt*, Don Mills, Ont.: Musson Book Company.

Léry, J. de (1992) *History of a Voyage to the Land of Brazil, Otherwise called America...* translated and introduction by Janet Whaley, Berkeley: University of California Press.

Lévi-Strauss, C. (1974) *Tristes Tropiques*, New York: Atheneum.

Lever, M. (1985) *Les Bûchers de Sodome: histoire des 'infâmes'*, Paris: Fayard.

Levin, E. (1989) *Sex and Society in the World of the Orthodox Slavs, 900–1700*, Ithaca, NY: Cornell University Press.

Levine, L. (1995) *Men in Women's Clothing: Anti-Theatricality and Effeminization, 1579–1642*, Cambridge: Cambridge University Press.

Levine, M.P. (1979) *Gay Men: The Sociology of Male Homosexuality*, New York: Harper and Row.

Levine, M.P. (1998) *Gay Macho: The Life and Death of the Homosexual Clone*, edited by Michael S. Kimmel. New York: New York University Press.

Levine, M.P., Nardi, P.M. and Gagnon, J.H. (eds) (1997) *In Changing Times: Gay Men and Lesbians Encounter HIV/AIDS*, Chicago: University of Chicago Press.

Lieshout, M. van and Hafkamp, H. (eds) (1988) *Pijlen van naamloze liefde. Pioniers van de homobeweging*, Amsterdam: SUA.

Limpricht, C., Müller, J. and Oxenius, N. (eds) (1991) *'Verführte' Männer. Das Leben der Kölner Männer im Dritten Reich*, Köln: Volksblatt Verlag.

Lockwood, C. (1978) *Suddenly San Francisco: The Early Years of an Instant City*, San Francisco: A California Living Book.

Loja, A.E.F. (1986) *A Luta do Poder Contra a Maçonaria: Quatro Perseguições no Século XVIII*, Lisbon: Imprensa Nacional.

Lotchin, R.W. (1974) *San Francisco, 1846–1856: From Hamlet to City*, New York: Oxford.

Lyons, F.J. (1936) *Jonathan Wild*, London: M. Joseph Ltd.

McCaffrey, J.A. (ed.) (1972) *The Homosexual Dialectic*, Englewood Cliffs, NJ: Prentice-Hall.

MacGregor, W.L. (1876) *San Francisco in 1876*, Edinburgh: Thomas Laurie.

McIntosh, M. (1968) 'The homosexual role,' *Social Problems* 16, 2, 182–92.

Maillard, C. (1967) *Les Vespasiennes de Paris ou les précieux édicules*, Paris: La Jeune Parque.

Mains, G. (1984) *Urban Aboriginals: A Celebration of Leathersexuality*, San Francisco: Gay Sunshine Press.

Male Escorts of San Francisco (1992) Matthew Link, (dir.), videocassette.

Mansel, P. (1995) *Constantinople: City of the World's Desire 1453–1924*, London: John Murray.

Maroger, D. (ed.) (1955) *The Memoirs of Catherine the Great* London: Hamish Hamilton.

Marotta, T. (1981) *The Politics of Homosexuality*, Boston: Houghton Mifflin.

Martel, F. (1996) *Le Rose et le noir: les homosexuels en France depuis 1968*, Paris: Seuil.

Matiushenskii, A.I. (1908) *Polovoi rynok i polovye otnosheniia*, St Petersburg.

Maupin, A. (1990) *28 Barbary Lane: A Tale of the City Omnibus*, New York: Harper and Row.

Maupin, A. (1991) *Back to Barbary Lane: The Final Tales of the City Omnibus*, New York: Harper Collins.

May, A. and Appleby, V. (1994) *Voices of San Francisco: Speaking Out from the City by the Bay*, New York: Harper Collins.

Mayeur Saint-Paul, F.M. (1781) *Le Désoeuvré, ou l'espion du Boulevard du Temple*, London: no pub.

Mayne, X. (?1908)/1975) [pseudonym of Edward Irenaeus Prime Stevenson] *The Intersexes: A History of Similisexualism as a Problem in Social Life*, reprinted New York: Arno Press.

Meer, T. van der (1984) *De wesentlijke sonde van sodomie en andere vuyligheeden. Sodomietenvervolgingen in Amsterdam*, Amsterdam: Tabula.

Meer, T. van der (1995) *Sodoms zaad in Nederland. Het Ontstaan van Homoseksualiteit in de Vroegmoderne Tijd*, Nijmegen: SUN.

Melville, H. (1962) *Billy Budd, Sailor*, Chicago: University of Chicago Press.

Melville, H. (1846) *Typee 1846, Narrative of a Four Months Residence among the natives of the Marquesas Islands*, London: Murray.

Merzheevskii, V. (1878) *Sudebnaia ginekologiia. Rukovodstvo dlia vrachei i iuristov*, St Petersburg:

Messian, A. and Mouret-Fourme, E. (1993) 'Homosexualité, bisexualité: éléments de socio-biographie sexuelle,' *Population* 48: 1353–80

Miller, R. (1977) *Bohemia: The Prototype Then and Now*, Chicago: Nelson Hall.

Minella, A.G. and Angelotti, P. (1996) *Générations Gay*, Paris: Éditions du Rocher.

Monteiro, A.C. (1922) *Amor Sáfico e Socrático: Estudo Médico-forense*, Lisbon: Instituto de Medicina Legal de Lisboa.

Morton, D. (ed.) (1996) *The Material Queer: A Lesbigay Cultural Studies Reader*, Boulder: CO: Westview.

Moss, K. (ed.) (1996) *Out of the Blue: Russia's Hidden Gay Literature* San Francisco: Gay Sunshine Press.

Mosse, G.L. (1985) *Nationalism and Sexuality: Respectability and Abnormal Sexuality in Modern Europe*, New York: Howard Fertig.

Mott, L.R.B. (1988a) 'Pagode português: a subcultura *gay* em Portugal nos tempos inquisitoriais,' *Ciência e Cultura* (February) 40, 1.

Mott, L.R.B. (1988b) *O Sexo Proibido: Escravos, Gays e Virgens nas Garras da Inquisição*, Campinas: Papirus Editora.

Muhleisen, L. (1995) '80,000 raisons d'être fier(e)s,' *3 Keller*, July/Aug., 7.

Murphy, J. (1795) *Travels in Portugal…in the Years 1798 and 1790…*, London: A. Strahan.

Murray, S.O. (1979) 'The institutional elaboration of a quasi-ethnic community,' *International Review of Modern Sociology* 9 (July–Dec.), 165–77.

Murray, S.O. (1995) *Latin American Male Homo-sexualities*, Albuquerque: University of New Mexico Press.

Murray, S.O. (1996) *American Gay*, Chicago: University of Chicago Press.

Muscatine, D. (1975) *Old San Francisco: The Biography of a City*, New York: G.P. Putnam's Sons.

Naerssen, A.X. van (ed) (1987) *Interdisciplinary Research on Homosexuality in the Netherlands*, New York: Haworth.

Needell, J.D. (1987) *A Tropical Belle Époque: Elite Culture and Society in Turn-of-the-century Rio de Janeiro*, Cambridge: Cambridge University Press.

Newton, E. (1979) *Mother Camp: Female Impersonation in America*, Chicago: University of Chicago Press.

Newton, E. (1993) *Cherry Grove, Fire Island: Sixty Years in America's First Gay and Lesbian Town*, Boston, MA: Beacon.

Noordam, D.J. (1995) *Riskante Relaties. Vijf Eeuwen Homoseksualiteit in Nederland 1233–1733*, Hilversum: Verloren.

Norton, R. (1992) *Mother Clap's Molly House: The Gay Subculture in England 1700–1830*, London: GMP.

Norton, R. (1997) *The Myth of the Modern Homosexual: Queer History and the Search for Cultural Unity*, London: Cassell.

Nunes, R.B. (1998) 'Portuguese migration to Rio de Janeiro 1822–1850,' unpublished PhD thesis, Toronto: University of Toronto.

Oosterhuis, H. (1992) *Homoseksualiteit in Katholiek Nederland. Een Sociale Geschiedenis 1900–1970*, Amsterdam: SUA.

Oosterhuis, H. (1997) 'Medicine, male bonding and homosexuality in Nazi Germany,' *Journal of Contemporary History* 32, 2, 197–205.

O'Reilly, J., Habegger, L. and O'Reilly, S. (eds) (1996) *Travelers' Tales: San Francisco*, Sebastopol, CA: O'Reilly and Associates.

Orwell, G. (1970) *The Collected Essays, Journalism and Letters of George Orwell, vol. 1: An Age Like This – 1920–1940*, London, Penguin.

Ostwald, H. (1906) *Männliche Prostitution*, Berlin: republished with a new subtitle (*im Kaiserlichen Berlin*) and illustrations, Berlin, Janssen, 1991.

Parker, G. and Smith L.M. (eds), (1997) *The General Crisis of the seventeenth century*, 2nd edn, London, Routledge.

Parker, R.G. (1991) *Bodies, Pleasures and Passions: Sexual Culture in Contemporary Brazil*, Boston, MA: Beacon Press.

Peniston, W. (1996) 'Love and death in gay Paris: homosexuality and criminality in the 1870s,' in Jeffrey Merrick and Bryant T. Ragan (eds) *Homosexuality in Modern France*, New York: Oxford University Press, 135–6.

Peniston, W. (1997) ' "Pederasts and Others": A Social History of Male Homosexuals in the Early Years of the French Third Republic,' PhD thesis, University of Rochester, New York.

Pennington, G. (compiler) (n.d.) 'San Francisco gay chronology [1882–1986],' typescript, GLHSNC Archives.

Penteado, D. (1976) *A Meta*, São Paulo: Edições Simbolo.

Persky, S. (1995) *Then We Take Berlin: Stories from the other Side of Europe*, Toronto: Knopf.

Petrow, S. (ed.) (1990) *Ending the HIV Epidemic: Community Strategies in Disease Prevention and Health Promotion*, Santa Cruz, CA: Network Publications.

Phillips, L. (1990) *Paris Scene: The Gay Man's Guide*, London: Gay Men's Press.

Pickelhaupt, B. (1996) *Shanghaied in San Francisco*, San Francisco: Flyblister Press.

Pieroni, G. (1996) 'Les Exclus du royaume: l'inquisition portugaise et le bannissement au Brésil XVII siècle,' unpublished doctoral thesis, Nouveau Régime, Université de Paris-Sorbonne (Paris IV) 2 vols.

Pires de Almeida, J.R. (1906) *Homossexualismo (a Libertinagem no Rio de Janeiro): Estudo sobre as Perversões do Instincto Genital*, Rio de Janeiro: Laemmert.

Pol, L. van de (1996) *Het Amsterdams Hoerdom. Prostitutie in de Zeventiende en Achttiende Eeuw*, Amsterdam: Wereldbibliotheek.

Pollak, M. (1985) 'Male homosexuality – or happiness in the ghetto,' in P. Ariès and A. Bejin, *Western Sexuality: Practice and Precept in Past and Present Times*, Oxford: Blackwell.

Ponte, A. (1992) 'Architecture and phallocentrism in Richard Payne Knight's theory,' in Beatriz Colomina (ed.) *Sexuality and Space*, Princeton, NJ: Princeton University Press, 273–305.

Portal, G. (n.d.) *The Tunic of Nessus, Being the Confessions of an Invert*, trans. Eric Wensleydale, Paris (originally published as *Un Protestant* Paris: Éditions Astra, 1936).

Porter, K. and Weeks, J. (1991) *Between the Acts: Lives of Homosexual Men 1885–1967*, London: Routledge.

Poznansky, A. (1991) *Tchaikovsky: The Quest for the Inner Man*, New York: Schirmer.

Poznansky, A. (1996) *Tchaikovsky's Last Days: A Documentary Study*, Oxford: Clarendon.

Pronger, B. (1990) *The Arena of Masculinity: Sports, Homosexuality, and the Meaning of Sex*, Toronto: Summerhill Press.

Raffalovich, M.-A. (1895) 'L'Affaire Oscar Wilde,' *Archives d'Anthropologie Criminelle* 10, 445–77.

Raffo, S. (ed.) (1996) *Queerly Classed: Gay Men and Lesbians Write about Class*, Boston, MA: South End Press.

Raven, S. (1960) 'The male prostitute in London,' *Encounter* November.

Raynaud, E. (1934) *La Police des moeurs*, Paris: Société Française d'éditions littéraires et techniques.

Reed, P. (1988) *Longing*, Berkeley, CA: Celestial Arts.

Reeves, T. (1973) 'Red and gay: oppression east and west,' *Fag Rag* 6 (Fall), 3–6.

Rey, M. (1979–80) 'Les Sodomites parisiens au XVIIIème siècle,' unpublished Mémoire de maîtrise d'histoire, Université de Paris VIII.

Rey, M.(1994) '1700–1750, les sodomites parisiens créent un mode de vie,' in *Cahiers* No. 24, Lille: Gai-Kitsch-Camp, xvi–xxxiii.

Ribeiro, L.(1938) *Homosexualismo e Endocrinologia*, Rio de Janeiro: Livraria Francisco Alves.

Richards, R. (1995) *Historic San Francisco: A Concise History and Guide*, San Francisco: Heritage House.

Robinson, C. (1995) *Scandal in the Ink: Male and Female Homosexuality in Twentieth-century French Literature*, London: Cassell.

Rocke, M. (1996) *Forbidden Friendships: Homosexuality and Male Culture in Renaissance Florence*, New York: Oxford.

Rodgers, B. (1972) *The Queens' Vernacular: A Gay Lexicon*, London: Blond and Briggs.

Rohrbough, M.J. (1997) *Days of Gold: The California Gold Rush and the American Nation*, Berkeley: University of California Press.

Rollison, D. (1981) 'Property, ideology and popular culture in a Gloucestershire village 1660–1740,' *Past and Present*, 93, 70–97.

Roodenburg, H. (1990) *Onder censuur. De kerkelijke tucht in de gereformeerde gemeente van Amsterdam, 1578–1700*, Hilversum: Verloren.

Rosario, V.A.(ed.) (1997) *Science and Homosexualities*, New York, Routledge.

Ruadze, V.P. (1908) *K sudu!.. Gomoseksual'nyi Peterburg* St Petersburg.

Rubinov, A. (1990) *Sanduny: kniga o Moskovskikh baniakh*, Moscow: Moskovskii rabochii.

Rudorff, R. (1969) *The Paris Spy: A Discreet Guide to the City's Pleasures*, London: Anthony Blond.

Russo, V. (1981) *The Celluloid Closet: Homosexuality in the Movies*, New York: Harper and Row.

Rybczynski, W. (1995) *City Life*, Toronto: Harper Collins.

Sá-Carneiro, M. (1993) *Lucio's Confession*, translated by Margaret Jull, Sawtry, UK: Dedalus.

Schenk, Johan (1982) 'Homoseksualiteit in de Nederlandse beeldende kunst voor 1800,' *Spiegel Historiael* 17, 11, 576–83.

Schleiner, W. (1994) ' "That matter which ought not to be heard of" homophobic slurs in Renaissance cultural politics,' *Journal of Homosexuality* 26, 4, 41–74.

Schmiechen, R. and Epstein, R. (producers) (1986) 'The times of Harvey Milk,' Beverley Hills: Pacific Arts Video.

Schwarz, L.D. (1992) *London in the Age of Industrialization: Enterpreneurs, Labor Force and Living Conditions, 1700–1850*, Cambridge: Cambridge University Press.

Senelick, L. (1990) 'Mollies or men of mode? Sodomy and the eighteenth-century London stage,' *Journal of the History of Sexuality* 1, 33–67.

Sex Is… (1993) Marc Huestis (dir.) videocassette.

Seymour, G. (1985) 'The trial and its aftermath,' in *Solomon: A Family of Painters*, London: Geffrye Museum.

Shepard, B. (1997) *White Nights and Ascending Shadows: A History of the San Francisco AIDS Epidemic*, New York: Cassell.

Shilts, R. (1982) *The Mayor of Castro Street: The Life and Times of Harvey Milk*, New York: St Martin's Press.

Shilts, R. (1987) *And the Band Played On: Politics, People, and the AIDS Epidemic*, New York: St Martin's Press.

Shinoff, P. (1982) 'City's gay population peaks in '70s, levels off, surveys reveal,' *San Francisco Examiner* 29 April, A6.

Shiveley, C. (1997) 'Harry Hay,' in M.J. Tyrkus (ed.) *Gay and Lesbian Biography*, Detroit: St James Press.

Sibalis, M. (1996) 'The regulation of male homosexuality in Revolutionary and Napoleonic France, 1789–1815,' in Jeffrey Merrick and Bryant T. Ragan (eds) *Homosexuality in Modern France*, New York: Oxford University Press, 80–101.

Signorile, M. (1997) *Life Outside. The Signorile Report on Gay Men: Sex, Drugs, Muscles, and the Passages of Life*, New York; HarperCollins.

Silva, H.R.S. (1993) *Travesti: a Invenção do Feminíno*, Rio de Janeiro: Relume Dumara.

Simpson, C., Lewis, C. and Leitch, D. (1976) *The Cleveland Street Affair*, Boston: Little Brown

Sjoberg, Gideon (1960) *The Preindustrial City Past and Present*, New York: The Free Press.

Spate, O.H.K. (1936) 'The growth of London AD 1600–1800,' in H.C. Darby (ed.) *An Historical Geography of England*, Cambridge: Cambridge University Press.

Stansky, P. and Abrahams, W. (1994) *London's Burning: Life, Death and Art in the Second World War*, London: Constable.

Starr, K. (1973) *Americans and the California Dream, 1850–1915*, New York: Oxford University Press.

Steegmuller, F. (1970) *Cocteau: A Biography*, Boston, MA: Constable.

Steinberg, L. (1983) *The Sexuality of Christ in Renaissance Art and in Modern Oblivion*, New York: Pantheon.

Stoddard, C.W. (1903) *For the Pleasure of His Company*, San Francisco: A.M. Warren.

Stryker, S. and Buskirk, J. van (1996) *Gay by the Bay: A History of Queer Culture in the San Francisco Bay Area*, San Francisco: Chronicle Books.

Summers, C.J. (1995) *The Gay and Lesbian Literary Heritage*, New York: Henry Holt.

Suttles, G.D. (1972) *The Social Construction of Communities*, Chicago: University of Chicago Press.

Symanski, R. (1981) *The Immoral Landscape: Female Prostitution in Western Societies*, Toronto: Butterworth.

Symonds, J.A. (1984) *The Memoirs of John Addington Symonds*, edited and introduced by Phyllis Grosskurth, New York: Random House.

Tarnovskii, V.M. (1885) *Izvrashchenie polovogo chuvstva. Sudebno-psikhiatricheskii ocherk*, St Petersburg.

Teyssier, P. (1982) 'La comédia do fanchono d'António Ferreira: que signifie ce titre?', *Arquivos do Centro Cultural Português*, 17, 65–78.

Thomas, K. (1994) 'As you like it,' *New York Review of Books*, 41, 15 (22 September), 9–12.

Thompson, M. (ed.) (1991) *Leatherfolk: Radical Sex, People, Politics, and Practice*, Boston: Alyson.

Tielman, R.A.P. (1982) *Homoseksualiteit in Nederland. Studie van een Emancipatiebeweging*, Meppel: Boom.

Tongues Untied: Black Men Loving Black Men (1989) Marlon Riggs (dir.) videocassette.

Torchia, J. (1983) *As If After Sex*, New York: Holt, Rinehart and Winston.

Tremblay, M. (1995) *La Nuit des princes charmants*, Montréal: Leméac.

Trevisan, J.S. (1986) *Perverts in Paradise*, translated by Martin Foreman, London: GMP.

Trexler, R.C. (1995) *Sex and Conquest: Gendered Violence, Political Order and the European Conquest of the Americas*, Ithaca, NY: Cornell University Press.

Trüeb, K. and Miescher, S. (eds) (1988) *Männergeschichten. Schwule in Basel seit 1930*, Basel: Buchverlag Basler Zeitung.

Trumbach, R. (1978) *The Rise of Egalitarian Family: Aristocratic Kinship and Domestic Relations in Eighteenth-Century England*, New York: Academic Press.

Trumbach, R. (1988) 'Sodomitical assaults, gender role, and sexual development in eighteenth-century London,' in K. Gerard and G. Hekma (eds) *The Pursuit of Sodomy: Male Homosexuality in Renaissance and Enlightenment Europe*, New York: Harrington Park Press.

Trumbach, R. (1989a) 'The birth of the queen: sodomy and the emergence of gender equality in modern culture, 1660–1750,' in M. Duberman, M. Vicinus and G. Chauncey Jr (eds) *Hidden from History: Reclaiming the Gay and Lesbian Past*, New York: New American Library.

Trumbach, R. (1989b) 'Gender and the homosexual role in modern western culture: the eighteenth and nineteenth centuries compared,' in Dennis Altman *et al. Homosexuality, which Homosexuality?: International Conference on Gay and Lesbian Studies: Papers* London: GMP.

Trumbach, R. (1990) 'Sodomy transformed: aristocratic libertinage, public reputation and the gender revolution of the eighteenth century,' in Michael S. Kimmel (ed.) *Love Letters between a Certain Late Nobleman and the Famous Mr. Wilson*, New York: Harrington Park Press.

Trumbach, R. (1994a) 'London's sapphists: from three sexes to four genders in the making of modern culture,' in Gilbert Herdt (ed.) *Third Sex, Third Gender*, New York: Zone.

Trumbach, R. (1994b) 'The origins and development of the modern lesbian role in the western gender system: northwestern Europe and the United States, 1750–1990,' *Historical Reflections / Réflexions Historiques* 20, 287–320.

Trumbach, R. (1997) 'Are modern lesbian women and gay men a third gender?' in Martin Duberman (ed.) *A Queer World, The Center for Lesbian and Gay Studies Reader*, New York: New York University Press.

Trumbach, R. (1998) *Sex and the Gender Revolution: Heterosexuality, and the Third Gender in Enlightenment London*, Chicago: University of Chicago Press.

Tuller, D. (1996) *Cracks in the Iron Closet: Travels in Gay and Lesbian Russia*, Boston and London: Faber and Faber.

Upchurch, C.J. (1996) 'Becoming invisible: layers of silence in the case of the Queen versus Boulton and others,' MA thesis, University of North Carolina at Wilmington.

Urville, F. d'(1874) *Les Ordures de Paris*, Paris: Librairie Sartorius.

Vance, J.E. (1977) *This Scene of Man: The Role and Structure of the City in the Geography of Western Civilization*, New York: Harper and Row.

Varias, A. (1996) *Paris and the Anarchists: Aesthetes and Subversives during the Fin de Siècle*, New York: St Martin's Press.

Venciguerra, M. (1988) *O pecado de Adão: Crimes Homossexuais no Eixo Rio – São Paulo*, São Paulo: Icone.

Vichit-Vadakan, V. (1995) *Guide: Gay Paris*, Paris: R. G. A Editions.

Vieira, A. (1937) *Arte de Furtar, Espelho de Enganos, Teatro de Verdades*, Lisbon: Peninsular Editora.

Vries, P. de (1997) *Kuisheid voor Mannen, Vrijheid voor Vrouwen. De Reglementering en Bestrijding van Prostitutie in Nederland, 1850–1911*, Hilversum: Verloren.

Walser, E. (1991) 'Milieu und Maskenzwang. Geschlechterrolle und Disziplinierung. Lebensgeschichten homosexueller Männer in Bern 1935–1960,' in B. Bietenhard *et al.* (eds) *Ansichten von der rechten Ordnung. Bilder über Normen und Normenverletzungen in der Geschichte. Festschrift für Beatrix Mesmer*, Bern: Haupt, 20–42.

Ward, E. (1709) *The Secret History of Clubs*, London:

Wardlow, D.L. (1996) 'Gays, lesbians and consumer behavior: theory, practice, and research issues in marketing,' special issue of *Journal of Homosexuality* 31, 1–2.

Warmerdam, H. and Koenders, P. (1987) *Cultuur en ontspanning. Het COC 1946–1966*, Utrecht: Homostudies.

Weeks, J. (1977) *Coming Out: Homosexual Politics in Britain from the Nineteenth Century to the Present*, Totowa, NJ: Barnes and Noble.

Weinberg, T.S. (1994) *Gay Men, Drinking, and Alcoholism*, Carbondale, IL: Southern Illinois University Press.

Weston, K. (1991) *Families We Choose: Lesbians, Gays, Kinship*, New York: Columbia University Press.

Weston, K. (1995) 'Get Thee to a Big City: Sexual Imaginary and the Great Gay Migration,' *Gay and Lesbian Quarterly* 2, 3, 253–77.

Whitam, F.L. (1986) *Male Homosexuality in Four Societies: Brazil, Guatemala, the Philippines, and the United States*, New York: Praeger.

White, E. (1981) *States of Desire: Travels in Gay America*, New York: Bantam.

White, E. (1986) *States of Desire: Travels in Gay America*, with a new Afterword by the author, London: Picador.

White, E. (1993) *Genet: A Biography*, New York: Vintage Books.

Wild, J. (1718) *An Answer to a Late Insolent Libel*, London:

Willette, A. (1919) *Feu Pierrot 1857–19?*, Paris: H. Fleury.

Willy [Gauthier-Villars, H.] (1927) *Le Troisième Sexe*, introduction de Louis Estève, Paris: Paris-Édition.

Wilson, M. (1991) ' "Sans les femmes, qu'est-ce qui nous resterait?" Gender and transgression in Bohemian Montmartre,' in Julia Epstein and Kristina Staub (eds) *Body Guards: The Cultural Politics of Gender Ambiguity*, New York: Routledge, 195–222.

Word is Out: Stories of Some of Our Lives (1977) Mariposa Film Group, videocassette.

Wotherspoon, G. (1991) *City of the Plain: History of a Gay Sub-culture*, Sydney: Hale and Iremonger.

Wray, M. and Newitz, A. (eds) (1996) *White Trash: Race and Class in America*, New York: Routledge.

Wright, F.B. (1816) *A History of Religious Persecutions, from the Apostolic Age to the Present Time, and of the Inquisition of Spain, Portugal, and Goa*, Liverpool: Robinson.

Wright, L.K. (1997) *The Bear Book: Readings in the History and Evolution of a Gay Male Subculture*, New York: Harrington Park Press.

Wright, (forthcoming) 'Clone culture,' in *Encyclopedia of Homosexuality*, 2nd edn, revised.

Index